Sunset

SUCCESSFUL GARDENING

Month-by-Month

BY THE EDITORS OF SUNSET BOOKS

SUNSET BOOKS • MENLO PARK, CALIFORNIA

SUNSET BOOKS

Vice President, General Manager: Richard A. Smeby

Editorial Director: Bob Doyle

Production Director: Lory Day

Art Director: Vasken Guiragossian

Cover Photography: Jerry Black (front cover, top left), Claire Curran (front cover, bottom right), Norman Plate (front cover, top right; back cover), and Michael Thompson (front cover, bottom left)

ROUNDTABLE PRESS, INC.

Directors: Marsha Melnick, Julie Merberg, Susan Meyer

Project Editor: Laura Tringali

Managing Editor: John Glenn

Design and Production: Smythtype

Editorial Assistants: Carrie Glidden, Erica Toth

First printing August 1999
Copyright © 1999 Sunset Publishing Corporation,
Menlo Park, CA 94025.

Library of Congress Catalog Card Number: 99-66003
ISBN 0-376-03159-X

Printed in the United States

Contents

How to Use this Book

Everybody loves gardens. They enhance our homes, put us in touch with nature, delight us with their sights and smells, and provide us with fresh produce and seasonings for our kitchens. Yet in the busyness of everyday life, it is all too easy to run out of gardening time and energy, leaving the dream landscape to turn into a nightmare. This book, *Successful Gardening Month-by-Month,* was designed to help busy western gardeners focus their time and effort where they can have the greatest impact. In addition, the book gives gardeners the information they need to create and maintain attractive, productive gardens and outdoor spaces all year round.

Look at *Successful Gardening Month-by-Month* as a road map to great results in your garden. Since the book is organized by months, it's easy to jump right in and get to work. Simply find your climate zone (pages 6 to 7), then locate the checklist for that zone for the current month. (It's a good idea to scan the headings of the other climate zones, too. Often you'll find nuggets of information that you can use in your own region—either at that time or at a later date.) Just behind the checklist section you'll find features that offer practical information, handy tips, and glorious inspiration—all relating to the main concerns of the month.

Because the West has a variety of climate zones, gardeners will naturally need to do different things at different times of the year, depending on where they live. While Denver gardeners are preparing to set out the first of their one-season plantings, for example, desert gardeners are getting ready to pack it in for the summer. Gardeners may need the same information—but they'll need it at different times of the year. Therefore, you will sometimes find that information that would be of use to you in a particular month has been included under a different month in the book. For instance, if you live in Northern California, the checklist will advise you to shop for bare-root roses in December, but the feature on planting bare-root stock appears in the February section, where it is relevant to more western gardeners. Use the index to find the information you need, or just thumb through the book, feasting your eyes on all that you see.

—*Laura Tringali*

Climate Zones / 1 2 3 4 5 6 7 8 9 10 11 12 13 14 15 16 17 18 19 20 21 22 23 24

The West's 24 Climate Zones

To garden successfully in the West, it is essential to understand the attributes of the climate zone in which you live. This book uses 24 climate zones, numbered from harshest (Zone 1) to mildest (Zone 24). The boundaries of each of these unique zones are a function of six geographic and climatic factors: latitude, elevation, ocean influence, continental air influence, mountains and hills, and local terrain. Taken together, these factors determine what will grow well in your garden and what won't; knowing them makes clear any extra steps you may need to take to make sure your plants thrive.

Zones 1–3 are cold and snowy. The snow-covered peaks of the Rocky Mountains and the Sierra Nevada are the dominant features of these zones.

If you live in these areas, the short growing season means it's critical to get a garden off to a good start.

Zones 4–6 are the rainy northern zones. Rain dominates the winter and spring seasons, but the area also boasts some of the longest and mildest summer and fall growing seasons in the country. Drought can be a problem here, as can the soil, whose nutrients must be continually replenished after being leached out by heavy rains.

Zones 7–9 and 14–17 are the northern and interior-valley California zones. Mild climate and fertile soils make much of Northern California and the Central Valley a gardener's paradise. All these zones can be found within a 50-mile radius of San Francisco.

Zones 10–13 are the southwest desert zones, from California to New Mexico. They include hot low-desert areas and colder high-desert areas that abut nearby snowy and wintry mountain areas. In these zones, you must be aware of the best time to plant—or even to attempt to work in the garden.

Zones 18–24 are the Southern California zones. These zones aren't always consistent, particularly in areas that are influenced by both the ocean and interior winds. If you garden within these zones, you must know the full temperature range of your particular zone to figure out whether it is possible to grow tropical or subtropical ornamental plants, citrus, and avocados.

The lush cottage gardens typical of the Pacific Northwest (left) couldn't be more different from those found in the southwest desert zones (right).

Primroses add sparkle to the winter garden in mild-winter areas of California and the Southwest.

January

Pacific Northwest Checklist

PLANNING & PLANTING

☑ **PLAN FOR A HEALTHY GARDEN.** A well-tended garden—with appropriate plants, healthy soil, and a balanced ratio of beneficial insects to pests—rarely, if ever, will need heavy-handed pest control. Take the opportunity during this quiet season to learn what you can about Integrated Pest Management (IPM), a strategy that encourages gardeners to work closely with nature to minimize common garden problems.

☑ **ORDER SEEDS.** Look through catalogs and order seeds now so you won't be stuck with substitutions later in the season.

☑ **BARE-ROOT STOCK.** Zones 4–7: Shop for bare-root berries, fruit and shade trees, grapes, ornamental shrubs and roses, and perennial vegetables (asparagus, horseradish, and rhubarb). Plant them whenever the soil is workable. If you can't plant right away, keep the roots from drying out by heeling in plants: Place them on their sides in a shallow trench and cover with moist sawdust or light soil.

☑ **HARDY PERENNIALS.** For frost-tolerant perennials such as columbine, delphinium, hellebore, veronica, and viola, start seeds now in cold-frames or greenhouses. Set plants outside when they develop one or two true sets of leaves, but not more than a month before the last frost.

☑ **WINTER-BLOOMING SHRUBS.** Zones 4–7: A feast of color awaits you at your local nursery. Among other shrubs, you'll be tempted by hybrid camellias, cornelian cherry (*Cornus mas*), *Prunus subhirtella* 'Autumnalis', stachyurus, wintersweet, and witch hazel. Plant shrubs immediately or slip them into decorative pots for patio or deck display.

MAINTENANCE

☑ **PRUNE FRUIT TREES & ROSES.** Zones 4–7: On a day when temperatures are well above freezing, prune roses and deciduous fruit trees. Prune hybrid tea roses to a vase shape made from the 3 to 5 strongest canes. Remove dead, diseased, crossing, and close parallel branches from fruit trees, then prune for form. In Zones 1–3, hold off on pruning fruit trees until early spring.

☑ **CHECK STORED BULBS.** Examine corms and tubers. Sprinkle water on any that are shriveled—they should rehydrate. Throw out any that show signs of rot. Dahlia tubers are the exception: Cut out any bad spots, dust with sulfur, and store away from other bulbs.

☑ **LAWNS.** Avoid walking on the lawn when it's wet or frozen.

☑ **CONTAINER PLANTS.** Bring containers indoors or into a sheltered spot to protect them from freezing.

PEST & WEED CONTROL

☑ **APPLY DORMANT OIL.** Spray dormant oil on deciduous trees and shrubs, including fruits, ornamentals, and roses, to kill larvae, eggs, and overwintering insects.

☑ **SLUGS.** Whenever there's a warm spell, slugs wake up and start nibbling. Poison bait and hand-picking are the most effective methods at this time of year. Place the bait near slugs' hiding places—under rocks, pavers, and large pots, along house foundations, and in dense ground covers like ivy. Keep children and pets well away from the bait. (See the June section for more information on pest control.)

☑ **PULL WEEDS.** Many plants are leafless, and planting beds are empty, making weeds easy to spot. Remove them now and they won't be around later to multiply.

Northern California Checklist

PLANNING & PLANTING

LEARN ABOUT INTEGRATED PEST MANAGEMENT. IPM stresses good gardening practices—amending the soil, proper irrigation, crop rotation, routine cleanup, and the like—to head off trouble before it begins and minimize the use of chemicals in the garden.

ORDER SEEDS. Thumb through catalogs and order varieties you can't find on the racks. Zones 7–9, 14–17: Sow seeds of cool-season vegetables such as chard, lettuce, and spinach for planting out in February. Zones 1–2: Sow seeds of cool-season crops such as broccoli and cauliflower 6 to 8 weeks before the soil can be worked.

BARE-ROOT STOCK. Zones 7–9, 14–17: Buy and plant dormant roses, shrubs, fruit and shade trees, and vines. Bare-root plants cost less and adapt more quickly than container plants.

PLANT BERRIES AND VEGETABLES. Zones 7–9, 14–17: Artichokes, asparagus, blackberries, grapes, raspberries, and strawberries are all available bareroot this month. 'Olallie' blackberries are taste treats—the huge 1½-inch-long berries are sweet and succulent, and the plant is well adapted to Northern California. 'Sequoia' strawberries are also rich in flavor.

PLANT ANNUALS. Zones 7–9, 14–17: For midwinter bloom, buy 4-inch-size instant color (smaller plants will just sit until spring). Stuff plants into containers or set them out in flower beds. Try calendula, candytuft, cineraria, dianthus, English daisies, English and fairy primroses, Iceland poppies, pansies, snapdragons, stock, and violas.

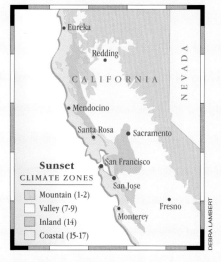

Sunset CLIMATE ZONES

- Mountain (1-2)
- Valley (7-9)
- Inland (14)
- Coastal (15-17)

DEBRA LAMBERT

MAINTENANCE

CARE FOR GIFT PLANTS. Zones 7–9, 14–17: Snip off spent blossoms on blooming plants and move hardier types such as azaleas, cineraria, cyclamen, cymbidiums, and living Christmas trees to protected spots outside. If the plant is rootbound, transplant it into a larger container or trim off some of the rootball and replant with fresh potting mix. Water thoroughly. Give plants partial sun to begin with, then move into full sun after a week or two. Zones 1–2: Keep all plants indoors until after the last hard freeze.

CUT BACK HYDRANGEAS. Zones 7–9, 14–17: Cut stems that have bloomed back to 12 inches. For the largest flowers next spring, reduce the number of stems; for more numerous medium-size blossoms, keep more stems.

PROTECT PLANTS FROM FROST. Zones 7–9, 14–17: If weather forecasts predict dry, still, clear nights and frost, water all plants well. Move tender container plants such as citrus, cymbidiums, hibiscus, and mandevilla beneath overhangs or into the garage. Protect other frost-tender plants with burlap or cloth coverings; do not let the cover touch the leaves. Remove covers first thing in the morning.

FEED CITRUS TREES. Zones 7–9, 14–17: Six to 8 weeks before they bloom, feed citrus trees according to their age. Give 2-year-old trees (trees planted last season) ¼ pound of actual nitrogen; 3-year-old trees ½ pound; 4-year-old trees ¾ pound; 5-year-old trees 1 pound; and trees more than 5 years old 1 to 1½ pounds. Or divide the total fertilizer into 2 feedings (January and February). For very sandy soils, divide the fertilizer into once-a-month feedings from late winter through summer.

PEST CONTROL

SPRAY ROSES. Zones 7–9, 14–17: To control overwintering insects such as aphids, mites, and scale, spray roses with a dormant oil. Thoroughly cover the trunk, branches, and twigs.

Southern California Checklist

PLANNING & PLANTING

PROACTIVE PROBLEM-SOLVING. Study the techniques of Integrated Pest Management (IPM) to learn how to incorporate commonsense gardening practices to ward off pests and diseases. Many books are available on the subject.

SHOP FOR SUCCULENTS. Winter-blooming succulents can brighten a winter garden. They look particularly at home in drought-tolerant Mediterranean-style settings. Look for flowering aloes, echeveria, and kalanchoe, among others, at your nursery.

BARE-ROOT PLANTS. January and February are bare-root planting time in all mild-weather climates. Take advantage of it. Bare-root plants are not only less expensive than leafed-out ones, but also take hold more quickly. Shop for roses, stone fruit and deciduous shade trees, strawberries and cane berries, and artichokes, asparagus, and other perennial vegetables. Plant them immediately if possible. If the soil is too wet to plant right away, cover the roots with soil or plant temporarily in containers.

PLANT WINTER ANNUALS. If the soil isn't soggy from rain, there's still time to plant Iceland poppies, pansies, primulas, and other winter annuals, especially along the coast. Low-desert gardeners (Zone 13) can also plant petunias.

PLANT SUMMER BULBS. Nurseries are well stocked with calla, canna, crinum, dahlia, gladiolus, lily, nerine, tigridia, and other summer-blooming bulbs. If you live in a frost-free area, this is also a good time to replant into the garden any amaryllis plants you forced or received for the holidays. They won't bloom this spring but should next year.

Sunset
CLIMATE ZONES
1-3 7-9 11 13 14-24

DEBRA LAMBERT

PLANT WINTER VEGETABLES. Germination will be slow, but it's still possible to start cool-season crops from seed—especially endives, lettuces, and other greens. Also try beets, carrots, peas, and radishes. Set out broccoli, Brussels sprouts, and cabbage seedlings.

MAINTENANCE

BEGIN PRUNING DORMANT PLANTS. Start with roses. Cut out all dead wood, crossing branches, and twiggy growth, leaving five to seven strong canes. Deciduous fruit trees should be pruned now, too. Apricots, peaches, and plums all require different pruning. Consult a good reference book and/or attend a fruit-tree pruning demonstration at an arboretum before proceeding. Hold off pruning trees, shrubs, and vines that flower in early spring; wait until after they bloom to shape them.

GROOM CAMELLIAS. If camellia blight is a problem (petals turn brown and rot in the center), keep ground beneath plants clean by removing fallen flowers and leaves promptly. Pick infected flowers from plants.

WATER NATIVE PLANTS. In winter, native plants can best absorb and store water for summer. If rains have been light or nonexistent, give plants slow, deep soakings now through early spring as needed.

FEED CITRUS. In frost-free areas, fertilize citrus this month; inland, wait until February. Where frost lingers, wait until March to avoid damage to new growth. Water first; a day later, sprinkle slow-release ammonium sulfate over entire root area, then water to wash into soil. Wait 2 months, then apply a second feeding.

PEST & WEED CONTROL

APPLY DORMANT SPRAY. Spray roses and deciduous flowering and fruit trees with horticultural oil to smother overwintering insects such as mites, scale, and sawfly larvae. For fungal diseases such as peach leaf curl or brown rot, mix lime sulfur or fixed copper into the oil. Spray the branches, crotches, trunk, and ground beneath the tree's drip line. Hold off spraying if rain is forecast or temperatures are expected to drop below 0.

MANAGE WEEDS. Mulch flower and vegetable beds to keep ahead of weeds encouraged by winter rains. Keep on top of areas seeded with wildflowers. Hand-pull or carefully hoe emerging weeds.

Mountain Checklist

PLANNING & PLANTING

☑ **FOCUS ON PREVENTION.** Plan to keep your garden healthy and beautiful with a minimum of pesticides. An approach called Integrated Pest Management (IPM for short) uses a commonsense garden strategy to help keep problems from occurring in the first place. Learn as much as you can about it, so you can apply IPM principles during the gardening season.

☑ **ORDER SEEDS AND PLANTS.** To ensure the best selection, place catalog orders early for seeds and plants, particularly if you want specialty varieties such as Chinese vegetables, rare plants, or antique roses. Start seeds indoors about 5 weeks before the date of the last frost in your area.

☑ **START HARDY PERENNIALS.** In milder parts of the intermountain West, start seeds of perennials such as delphinium, hellebore, veronica, and viola in a cold frame or greenhouse. Transplant seedlings when they have at least 2 sets of true leaves; in coldest areas, wait until the ground thaws and soil can be worked.

☑ **BRING COLOR INDOORS.** For a splash of cheery winter color, shop nurseries for cyclamen, Johnny-jump-ups, pansies, and primroses. Set the pots in a bright, cool spot.

Sunset
CLIMATE ZONES

☐ 1-3   ☐ 10-11

DEBRA LAMBERT

MAINTENANCE

☑ **CHECK STORED BULBS AND PRODUCE.** Inspect corms, tubers, and produce for shriveling and rot. Reverse shriveling by sprinkling on a little water. Discard any items that show signs of decay, except dahlia tubers: For these, cut out bad spots, dust with sulfur, and store apart from the other bulbs.

☑ **CARE FOR LIVING CHRISTMAS TREES.** After the holidays, move the tree outside as soon as possible. Start it off in a place that's shaded from midday and afternoon sun, moving it into full sun after a couple of weeks. If your tree is among the varieties that thrive in your area, plant it after the ground thaws; otherwise, keep the tree in the container and protect it from prolonged hard frost.

☑ **KNOCK SNOW OFF EVERGREENS.** If you live in an area that gets heavy snow, knock or sweep it off the branches of evergreen shrubs and trees before any accumulated weight causes damage.

☑ **PRUNE TREES AND SHRUBS.** In the mildest parts of the intermountain West, start pruning when daytime temperatures are well above freezing. Remove dead, diseased, crossing, and close parallel branches, then prune for shape.

☑ **FEED WILD BIRDS.** When winter diminishes their natural food supply, birds seek out backyard feeders. Insect-eating birds go for suet and peanut butter; seed-eaters prefer sunflower seeds, cracked corn, millet, and mixed birdseed.

☑ **MAINTAIN TOOLS.** Spring will be here before you know it. Get ready for it now by sharpening blades of shovels, hoes, and mowers. Rub down wood handles with linseed oil. Hone or replace the blades of pruning shears.

Southwest Checklist

PLANNING & PLANTING

☑ **PLAN FOR A HEALTHY GARDEN.** Avoid having to use heavy-handed disease and pest controls by adopting Integrated Pest Management (IPM) practices. These commonsense strategies encourage gardeners to work closely with nature to minimize common gardening problems.

☑ **BARE-ROOT STOCK.** Nurseries offer bare-root berries, fruit trees, grapes, roses, and shade and flowering trees now. Before you buy, decide what you want to grow and dig the planting hole. To keep bare roots from drying out, ask nursery staff to pack them in damp peat moss or sawdust and wrap them for the trip home.

☑ **PLANT BULBS.** If you've chilled crocus, hyacinth, and tulip bulbs in the refrigerator for 6 weeks, take them out and plant now in amended soil; water well. Shoots should emerge in a month or two.

☑ **START VEGETABLES.** Zones 12–13: Start seeds of eggplant, melons, peppers, and tomatoes indoors now for transplanting outside when the weather warms up. Also set out short-day onions.

☑ **WINTER COLOR.** Zones 10–13: Nurseries offer a big selection of cool-season flowers, including bachelor's buttons, calendulas, cinerarias, cyclamen, English daisies, pansies, primroses, snapdragons, sweet alyssum, and wallflowers.

MAINTENANCE

☑ **PRUNE ROSES.** For hybrid tea roses, prune plants back to the 3 to 5 strongest canes. Cut back top growth by about a third.

☑ **CARE FOR CITRUS TREES.** Apply fertilizer now, so nutrients will be available when citrus starts to bloom. Water trees first, then apply ammonium sulfate a day later at the following rates for mature, full-size trees: 2½ pounds for grapefruit trees; 4 pounds for oranges and tangerines; and 5 pounds for lemons. Water again after feeding. If temperatures below 28° are forecast, cover trees at night with a cloth (old sheets are fine); uncover them in the morning. When temperatures drop below 25° for longer than two hours, most citrus fruits will be damaged. Pick and juice damaged fruit within 24 hours.

☑ **WATER.** Zones 12–13: If winter rains are sporadic, deeply water trees and shrubs every 2 or 3 weeks.

☑ **SPREAD MULCH.** To keep weeds down and the ground moist, spread a thick layer of mulch around shrubs and trees, and in vegetable and flower beds.

☑ **LAWN CARE.** Zones 1–3: Avoid walking on lawns when the ground is wet or frozen. If you're tired of maintaining a lawn, consider planting drought-tolerant ground covers such as bearberry or low-growing rosemary.

PEST CONTROL

☑ **SPRAY OVERWINTERING INSECTS.** Spray dormant deciduous trees and shrubs with horticultural oil to kill insects, eggs, and larvae.

A Commonsense Approach to Garden Problems

In years past, the preferred solution to garden problems was to eradicate the trouble with pesticides. As we've since learned, however, it is neither possible nor desirable to completely eliminate every problem that besets our plants—and by trying to do so, we may cause immediate or long-term harm to people, animals, and the environment. Today, the focus is on prevention and management, not eradication. This approach, called Integrated Pest Management (IPM), had its origins in the agricultural industry, but it is just as applicable to home gardens.

You won't find many problems in this Santa Fe garden. The plants are appropriate for the climate, and the gardener gives them what they need to thrive. And because they're of many kinds and many heights, they offer a habitat for beneficials and birds—your partners in pest control.

Prevention

Whatever your garden's size or style, good plant health is your first line of defense against potential problems of any kind. Strong, vigorous plants are better able to resist pests that fly or crawl into the garden and disease spores that drift in on the wind; a thick, healthy lawn foils weed invasion before it can begin. Make it a priority to give each plant the water, fertilizer, and light it needs to thrive.

There are other steps you can take to keep problems away. Remember that landscaping choices can contribute to a healthy garden: If you include a variety of plants of different heights, you'll provide a habitat for insect-eating birds and other creatures that help keep pest populations under control. You'll also avoid monoculture, where one severe pest infestation can devastate the entire landscape as it spreads rapidly from plant to plant. In a diverse garden, however, even if a severe infestation comes through the neighborhood, some plants are likely to have greater resistance than others and survive.

Learn to ask questions about disease resistance when you make a purchase. For example, certain tree varieties are more resistant to fireblight than others. While that doesn't mean there's a guarantee, it does reduce the likelihood of your losing a mature tree to this disfiguring and eventually life-threatening disease. When you get the plants home, take the time to prepare the soil, water them regularly until you plant them, and monitor them through their post-planting transition. Otherwise you're adding stress to those plants and leaving them vulnerable to pest infestation or disease.

Finally, pay attention to maintenance: Keep an eye on the accumulation of debris such as old leaves, pieces of wood, pulled annual flowers, and fallen seedpods. Although such materials—if nondiseased—can act as a good natural mulch (and a source of nutrients as they decay and work into the soil), they also provide a favorite home for ground-dwelling pests. If pests of this sort are a nuisance for you, you may want to clear away their hiding places periodically.

This attractive, problem-free garden in California is composed entirely of native plants, which are less susceptible than imports to pests and disease.

For success with a plant, give it what it needs. The right location is a site that satisfies the plant's requirements. Failure to attend to the water requirements of these beans has stunted them and left them susceptible to a spider mite infestation (right). Compare them to their well-watered counterparts (far right). Rhododendrons are shade-loving shrubs, that thrive when sheltered from direct sun (below, right). The one planted in a sunny location has suffered sunscald (below, right).

Management

Preventing a problem is the first line of defense in keeping your garden free from pests, diseases, and weeds. Managing problems through early intervention—or with simple techniques—is the backup plan.

Often a simple barrier will solve a problem. If you live in deer territory, you may resort to fencing those parts of your garden that contain plants known to be deer favorites. Or you might place a row cover over a bed of lettuce to prevent flying insects from eating tender leaves.

Consider adding elements to your garden that will attract pest-eating allies. Certain flowering plants attract beneficial insects, which in turn consume plant-eating pests. Daisy family members are among the best at attracting helpful insects. A summer annual, such as sweet alyssum, can be another such ally. A simple bat house and an overturned pot near a water source to attract toads are other possible offensive tactics: Bats eat several hundred insects per hour, including mosquitoes, and toads help out by consuming small slugs.

Sometimes you'll find that a problem has taken hold in your garden and physical controls won't manage it. A range of products is at your disposal for reducing or eliminating problems, products that have varying impacts on you and your family, beneficial insects, and the environment.

Some of these are biological controls. Tiny nematodes, for example, feed on many kinds of soil-dwelling and plant-boring pests. (These are different from the nematodes that attack plant roots.) Previously available only through specialty mail-order suppliers, nematodes are now carried by some garden centers and hardware supply stores. To use them you just mix the nematode package with water and apply to the soil with a watering can.

Other controls are simple sprays that reduce or eliminate common pests and diseases. Baking-soda-and-water solutions that you make yourself or a lightweight oil-and-water mixture will manage many outbreaks of mildew. Soap-and-water solutions (which are commonly sold as insecticidal soap spray) will rid a plant of a variety of invading pests.

If a problem requires a more stringent solution, you will find a wide variety of pesticides available. Before you buy, make sure you have the right one for the job. Read its label carefully, and make sure to follow all the directions exactly.

Sometimes, even with the best of care, a plant simply won't thrive in your garden. Have you ever heard gardeners talk about shovel pruning? This isn't a fancy gardening technique but a tongue-in-cheek way of saying, "Dig up the plant and get rid of it." Experienced gardeners may give a plant one or two seasons—perhaps even move it to a new location—but if it doesn't thrive, there comes a time when it's best to consign it to the compost heap.

Many pests are a problem for only a short time, most often when plants are young and tender. It's a simple task to cover a bed with gauzelike cloth during this critical time. The gauze keeps out flying and crawling pests while letting light reach the plants.

Make time for planning

Planning is one of the most important things you can do to keep a garden healthy. No matter where you garden, there comes a time when most activities slow down or stop. For many, the dormant period occurs in January, when seed and plant catalogs begin to arrive. The catalogs stimulate thinking about what worked and what didn't work last year—and what you might do differently this time.

Before you begin planning for an upcoming season, do a walking inventory of your garden. Make notes as you go, recalling what happened in each area and planting bed. Perhaps your peaches were afflicted with peach leaf curl, aphids wreaked havoc with your roses, or spider mites caused problems in the dwarf conifers. These pest infestations can be remedied by preventive techniques during the dormant season, followed by prompt attention as they first become apparent next spring. If you kept a journal or made a few notes during the past season, refer to them to remind yourself which management methods worked.

Some problems might require structural solutions. Perhaps last season's cutting garden was a failure because a layer of hardpan just below the topsoil prevented proper root development. You make a note to construct raised planting beds to remedy this problem. Or you see some struggling shrubs and jot down a reminder to order soil amendments next spring.

If you have a vegetable and herb garden each year, you may decide to rearrange it, breaking up one large plot into several smaller ones dispersed throughout the garden to take better advantage of microclimates. If you have particular pest problems with a certain vegetable, you might diversify its planting among the various beds so that pests don't spread from one plant to another. In many western climate zones, you can also let some herbs, such as lavender and rosemary, do double duty as foundation shrubs.

Another aspect of planning ahead is preparing for later pest prevention. For example, if you lost an entire flat of transplanted vegetable seedlings to cutworms or earwigs the day after you planted them, make a note to start stockpiling milk cartons now. This season, surround each seedling with a cutoff carton at the time you plant. The carton will prevent cutworms from getting to the plants and eating them. (Make sure there's at least 1 inch between the outermost plant leaves and the edge of the carton and that the carton extends 1 inch below soil level and 2 inches above it.)

Taking inventory and doing advance planning doesn't mean that every task in your garden must be strictly governed by rules. In fact, a great deal of gardening's popularity is due to its relaxed nature—a refreshing change from the busy lives most of us lead. But your garden will be healthier and you'll be able to enjoy it more if you pay timely attention to a few key tasks.

Attracting beneficial insects

The following plants will draw beneficial insects to your garden and hold down populations of undesirable insects.

Annuals

Aegopodium podagraria. Bishop's weed. Low-growing, 6-inch-tall plant similar to Queen Anne's lace; blooms April to October. Attracts: parasitoid wasps, pirate bugs, syrphid flies.

Agrostemma. Corn cockle. Wispy, 2–3-foot plants with pink cup-like flowers; blooms November through April where winters are mild, May to August elsewhere. Attracts: ladybugs, parasitoid wasps.

Coriandrum sativum. Coriander. Small white flowers on fine-textured, 12–15-inch plant; blooms May and June. Attracts: parasitoid wasps, pirate bugs.

Cosmos bipinnatus. Cosmos. White works best; 1–4-foot fernlike foliage; blooms April to November. Attracts: insidious flower bugs, lacewings, ladybugs.

Layia platyglossa. Tidytips. Yellow-and-white flowers on plants 5–16 inches tall; blooms March to August. Attracts: parasitoid wasps, pirate bugs.

Lobularia maritima. Sweet alyssum. Tiny, white to purple flowers on 6–8-inch plants; blooms all year in mild-winter areas. Attracts: lacewings, parasitoid wasps, pirate bugs.

Nemophila menziesii. Baby blue eyes. Blue flowers on plants 6–10 inches tall; blooms March to May. Attracts: parasitoid wasps, pirate bugs.

Perennials

Achillea. Yarrow. Pink, yellow, red, lavender, and white flowers on plants ranging from a few inches to 3 feet tall; blooms April to September. Attracts: ladybugs, damsel bugs, big-eyed bugs, parasitoid wasps.

Coreopsis sp. Coreopsis. Yellow, orange, and maroon flowers on 1–3-foot plants; blooms May to September. Attracts: lacewings, ladybugs, parasitoid wasps.

Eriogonum. Buckwheat. White, yellow, pink, and rose flowers on 1–4-foot plants; blooms May to October or later. Attracts: pirate bugs.

Foeniculum vulgare. Common fennel. Soft, fernlike foliage and yellow, flat flower clusters on 3–5-foot plants; blooms April to November. Attracts: lacewings, ladybugs, paper wasps, soldier bugs.

Lychnis coronaria. Crown-pink. Soft, gray foliage on 2-foot plants; magenta, pink, and white flowers; blooms April to August. Attracts: parasitoid wasps.

Ruta graveolens. Rue. Blue-gray foliage and small yellow flowers on 2–3-foot plants; blooms in early summer. Attracts: mud wasps, parasitoid wasps, potter wasps.

Tanacetum vulgare. Tansy. Yellow flowers and fernlike foliage on 2–3-foot plants; blooms June and July. Attracts: lacewings, ladybugs, parasitoid wasps, pirate bugs.

Daisy and pink family members attract beneficials to this flower bed.

Soil and Amendments

Any discussion of garden soil starts with some basic geology. Soil includes rock that has been worn down into mineral particles of various sizes. Imagine your garden as a pile of boulders. Now imagine wind and water wearing away at those boulders over a very, very long time—until, eventually, they become the soil in which your plants are growing today.

Though soil may have started out as solid rock, it's usually relatively easy to work by the time we put a shovel to it. That's due both to the small size of the mineral particles and to the air and water contained in the pore spaces between them. In fact, a shovelful of soil is only about half mineral particles; the other half is almost equally divided between air and water. Only a very small amount is organic matter (decaying plant material, for example).

Turn over a shovelful of garden soil. If you see earthworms, your soil is healthy and "alive." Living creatures add humus to the soil, make nutrients available to plant roots, and help control harmful fungi.

Soil's living creatures

Besides minerals, air, and water, your garden soil comes complete with living creatures. The most visible one is the familiar earthworm—but besides a few hundred of these, the top several inches of a square yard of soil may include a million mites and mite-like creatures and over 10 million nematodes and protozoans. These creatures all help keep the soil healthy. They process minerals to make them available to plant roots; they keep harmful fungi under control. Their waste products (and later on, their remains) form humus, a soft, blackish brown material that improves the structure of any soil.

Because most of these creatures live in the upper few inches of soil, their habitat is destroyed if this layer has been scraped away (during the construction of a new home, for example) or is constantly worked. If you're starting out with poor or depleted soil, keep in mind that you will need at least a few years to revive it. Part of what happens during this time is that colonies of soil-dwelling organisms become established and begin to flourish.

Soil textures

What's the soil like in your garden? You'd probably describe it as sand, clay, loam, or something in between. To soil experts, these are all soil textures, determined by the percentage a soil contains of mineral particles of various sizes. Texture, in turn, influences drainage, a very important aspect of soil quality. Water applied to the soil surface percolates down through the pore spaces between soil particles. At first, it completely fills the pores. In time, however, it's drawn away—carried downward by gravity, absorbed by plant roots, drawn up from the soil surface and out through foliage. As water leaves the pores, air returns to them, until just a film of water remains on the soil particles.

Clay soil—whether you call it adobe, gumbo, or just plain "heavy" soil—is composed of many flattened, tiny particles packed tightly together to form a dense mass with microscopic pore spaces. (Clay soil can be so dense, in fact, that in some parts of the country it's used to make bricks!) Drainage is slow, since water and nutrients move through the pore spaces slowly. On the plus side, clay's slow drainage lets you water less often. And such soil is better able than others to attract, hold, and release certain nutrients. On the minus side, clay is difficult for plant roots to penetrate, and during rainy periods it can remain saturated and airless to the point of suffocating roots (which need air as well as water to live).

Claylike soils are produced by a number of factors. In parts of California, for instance, the particular series of geological events and climatic changes broke a high proportion of mineral particles down to microscopic size; due to the lack of summer rain, vegetation was sparse, and what there was tended to dry up and blow away rather than decaying to help loosen the soil.

At the opposite end of the spectrum from clay is sand, typically found in areas near oceans and rivers and in places where these once existed. Its large, irregularly rounded particles fit loosely together, with large pore spaces between them. Water and nutrients drain through sand quickly—so fast that it can be difficult to keep plants well watered in hot weather. Sand is less fertile than clay, but roots penetrate it easily, growing deeply and rapidly, and it's far easier than clay to work.

A third soil texture, midway between the extremes of sand and clay, is loam. This is the excellent soil often found in climates with ample summer rain and cold winters: The rainy summers encourage lush vegetation, while the harsh, freezing winters make for the slow decay of dead plants directly into the soil. This combination of conditions tends to break down mineral particles into a variety of sizes, ranging from quite large (as in sand) to almost microscopic (as in pure clay), with particles of an intermediate size (known as silt) in between. Loam typically contains about 40% sand, 40% silt, and 20% clay. Soil of this texture that also contains a relatively high proportion of organic matter (5% or more of the total volume) is the ideal that gardeners strive to achieve.

To identify the soil texture in your garden, thoroughly wet a patch

Testing your soil

A soil test may be in order if you're planning to put in a new lawn, a vegetable plot, or ornamentals. The time to correct fertility, pH, or other soil problems is before you put plants in the ground.

Before getting a test, ask neighbors about any problems they've had with their soil. Your county's Cooperative Extension Service or local nursery can let you know about soil problems common to your area. If your lawn or ornamental plants are dying, check first to make sure the cause is not overwatering, poor drainage, insects, or disease.

In some western states, you can have your soil tested through the Cooperative Extension Service. In other areas, the service can recommend a private soil laboratory. Before sending your sample, find out what tests are available, their cost, and whether the lab will recommend specific soil improvements.

Laboratory soil testing can be expensive, so be sure to get a reliable sample.

Here's how to get soil that is representative of your garden.

Dig samples from different areas of the garden separately, using a soil probe or shovel and scraping away surface residue such as rocks.

Cut a ½-inch-thick vertical slice; dig down about 12 inches for unplanted areas, 3 to 6 inches for turf. Cut out a 1-inch-wide core from each shovel slice. Place the samples in clean paper or plastic bags.

Collect 5 to 10 samples for each area, all similar in texture and type, per 1,000 square feet.

Thoroughly mix samples from one area, breaking up any clods. If soil is too wet to mix, spread it out to air-dry.

Label the sample with your name, address, phone number, general sample location, the types of plants that grow in the sample location, date and depth of sample, and any special problems you know about. Generally, the more information you provide, the more specific remedies the tester will provide.

---

of soil, then let it dry out for a day. Now pick up a handful of soil and squeeze it firmly in your fist. If it forms a tight ball and has a slightly slippery feel, it's predominantly clay-like. If it doesn't hold its shape at all but simply crumbles apart when you open your hand, it's sandy. If it is slightly crumbly but still holds a loose ball, it's close to loam.

A profusion of plants replaces a dull, thirsty lawn, but good soil is key to such exuberant bloom.

Improving soil structure

Most gardens have soil that provides something less than the ideal environment for many garden plants. Perhaps it's rocky or scraped bare; perhaps it's too claylike or too sandy to suit the plants you want to grow. While changing a soil's basic texture is very difficult, you can improve its structure—making clay more porous, sand more water retentive—by adding amendments. The best amendment for any soil is organic matter, the decaying remains of plants and animals. As it decomposes, organic matter releases nutrients that are absorbed by soil-dwelling microorganisms and bacteria. The combination of these creatures' waste products and their remains, called humus, binds with soil particles. In clay, it forces the tightly packed particles apart; drainage is improved, and the soil is easier for plant roots to penetrate. In sand, it lodges in the large pore spaces and acts as a sponge, slowing drainage so the soil stays moist longer.

Among available organic amendments are compost, well-rotted manure, and soil conditioners (composed of several ingredients); these and others are sold in bags at many full-service nurseries, or in bulk (by the cubic yard) at supply centers. Byproducts of local industries, such as rice hulls, cocoa bean hulls, or mushroom compost, may also be available.

Wood chips and sawdust are also used, but because they are "fresh" ("green") amendments, they'll take nitrogen as they decompose. To make sure your plants aren't deprived of the nitrogen they need, add a fast-acting nitrogen source such as ammonium sulfate along with the amendment (use about 1 pound for each

While many plants prefer loam, some come from regions with sandy or claylike soil and thrive in garden soils of the same texture. Shown here is Rosa rugosa, *native to the ocean shores of temperate-climate Asia. The species and its hybrids thrive in sandy coastal gardens like this one.*

To add amendments to unplanted beds, spread the material evenly over the soil, then work it in by hand or with a rototiller to a depth of about 9 inches. If your soil is mostly clay or sand, spread 4 to 5 inches of amendment over it; once this is worked in, the top 9 inches of soil will be about half original soil, half amendment. If the soil is loamy or has been regularly amended each season, add just a 2- to 3-inch layer of amendment; you'll have a top 9-inch layer of about three-quarters original soil, one-quarter amendment.

Permanent or semipermanent plantings of trees, shrubs, or perennials benefit from soil amendment too, but you need to do the job without damaging plant roots. It's often sufficient simply to spread the amendment over the soil surface as a mulch; earthworms, microorganisms, rain, and irrigation water will all carry it downward over time, gradually improving the soil's top layer. If the plant isn't a shallow-rooted type (that is, if it doesn't have many roots concentrated near soil level), you can speed up the improvement process by working the amendment into the top inch or so of soil, using a three-pronged cultivator.

Where the climate is generally mild and winters are rainy, amend the soil in established plantings annually after fall cleanup. In cold-winter regions with spring and summer rainfall, do the job as you begin spring gardening.

1-inch layer of wood chips or sawdust spread over 100 square feet of ground).

Though the particular organic amendment you use is often decided simply by what's available at the best price, many experts favor compost over all other choices. Vegetable gardeners in particular prefer compost, and they often also add plenty of well-rotted manure to their planting beds.

Adding amendments: when and how

New beds for landscape plants should be amended before planting. Choose an amendment that breaks down slowly. Shredded bark and peat moss hold their structure the longest, taking several years to decompose. Include compost in the mix as well; though it breaks down in just a few months, it bolsters the initial nutrient supply available to soil microorganisms—and these will contribute humus to the soil, improve soil aeration, and help protect your new plants from some diseases.

In beds earmarked for vegetables and annual flowers, amend the soil before each new crop is planted. Compost and well-rotted manure are preferred by most gardeners, since they dramatically improve the soil's structure, making it hospitable to the fine, tiny roots of seedlings. Unamended soil may dry into hard clods that small roots cannot penetrate, and plants may grow slowly, be stunted, or die as a result. Manure and compost break down rapidly—manure in a few weeks, compost in several months—so be sure to replenish these amendments before you plant each crop.

Shown above are six organic amendments. From left to right, the first two bags hold organic compost; the others contain shredded bark, redwood mulch, forest bark, and peat moss.

Basic Pruning

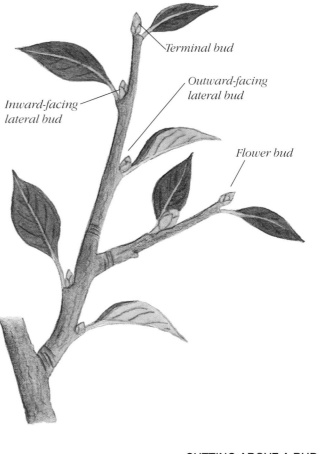

Terminal bud

Outward-facing
lateral bud

Inward-facing
lateral bud

Flower bud

Pruning encourages a plant to stop growing in one direction and start growing in another. How—and when—you prune depends on two factors: the effect you wish to achieve (such as prolonged bloom) and the growing characteristics of the plant. For the least maintenance, let plants grow according to their natural patterns. Prune young trees and shrubs just enough so they develop strong, shapely forms; prune flowering shrubs to produce more blossoms; and prune older shrubs to remove unhealthy or unwanted branches.

The illustration at right shows the main points of growth on a typical branch. Learning to recognize "growth buds" will help you identify where to make cuts, especially if you keep in mind one simple rule: Cutting a terminal bud forces the branch to develop in the direction of other growth buds. The result will be healthier, bushier, more long-lived plants.

Making the cut

Proper pruning calls for cutting back to a part that will continue to grow—to the trunk, to another branch, to a bud, or even to the ground, in the case of shrubs that send up new stems from the roots. Because clean cuts heal faster than ragged ones do, always use an appropriate, well-sharpened pruning tool. Never force a tool to cut a bigger branch than it is designed to handle. And remember, you can use your fingers to pinch tip growth, but never to snap or break off twigs or small branches.

The placement of a cut is crucial. If you cut too close to a bud, or make a flush cut at a branch base, you can cause injury. If you cut too far away from a bud, you leave a stub, which will wither and die, though still attached to the plant. In time it will decay and drop off, leaving an open patch of dead tissue.

When using hand shears or loppers with a hook-and-blade design, position the blade next to the stem or branch that will remain on the plant. If the hook is next to the plant, you'll leave a small stub. You may have to turn the pruners upside down to position them correctly.

When cutting back to a bud, look for a healthy specimen pointing in the direction you want the new shoot to grow. A proper cut will be about ¼ inch above the bud, sloping away at approximately a 45° angle. The lowest point of the cut should be opposite the bud and even with it; the cut should slant upward in the direction the bud is pointing.

When removing a branch, avoid making a flush cut. Position your shears or saw just outside the branch collar. This is the wrinkled area or bulge at the base of a branch where it meets another branch or the trunk. Also refrain from cutting into the branch bark ridge (the raised bark in the branch crotch). Leaving these areas intact will help keep decay to a minimum.

CUTTING ABOVE A BUD

Correct — Incorrect —

45° angle — Too angular — Too low — Too high

POSITIONING PRUNING SHEARS

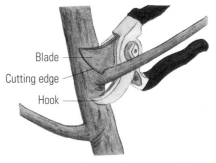

Blade

Cutting edge

Hook

For a proper close pruning cut, hold the pruning shears with the blade closer to the growth that will remain on the plant. Shears placed at the opposite angle will produce a stub.

Thinning cuts remove overcrowded branches and any weak or old stems. Cut to where a side branch joins the main stem; no new shoots will be produced below the cuts.

Heading cuts—removing the terminal buds—force the branch to produce a cluster of new shoots from buds below the cuts. Do this to growing plants to make them more bushy.

Removing the terminal buds of a growing plant (far left) forces it to fill out and become bushier.

Removing, or pinching, the spent flower heads of blooming shrubs (left) prevents the plant from putting energy into seed production. For rhododendrons, the effect is bushier growth or side branching.

Rejuvenate shrubs by removing a third of the oldest basal growth annually for 3 years (left). For shrubs that tolerate hard pruning (such as barberry and oleander), cut to a few stubs (right).

Clean up small trees by cutting off branches that are awkwardly crossed, diseased, broken, or damaged.

Pruning roses

Although it may seem like it, there's no mystery to pruning roses. Wait until late winter, as new leaf buds begin to swell on the branches, and you'll have an easy time finding the right places to cut. Make cuts at a 45° angle, always just above an outward-facing lateral bud. During the blooming season, help form new flower buds by cutting lanky stems and spent blossoms just above any five-leaflet leaf (below, left).

Arching shrub roses, rugosas, and climbers usually require only simple thinning. To prune bushy roses quickly, use sharpened hedge clippers to cut off the top of each plant by as much as one-third. Then use pruning shears to snip out the oldest, grayish canes and any that cross, look dead or diseased, or are thinner than a pencil. The stout stems of hybrid teas can be pruned back harder, 6 to 12 inches from the bumpy bud union or graft.

If you deadhead roses, or cut them for display, always cut above a five-leaflet leaf. Dotted lines show the best place to cut at different times during the growing season.

Remove dead wood and all weak, twiggy branches (darker ones shown above). Make these cuts flush with the bud union (the swelling at the base of the plant).

Cut out all branches that cross through the center of the plant. This opens up the bush and encourages it to grow into a vase shape.

In mild climates, shorten the remaining healthy growth by one-third. In cold climates, remove any stems that were injured or killed by winter freeze damage. (This may result in a shorter bush.)

Succulents

Many Westerners identify cacti and succulents with desert gardens. But these sturdy, drought-tolerant plants can easily be used in combinations with other garden plants to add exotic appeal to entranceways, patios, flower borders, terraced slopes, and containers.

The most appealing features of succulents are their color range—from golden barrel cactus to almost-black aeoniums—their interesting sculptural shapes, and their surprisingly showy flowers. Many multiply easily, and new plants are easily broken off the parent plant and re-rooted.

When planted in a suitable site, succulents rarely need to be pruned or checked for pests. Nearly all can survive weeks without water, but most look better if watered regularly during the spring and summer. To remove dust and city soot, simply hose down your plants now and then. A few species, such as the popular *Sedum telephium* 'Autumn Joy' will be quite at home in an irrigated flower bed. The range of succulents available for garden culture varies widely from region to region.

Planting succulents in containers

You can plant cacti and succulents in almost any kind of pot; just be careful not to overwater, especially if you use plastic or other nonporous pots. For round cactus plants, choose a container at least 2 inches wider than the plant; for more vertical plants, use a container as wide as half the plant's height to create visual balance. Small cacti and succulents also make delightful dish gardens.

You can buy a special soil mix for cacti and succulents or mix your own, using one part peat-moss–based soil mix (such as packaged house plant mix) and two parts builder's sand or fine gravel to provide the good drainage these plants need.

Place containers where they'll get full sun. Water regularly during their active spring-to-summer growth period. Soak the soil thoroughly, then

With its coral flowers and many species, aloes make striking, no-fuss garden plants. At top, an aloe and red-flowered Linum *are surrounded by a gravel mulch. An informal blending of textures (left) includes aloe and* Echeveria. *The powder-blue hen-and-chicks* (Echeveria imbricata) *makes an ideal front-of-border edging (below).*

wait until it's almost completely dry before watering again. Fertilize monthly during that period with ¼-strength liquid fertilizer. Cut back to about one watering a month and stop fertilizing during the autumn-winter rest period.

In very mild climates, these plants can live outdoors all year. In cold-winter areas, bring them indoors as house plants, placing them where they'll get plenty of light.

Most cacti and succulents need repotting every 2 to 3 years; do this in early spring.

What is a Succulent?

A succulent is any plant that stores water in juicy leaves, stems, or roots, enabling it to withstand periodic drought. Most succulents are native to desert or semi-arid lands, including South America and southern Africa. Many of those are frost-tender, but other species come from colder climates, such as cobweb houseleek (Sempervivum arachnoideum), *native to Europe. Succulent plants may be planted directly in the ground or in containers—arrange them in a strawberry pot for an easy, low-care display. This border planting of succulents includes dramatic agaves.*

What is a Cactus?

Cacti are succulent plants native only to the Western Hemisphere, their range covering climate extremes from the New England coastline to Death Valley. Generally leafless, cacti have stems modified into thick-skinned cylinders, pads, or jointed stems that store water during periods of drought. Most species have sharp spines to protect plants against browsing animals, and a great many offer large, colorful flowers. The golden barrel and saguaro cactus shown here are well suited to dry landscapes featuring other heat-lovers such as tall whiplike ocotillo (Fouquieria splendens) *and red bougainvillea.*

A few spiny tips

■ **Drainage.** Succulents and cacti will not survive without loose, well-draining soil that resembles the soil of their native habitats. Slopes, rock walls, terraces, and sandy or rocky soils make the best planting sites.

■ **Plant partners.** Although there's great variety in form and color, mixing a few species usually looks better than a mass of single plants. An exception is the striking look of several golden barrel cactus.

■ **Irrigation.** Group drought-tolerant, desert species together in areas you prefer not to irrigate; for many of these plants, winter rains provide all the irrigation they need.

■ **Safety.** Use heavy rubber gloves or long-handled tweezers to weed or work around spiny plants. Even the tiny prickles of innocuous-looking prickly pear cactus can irritate the skin for hours and are frustratingly difficult to extract.

■ **Weeds.** To cut down weeding chores, set plants into holes cut through a layer of a permeable landscape fabric. Cover the fabric with sand, soil, or crushed stones.

■ **Security.** Use prickly cacti as barrier plants to keep intruders away from fences or low windows.

■ **Containers.** Try smoother-leaved succulents, such as jade plant, kalanchoe, or sedums, in window boxes or pots.

Desert sun sparks a ghostly glow over spines of teddybear cactus (Opuntia bigelovii), *a sculptural, treelike Arizona native.*

Plant Swiss chard from February through mid-July. It's nutritious, delicious, and easy to grow.

February

Pacific Northwest Checklist

PLANNING & PLANTING

☑ **BARE-ROOT STOCK.** Zones 4–7: Plant roses, trees, shrubs, vines, and cane berries. It's best to put them in the ground as soon as you get them, but if you can't, pack the roots in damp compost, sawdust, or soil, and keep them out of direct sun. In Zones 1–3, bare-root planting comes later in the spring.

☑ **FLOWERING SHRUBS AND TREES.** Shop nurseries for winter-blooming shrubs and trees, including coast silk-tassel *(Garrya elliptica)*, Cornelian cherry *(Cornus mas)*, February daphne *(D. mezereum)*, fragrant winter hazel *(Corylopsis glabrescens)*, *Stachyurus praecox,* and wintersweet *(Chimonanthus praecox)*.

☑ **PEAS.** Zones 4–7: You can plant peas outside this month. Give them a head start by soaking seeds in water overnight, then place them between layers of damp paper towels on a cookie sheet and set in a warm place. Use a spray bottle of water to keep the towels damp. Once the peas have sprouted, plant them.

☑ **PRIMROSES.** Zones 4–7: Plant primroses outdoors in beds or in pots. Keep plants evenly moist to prolong bloom.

☑ **LAWNS.** In mild coastal regions, prepare planting areas for grass sod; choose a tough, drought-tolerant type, or consider installing a meadow with ornamental grasses.

MAINTENANCE

☑ **CHECK STORED BULBS.** Look over the bulbs you've been storing through the winter. If any are shriveled, sprinkle a bit of water on them to rehydrate them. If any show signs of rot, toss them out. Dahlia tubers are the exception: Cut out the bad spots, dust wounds with sulfur, and store tubers apart from the rest.

☑ **PRUNE ROSES.** Zones 4–7: George Washington's birthday is the traditional time for pruning roses. Remove injured or dead canes, cut the remaining ones back to 6 to 8 inches long, then prune plants so canes form a vase shape. Each cut cane should have one strong, outward-facing bud. For climbing roses, a light pruning is all that's needed. In Zones 1–3, wait until April to prune.

☑ **INSPECT PERENNIALS.** Zones 4–7: Look over early-blooming perennials, such as basket-of-gold, and shear dead leaves and flowers. This will encourage another round of bloom.

PEST & WEED CONTROL

☑ **BATTLE SLUGS.** When the temperatures rise, slugs crawl out to eat—primroses are a prime target. Spread bait around plants and rocks, in ground covers, and along the foundation of the house. Make sure children and pets can't get at the poison bait.

☑ **WEED.** The weeds you pull now will never get the chance to steal soil nutrients from valuable plants.

Northern California Checklist

PLANNING AND PLANTING

☑ **BUY FLOWERING PLANTS.** Zones 7–9, 14–17: Nurseries should have a good selection of early-spring-blooming shrubs and vines. Try azalea, camellia, Carolina jessamine, daphne, flowering quince, forsythia, hardenbergia, heath, or primrose jasmine.

☑ **PLANT BARE-ROOT ROSES.** Zones 7–9, 14–17: It's not too late to buy and plant several of these beauties to enjoy later in the year.

☑ **PLANT BARE-ROOT LILACS.** Zones 7–9, 14–17: The most economical way to purchase lilacs is to buy them bareroot. Call around to nurseries this month to find out who still sells bareroot plants. If you can't find them bare-root, buy them in containers, a form that most nurseries carry this time of year.

☑ **PLANT GLADIOLUS CORMS.** Zones 7–9, 14–17: For gladiolus from spring through fall, begin planting corms this month and make successive plantings every 15 to 25 days through July.

☑ **PLANT VEGETABLES.** Zones 7–9, 14–17: Set out artichokes and asparagus, and seedlings of broccoli, cabbage, cauliflower, celery (only in Zones 15–17), green onions, kohlrabi, and lettuce. Sow seeds of beets, carrots, chard, lettuce, peas, and spinach. Indoors, sow seeds of eggplant, pepper, and tomato using bottom heat (from a heating coil, or set containers on a water heater until seeds germinate, then move them into bright light); allow 6 to 8 weeks for seedlings to reach transplant size.

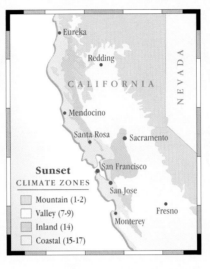

Sunset
CLIMATE ZONES
☐ Mountain (1-2)
☐ Valley (7-9)
☐ Inland (14)
☐ Coastal (15-17)

☑ **START VEGETABLES.** Zones 1–2: To get a jump on the season, start seeds of broccoli, cabbage, and cauliflower indoors or in a greenhouse at the end of the month. When seedlings are ready to plant (in 6 to 8 weeks), and the ground can be worked, set them out and drape with floating row covers.

☑ **PLANT SPRING-BLOOMING PERENNIALS.** Zones 7–9, 14–17: Plant common bleeding heart, catmint, coral bells, and other early-blooming perennials.

☑ **START SPECIALTY TOMATOES.** Zones 7–9, 14–17: Some of the tastiest varieties for Northern California are 'Brandywine', 'Gardener's Delight', 'Green Grape', and 'Stupice'. Start seeds this month for planting outside during April.

MAINTENANCE

☑ **CUT BACK WOODY PLANTS.** Zones 7–9, 14–17: To stimulate new lush growth on artemesia, butterfly bush, fuchsia, and Mexican bush sage, cut back woody stems close to the ground. If left unpruned, plants get leggy and scraggly-looking.

☑ **RECYCLE GARDEN CONTAINERS.** Many nurseries reuse plastic flats and containers or return them to growers. Instead of throwing them away after setting out plants, ask your nursery if it takes them back. If it doesn't, you can probably take the ones marked with a 1 or 2 on the bottom to your local recycling center.

PEST CONTROL

☑ **SLUG CONTROL.** Slug and snail eggs begin to hatch now; keep after them by hand-picking them at night or use traps or commercial baits.

☑ **SPRAY FOR PEACH LEAF CURL.** Zones 7–9, 14–17: Around mid- to late-February, when buds are beginning to swell on your peach trees but before any green foliage appears, apply a dormant spray to prevent peach leaf curl. This fungus distorts peach leaves and destroys the fruit. Use lime sulfur with a spreader-sticker to improve coverage; do not spray when rain is predicted to fall with 36 hours.

Southern California Checklist

PLANNING AND PLANTING

☑ **BARE-ROOT ROSES.** Finish planting bare-root roses in Zones 7–9 and 14–24.

☑ **PLANT PERENNIAL WILDFLOWERS.** In the low desert (Zone 13), it's time to set out coreopsis, evening primrose, penstemon, salvia, and *Tagetes lemmonii*.

☑ **PLANT SUMMER BULBS.** If you get glads into the ground now in Zones 14–24, they'll bloom before thrips attack and disfigure foliage and flowers. Nurseries are well stocked with gladiolus corms this month. Other summer bulbs to look for and plant now are callas, crinums, dahlias, daylilies, glory lilies, tigridia, and tuberoses.

☑ **PLANT WINTER BEDDING PLANTS.** In frost-free areas, it's not too late to set out African daisies, calendulas, cineraria, dianthus, Iceland poppies, lobelia, pansies, primroses, snapdragons, and violas. If the soil is too soggy, plant in containers.

☑ **SHOP FOR WINTER-BLOOMING SHRUBS.** Select camellias and azaleas at nurseries while in flower, but resist planting them if the ground is still soggy. Wait until the soil dries out enough to be crumbly, then plant. Other winter-blooming shrubs to look for include *Erica canaliculata*, Geraldton waxflower, and New Zealand tea tree *(Leptospermum scoparium)*. February is also an excellent time to add to your orchid collection—cymbidiums are in peak bloom this month.

Bishop
NEVADA
CALIFORNIA
San Luis Obispo
Bakersfield
Tehachapi
Santa Barbara
Lancaster
Los Angeles
Palm Springs
Sunset
CLIMATE ZONES
San Diego
1-3 7-9 11 13 14-24
MEXICO

MAINTENANCE

☑ **DRAIN STANDING WATER.** If water is pooling around plants, dig small, temporary trenches to let the water flow away. Few plants tolerate soggy roots for very long.

☑ **FINISH DORMANT-SEASON PRUNING.** Before spring growth appears, finish pruning stone-fruit trees, rosebushes, grapes, and other deciduous shrubs, trees, and vines. Consult a good pruning reference for specific instructions for each plant.

☑ **FEED PERMANENT PLANTS.** Feed ground covers, roses, shrubs, perennials, and trees. One quick method is to scatter all-purpose granular fertilizer before a storm is expected and let the rain do the watering-in. For more gradual feeding, apply a slow-release food such as cottonseed meal, bonemeal, or well-rotted manure.

☑ **TEND LAWNS.** Cool-season lawns such as tall fescue and ryegrasses grow quickly this time of year. Cut them frequently, weather permitting, with mower blades set low—1½ to 1¾ inches. Feed lawns this month, too.

PEST AND WEED CONTROL

☑ **APPLY DORMANT SPRAY.** To eliminate a lot of pesky problems later this spring, spray deciduous plants with horticultural oil. Spray rosebushes early this month, before they leaf out, to smother mites, sawfly larvae, scale, and other overwintering insects. To prevent peach leaf curl and other fungal diseases in deciduous fruit trees, add lime sulfur or fixed copper to the oil, following label directions, and spray trees before flower buds open. Spray branches, crotches, trunk, and the ground beneath the tree's drip line.

☑ **CONTROL CRABGRASS.** To prevent seeds of crabgrass and other annual weeds from germinating later this spring, apply a preemergence herbicide to lawns early this month.

☑ **TRAP GOPHERS.** The reproductive season is just beginning for gophers, so trapping now means fewer to deal with this summer.

☑ **PICK WEEDS.** Start to control weeds such as oxalis now, while the plants are still small, to prevent infestations later on in the season.

Mountain Checklist

PLANNING AND PLANTING

☑ BARE-ROOT PLANTS. If the soil can be worked where you live, you can plant bare-root stock. Nurseries carry small fruits like grapes and strawberries; cane fruits like blackberries and raspberries; all kinds of ornamental, fruit, and shade trees; and even vegetables like asparagus and horseradish.

☑ HARDY PERENNIALS. In milder parts of the intermountain West, start seeds of delphinium, hellebore, veronica, and viola in a cold frame or greenhouse for transplanting when at least two sets of true leaves appear (and when ground can be worked).

☑ SEED. Place your seed orders for spring planting this month, before suppliers run out of popular or unusual varieties.

☑ VEGETABLES. Indoors or in a greenhouse, start the seeds of cool-season vegetables such as broccoli, cabbage, cauliflower, Chinese vegetables, kale, and lettuce about 6 weeks before planting time in your region. In many areas, indoor sowing should be done late this month.

☑ LAWNS. If you're tired of maintaining a turfgrass lawn, consider planting ground covers such as bearberry or cape weed, or planting a meadow instead.

Sunset CLIMATE ZONES

☐ 1-3 ☐ 10-11

☑ WILDFLOWERS. Sow seeds of hardy wildflowers in prepared, weed-free soil. Most will bloom this season, but some of the perennials and biennials common to most wildflower mixes won't bloom until their second growing season.

MAINTENANCE

☑ CHECK STORED BULBS AND PRODUCE. Look over stored corms, tubers, and produce for shriveling and rot. You can usually rehydrate shriveled bulbs by sprinkling them with a little water. Discard any that show signs of decay except dahlia tubers: Cut the bad spots out of those, dust with sulfur, and store apart from the rest.

☑ PROTECT PLANTS FROM FROST. In the coldest parts of the West, late frost can come anytime and nip tender seedlings. Order cloches or row covers now so you'll have them when you need to cover plants.

☑ PREPARE BEDS. As soon as the ground can be worked, dig or till compost or other organic material into the soil to prepare flower and vegetable beds for spring planting. If spring comes late in your area, you can even dig in manure that's not rotted yet; by planting time it will have aged enough to fertilize plants without burning them.

☑ PRUNE TREES AND SHRUBS. Start pruning when daytime temperatures are well above freezing. First remove dead, crossing, and closely parallel branches, then prune for shape.

☑ WASH SEED-STARTING POTS. Before you start spring-blooming vegetables and flowers, wash pots and flats with a mild mixture of household bleach and water.

Southwest Checklist

PLANTING

☑ **BARE-ROOT STOCK.** Plant bare-root grapes, strawberries, blackberries, and raspberries; all kinds of ornamental, fruit, and shade trees; and even vegetables like asparagus and horseradish. It's also a good time to plant bare-root roses in Zones 12–13.

☑ **GROUND COVERS AND VINES.** Zone 11 (Las Vegas): Set out Hall's honeysuckle and *Vinca major* or *V. minor.* Zones 12–13: Set out these as well as perennial verbena, star jasmine, and trailing indigo bush *(Dalea greggii).*

☑ **PERENNIAL WILDFLOWERS.** Zones 1–2, 10–11: You can still scatter wildflower seed mixes now for bloom this summer. Zones 12–13: Set out desert marigold, evening primrose, paperflower *(Psilostrophe, cooperi),* penstemon, and salvia for bloom this spring.

☑ **BULBS.** Zones 10–13: Plant summer-blooming bulbs such as ornamental onion and montbretia. Feed established bulbs with a complete fertilizer later in the month.

☑ **VEGETABLES.** Zones 1–2: Order seed now for sowing when the weather warms up. Zones 10–11: Start seeds of cool-season crops (broccoli, cabbage, cauliflower, Chinese vegetables, and lettuce) indoors after mid-month. Zones 12–13: Start seeds of season-warm crops, including cucumbers, eggplant, melons, peppers, squash, and tomatoes, indoors for transplanting when danger of frost is past. Sow seeds of root crops (beets, carrots, radishes), peas, and spinach in prepared soil.

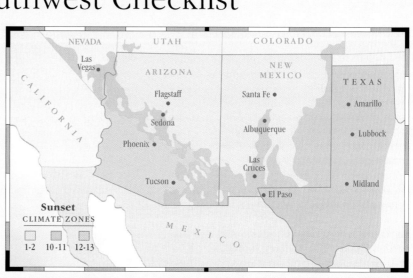

MAINTENANCE

☑ **FEED BEARDED IRISES.** Late in the month, scratch a complete fertilizer into the soil over iris rhizomes; water it in well.

☑ **FEED CITRUS.** If you didn't feed citrus last month, scatter a complete fertilizer over the entire root zone of each tree; water it in thoroughly.

☑ **FEED ROSES.** On a late-February day when nighttime temperatures are forecast to remain above freezing, water established plants, let the soil drain, apply a complete fertilizer, and water again.

☑ **FEED WINTER RYEGRASS.** Zones 12–13: Apply 2½ pounds of ammonium sulfate per 1,000 square feet of lawn and water it in well.

☑ **MAINTAIN DRIP SYSTEMS.** Clean or replace your drip system's filters and check each emitter. If you find one that can't be unclogged, install a new emitter next to it.

☑ **PREPARE SOIL.** Get beds ready for spring planting by digging compost or other organic matter into the soil. If the soil is very alkaline in your garden, you can adjust its pH and increase fertility by adding 2 pounds of ammonium phosphate and 3 pounds of soil sulfur per 100 square feet.

PEST CONTROL

☑ **CONTROL APHIDS.** Zones 12–13: Check new growth for aphids. When you see them, blast them off with a jet of water and, if necessary, follow up with a spray of insecticidal soap.

Strawberries

Sweet, juicy strawberries are among the easiest fruits for home gardeners to grow—and one of the most productive, too. June-bearing types bear one crop of high-quality berries each year in late spring or early summer. Everbearing (day-neutral) varieties peak in summer and continue to produce into autumn; though they bear fruit for a longer period than June-bearing sorts, they tend to be less vigorous.

Strawberries are planted anytime from now to early spring; where winters are mild, you can also plant in autumn. Plants are usually sold bareroot. Take care that the roots don't dry out. Just before you set plants out, trim roots to 6 inches to make planting easier. Space plants 14 to 18 inches apart in rows 2 to 2½ feet apart.

Most strawberries spread by runners. To get large plants with smaller yields of big berries, pinch off all the runners. For a heavier yield of smaller berries, allow some of the runners to grow and fruit; space them 7 to 10 inches apart in a circle around the mother plant, cutting off extras so the bed doesn't become too crowded.

Fertilize June bearers twice a year—very lightly when growth begins, then more heavily after fruiting. Everbearing types prefer consistent light fertilizing; feed them every 2 weeks. Note that heavy feeding of either type in spring leads to excessive leafy growth, soft fruit, and reduced sweetness.

Where winters are cold, it's crucial to mulch strawberries to prevent winter damage. In late November, after temperatures have dipped to freezing several times, lay straw loosely over the plants.

Replace plants with new ones as they begin to decline, usually after 3 years.

Pests and diseases

Strawberries are subject to mites, rose chafers, strawberry root weevils, and verticillium wilt. To reduce problems, plant only certified disease-free plants; also remove and dispose of diseased foliage and rotten fruit.

PLANTING DEPTH FOR STRAWBERRIES

Plant strawberries so that the crown is just above soil level (a buried crown will rot) and the topmost roots are at least ¼ inch beneath the soil (exposed roots will dry out).

Crown

Correctly planted strawberry

Too low   Too high

Berries by the barrel

Strawberries are easy to grow in containers. They will flourish in a half-barrel, tub, or, of course, the ever-popular strawberry jar—the classic pocket planter.

Set out about a dozen plants if you're planting in a barrel; to plant in a pocket planter, insert one plant per pocket and a couple at the top. Plant in standard potting soil, with the container placed where berries will get at least 6 hours of full sun daily.

To make the plant stronger, pinch off the first flowers. Water regularly so that soil stays moist, but don't overwater or the fruit will taste weak. Fertilize the same way you would strawberries in the garden. Plants usually bear a small harvest the first year, more in years to follow.

Growing and Caring for Vines

Gardeners with space limitations often turn to vines as a way to include more plants in a pocket-handkerchief garden. Many choices grow happily in containers, adding color and privacy to decks and patios.

Other than the fact that all have long, pliable stems (when they're young, in any case), vines differ greatly. They may be evergreen, semievergreen, or deciduous; they may be modest in size or rampant enough to engulf trees or scale high walls. Many grow well in ordinary garden soil with an annual springtime application of fertilizer, but a few need rich, well-amended soil and regular fertilizer throughout the growing season. Some require ample moisture, but a great many perform well with little additional water once established.

Climate preferences vary too, so always match your climate zone to the vines you want to grow. Many are native to semitropical parts of the world and cannot tolerate cold temperatures—or they may remain lush and green all year where winters are mild, but drop their foliage or die to the ground during winter in colder areas. Some vines are well behaved in temperate zones but grow with great vigor in warmer regions, overwhelming their support (and possibly the entire garden, too!).

Though most vines are quite easy to grow, they do need an appropriate support structure and some attention to training while young. Once they obtain the right size for their location, they'll usually require periodic pruning to stay in bounds.

The stems of vigorous twiners like this clematis tend to become snarled. Often the best way to sort out the problem is just to snip through the tangles. Resultant dead growth will be easier to identify and remove later on.

Vines can do many things

Soften a fence. Weave vigorous growers such as clematis (above), passion vine, or honeysuckle through an openwork fence to hide unsightly chain link or disguise old or sagging wood.

Another option is to plant vines beside the fence and allow them to grow and dangle over the top in lavish sprays. Danglers with showy flowers include rambler roses, potato vine, and clematis.

Brighten an entry. Train woody vines such as wisteria, trumpet vine, climbing roses, or bougainvillea (above) to frame entryways, gables, and balconies. Their beautiful flowers can dress up plain house walls or soften an angular deck or unattractive railings. Wires fastened to eye screws will hold main branches to the wall, or the vine may be run up porch or deck posts.

Create screens and boundaries. Quick climbers such as morning glory or more permanent perennials such as ivy, trumpet vine (above), or Virginia creeper can cover plain fences and walls with color. Vines covering a boundary fence increase the feeling of enclosure on the garden side, while the thick cover of greenery also serves as an attractive windbreak or privacy screen.

Training and pruning vines

Until a vine gets a firm hold on its support, you may need to tie it in place with twine. (For heavy vines, you can use thin rope or canvas strips.) For clinging vines, you might tack plastic mesh over the stems until they adhere. Once the stems of twining and sprawling vines lengthen, you can weave them through any openwork support, such as a trellis or wire fence.

To encourage bushy growth on young vines, pinch out the stems' terminal buds. If you want just a few vertical stems, though (for a tracery of growth around a column, for example), don't pinch. Instead, remove all but one or two long stems at the base.

Once a vine is established, you'll need to prune it periodically. The job is often done late in the dormant season, just before new growth begins, though you may want to wait to prune early-spring bloomers such as Carolina jessamine *(Gelsemium sempervirens)* until flowering has finished. Some vines are so vigorous they can be pruned at any time.

All vines are pruned by similar methods. Start by removing dead and damaged growth. If the stems are so tangled that you can't tell what to remove, snip through the mat of stems here and there; later on, remove those that have died. If the vine is such a haystack of growth that you can hardly find the support, make heading cuts low enough to reduce the vine's length by half. Then untangle the stems and make thinning cuts to remove unwanted growth at ground level. As a last resort, cut the entire vine to the ground in late winter or early spring and start training it all over again.

Clinging vines need regular monitoring. If you don't keep them under control, they'll crawl under eaves and wood shakes, causing structural damage; if removed, they'll take paint and plaster with them. Prune out any stems growing out of bounds. Once every few years, prune more extensively, cutting out wayward branches and any that have pulled away from their support.

FOUR TYPES OF VINES

How a vine climbs will influence your choice of supports and training.

- **Twining vines.** New growth twists or spirals as it grows around other growth, new or old, or around itself and nearby plants as well. Most twining vines are best supported by a cord or wire.
- **Vines with twining tendrils.** Specialized growths along the stems or at the ends of leaves reach out and wrap around whatever is handy. Tendrils grow out straight until they make contact, then they contract into a spiral.
- **Clinging vines.** Some have tendrils with suction-cup discs at the ends; others have hooklike claws or tips on tendrils that hook into small irregularities of a flat surface. Still others possess small roots along the stems; these roots cling fast even to vertical surfaces.
- **Vines that require tying.** These vines must be tied to a support. Some—climbing roses, for example—can stabilize themselves in adjacent shrubs or trees with their thorns. Others are naturally sprawling but will grow reasonably flat as long as you tie and train them.

Clinging vines are notorious trespassers; be sure to remove poorly placed growth while it is young.

The showy red blossoms of scarlet runner bean vine are followed by tasty beans. This is a twining vine and needs strong support.

Sowing Seeds

Many annuals, wildflowers, and vegetables can be seeded directly in the garden, either broadcast over a bed to give a planted-by-Nature look (see instructions on facing page) or sown in the traditional rows of a vegetable or cutting garden. Many other plants, however, are best raised from seed sown in containers. These include slow-growing perennials, plants with expensive or very fine seed, and warm-season vegetables and annuals that you want to start when the garden soil is still too cold and wet for in-ground planting.

Various seed-starting trays and pots are available at nurseries and through mail-order catalogs.

Preparing the soil

Whether you're sowing a wildflower mixture or several kinds of annuals for a showy border, start by preparing the soil. Remove weeds, then loosen the soil and work in amendments with a spading fork, shovel, or rototiller. Add a complete fertilizer in the amount directed on the label. Finally, smooth the soil with a rake. If rain doesn't do the job for you, moisten the bed thoroughly a few days before you intend to plant. At sowing time, the soil should be moist but not soggy.

What's a hill?

"Hill" is a term that causes a lot of misunderstanding. In gardening, a "hill" refers to a grouping of seeds or plants in a cluster, not necessarily on a mound. A hill of squash or corn can consist of two or three plants growing together, level with the rest of the garden. Hills, or clusters, are usually contrasted with rows, in which plants are spaced equal distances apart in a line.

Planting in rows

To grow vegetables or annuals in rows, prepare the soil as described above, but do not dig in fertilizer; it will be applied later.

Next, make furrows for the seeds, following the packet instructions for depth of furrows and spacing between them. If possible, lay out the rows in a north-south direction, so that both sides will receive an equal amount of sunlight during the day. Form the furrows with a hoe, rake, or stick; for perfectly straight rows, use a board or taut string as a guide, as shown below. Now dig two furrows alongside each seed furrow—one on either side, each 2 inches away from and 1 inch deeper than the seed furrow. Apply fertilizer in these furrows, following label recommendations for amount of fertilizer per foot of row. This technique puts the fertilizer where plant roots can best use it.

Sow seeds evenly, spacing them as the packet directs. You can tear off a small corner of the packet and tap the seeds out as you move along, or pour a small quantity of seed into your palm and scatter pinches of seed as evenly as possible. Larger seeds, such as beans, can be placed individually by hand.

Water the furrows with a fine spray, then keep the soil surface moist but not dripping wet until the seeds sprout. Thin overcrowded seedlings while they're still small; if you wait too long to thin, the plants will develop poorly, and you'll have a harder time removing an individual plant without disturbing those around it.

Sowing seeds in containers

Many plants get off to a better start when sown in containers and transplanted to garden beds later in the season. It's easier to provide plants in containers with the warm temperatures and bright light they need for quick growth, and easier to protect them from insects and birds as well. The seed packet information will help you decide when to plant; most annual flowers and vegetables should be sown 4 to 8 weeks before it's time to transplant them to the garden.

KEEPING ROWS STRAIGHT

Lay a board on the soil surface; then plant or make a furrow along its edge.

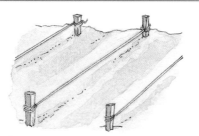

Or stretch string between two stakes and plant beneath it.

Container choices

Convenience, cost, and reusability will determine which containers you use. If you won't be around to water daily or don't plan to transplant seedlings into another container before planting them out, use 2- to 4-inch-diameter containers or flats with individual cells.

Plastic flats with no dividers are an old favorite. They're readily available from garden supply stores and mail-order catalogs, and free when you buy seedlings at nurseries.

Plastic cell-packs and 2- to 4-inch plastic pots, recycled from nursery purchases, are easy to obtain and use.

Peat pots are inexpensive, and because you plant out seedlings pot and all, such pots minimize disturbance to roots. Keep them moist (so roots can penetrate them easily).

Plastic foam flats with tapered individual cells are sold by nurseries and seed catalogs. They come in several cell sizes; some have capillary matting that draws water from a reservoir, making care much easier.

In addition to the containers already discussed, you can use any appropriate household items—plastic cups, yogurt containers, cut-down milk cartons, or foil baking pans. Be sure to punch several drainage holes in any container that lacks them, since seedlings will die if water collects around their roots.

If you're reusing old pots, scrub them out and soak them for 30 minutes in a solution of 9 parts water to 1 part household bleach to destroy any disease organisms.

Top: To help peat pots retain moisture after seeding, set them in 1½ inches of moist soil in a flat. Bottom: Plant two seeds in each cell of a plastic foam flat; later, thin to one seedling per cell.

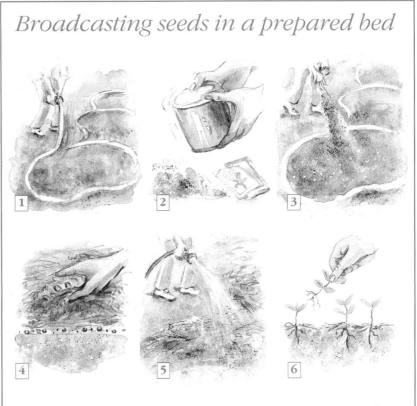

Broadcasting seeds in a prepared bed

1 For a patterned planting, outline the areas for each kind of seed with lime, flour, or stakes and string. You may want to put a label in each area.

2 To achieve a more even distribution, shake each kind of seed (or an entire wildflower seed mixture) in a covered can with several times its bulk of white sand.

3 Scatter the seed-sand mixture as evenly as possible over the bed or individual planting areas; then rake lightly, barely covering the seeds with soil. Take care not to bury them too deeply.

4 Spread a very thin layer of mulch (such as sifted compost) over the bed to help retain moisture, keep the surface from crusting, and hide the seeds from birds.

5 Water with a fine spray. Keep the soil surface barely damp until the seeds sprout; once seedlings are up, gradually decrease watering frequency.

6 When seedlings have two sets of true leaves, thin those that are too closely spaced. Transplant the thinned seedlings to fill empty spaces in the bed.

Growing medium, planting, and aftercare

Use the seed-starting mixes or potting soil sold at nurseries, or make your own by combining equal parts of peat moss, vermiculite, and perlite. Dampen the mix before use—it should be moist but not soggy.

Fill each container to within ½ inch of the rim with damp mix, firming it gently. Check the seed packet for recommended planting depth. You can make furrows or scatter the seeds over the soil surface. If using containers with individual cells, plant two seeds per cell. Cover the seeds with mix, taking care not to cover them too deeply, then label each container with the plant name and sowing date. Loosely cover the containers with wet newspaper, damp burlap, or foil; this keeps the soil moist but allows air to get in, preventing fungal growth.

If the seeds need light to germinate (this will be noted on the packet), gently press them into the potting mix, but do not cover them with more mix. Loosely cover the containers with a sheet of clear plastic.

Place the containers in a warm spot. After 3 days, check daily for germination. As soon as green leaves arch out of the soil, uncover the containers and move them into bright light (but not direct sunlight); otherwise, the seedlings will become spindly and weak. Use a greenhouse, a sunny south window, or fluorescent light. Set fluorescents 6 to 8 inches above the tops of the plants and turn them on 12 to 14 hours a day.

Water plants when the mix feels dry, spraying with a fine mist. Or place the containers in a tray or sink holding a few inches of water; the mix will absorb adequate moisture within a few hours.

After the seedlings form their first set of true leaves, fertilize them weekly, using a fertilizer sold for starting seeds or a liquid type diluted to half strength.

When the seedlings have developed their second set of true leaves, transplant or thin them, as shown below. Thin seedlings in individual pots or cells to one plant. If you want to save most of the germinated plants, transplant the seedlings to larger individual containers for growth to planting-out size.

To transplant seedlings, fill each new container with moist planting mix. Loosen the soil around the seedlings with a kitchen fork or spoon then carefully lift each one out. Or lift a clump of seedlings and carefully tease apart the tangled roots. Handle seedlings by their leaves to avoid damaging the tender stems. Poke a hole in the new container's planting mix, insert the seedling, and firm soil around it. Water the transplant right away. Keep the containers out of direct sunlight for a few days to let the transplants recover from the move.

HARDENING OFF

About 10 days before the seedlings are ready to plant outside, harden them off so they can withstand bright sun and cooler temperatures. Stop fertilizing them, and set them outdoors for several hours each day in a wind-sheltered spot that receives filtered light. A cold frame is useful. Over the next week or so, gradually increase exposure until the plants are in full sun all day (shade lovers are an exception; they shouldn't be exposed to day-long sun). Then set them out in the garden.

DAMPING OFF

If your seedlings suddenly collapse and die, a fungal disease called "damping off" or "seed and seedling rot" may be to blame. In one type of damping off, the seedling's stem collapses at or near the soil surface; in another type, the seedling rots before it emerges from the soil, or the seed decays before it even sprouts.

To prevent these problems, use pasteurized potting mix and new or thoroughly washed and disinfected containers. Try using seeds treated with a fungicide. Take care not to overwater seedlings; be sure to provide good air circulation and ventilation, so tops of seedlings stay dry and standing moisture is kept to a minimum. Thinning seedlings to eliminate crowding is also helpful.

THINNING SEEDLINGS

Thin seedlings to 1 to 2 inches apart by pinching them off with your fingers or snipping them off with scissors.

TRANSPLANTING SEEDLINGS

Transplant seedlings to the garden or to a larger container when they have at least their second set of true leaves.

Cold Frames and Hotbeds

Used to protect tender plants or rooted cuttings during the colder months, a cold frame is simply a box with a transparent lid or cover. It acts as a passive solar energy collector and reservoir. During the day, the sun's rays heat the air and soil in the frame; at night, the heat absorbed by the soil radiates out, keeping the plants warm.

A cold frame is useful at other times of the year as well. In spring, it provides an ideal environment for hardening off seedlings started indoors. Seeds of many plants can be sown directly in the frame and grown until it's time to transplant them. In summer, you can replace the cover with shade cloth or lath, creating a nursery for cuttings.

Set up your cold frame in a site protected from harsh winds. To ensure that the frame receives as much sunlight as possible, orient it to face south or southwest. Sinking the frame 8 to 10 inches into the ground increases heat retention significantly. Make sure the location has good drainage, since you don't want water to collect around the frame after every rain. To speed the germination of seeds and the rooting of some kinds of cuttings, convert your cold frame to a hotbed, as shown below.

Building a cold frame and a hotbed

1 Start by selecting a cover, since its size will determine the dimensions of the frame. Good choices include an old window sash or storm window. You can also make a cover out of clear acrylic or fiberglass sheets sandwiched between narrow strips of wood and reinforced at the corners with metal corner plates. Polyethylene film stapled to a wooden frame is another option; it's quick and inexpensive, though it lasts only a year or so. Make sure the cover isn't too heavy to lift easily. Don't make it too wide or you'll have a hard time reaching the plants inside the frame; a width of 2½ to 3 feet is ideal. A length of at least 4 feet will allow you to grow a variety of plants.

Build the frame from lumber, such as rot-resistant redwood or cedar or less expensive plywood or scrap lumber. The frame should slope from about 1½ feet high at the back to a foot high at the front; this traps the most heat and lets rainwater run off. For strength, reinforce the corners of the box with vertical posts. Attach the cover with galvanized steel hinges and apply weather stripping around the top edges of the box.

2 Ventilation is vital to prevent overheating. A minimum-maximum thermometer is useful for keeping track of temperature fluctuations. Plan to prop open the cover when the temperature inside reaches 70° to 75°F. Close the cover in late afternoon to trap heat. (If you won't be around during the day, you can buy a nonelectric vent controller that will automatically open and close the cover at a preset temperature.) On very cold nights, drape the frame with an old blanket or piece of carpet to provide extra insulation.

To convert your cold frame to a hotbed, add an electric heating cable. Make a base for the cable by spreading a 2- to 3-inch layer of sand or vermiculite. Lay the cable, spacing the loops 6 to 8 inches apart and keeping it 3 inches away from the sides of the frame. Add another inch of sand, then a sheet of window screen or hardware cloth to protect the cable. Most growers add another, 4- to 6-inch-thick layer of sand in which to sink pots of plants.

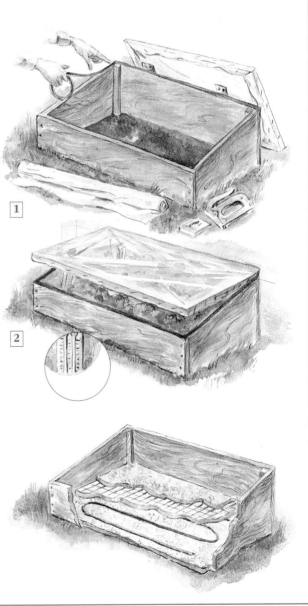

Roses

The classification of roses can be bewildering, but it's important to know what you're getting. Simply put, the three main groups are the modern roses (hybrid teas, grandifloras, floribundas, polyanthas, miniatures, climbing roses, and shrub roses); old roses (albas, centifolias, damasks, gallicas, Chinas, moss roses, Bourbons, damask perpetuals, hybrid perpetuals, Noisettes, and teas); and the wild species and their hybrids.

The best known of these are modern hybrid teas, which bear large, usually full-petaled flowers, mostly one to a long stem. They are favorites for cut flowers and generally grow 3 to 6 feet high. Floribundas are shrubby roses that produce large clusters of flowers. Most bloom over a long period and are excellent, easy-care landscape plants. They generally grow 3 to 6 feet high, but can be upright or spreading. Grandifloras are a diverse group of roses with flowers borne singly or in clusters. They most resemble hybrid teas in form but can be larger and more vigorous growing. Miniature roses have small leaves and tiny flowers. They grow anywhere from 12 inches to 4 feet high and are ideal for containers or as edgings. Climbers need to be tied to a strong support like an arbor or trellis to stay upright. They grow 8 to 20 feet high.

Shrub roses are a catch-all category. They vary in size and form, and include hybrid musks, David Austin's English roses, ground cover roses, and hardy Canadian roses.

Old-fashioned roses, also called old, antique, heirloom, or heritage roses, are shrubby (4 to 8 feet) and can be tough as nails. Many can be discovered in old cemeteries, still blooming despite decades of neglect. On the downside, most bloom only once a year, but their green foliage (and thorns) still make them useful as backdrops, boundary hedges, and fence coverings.

Many climbing roses, including 'Kathleen', need only enough pruning to keep them in shape. They'll happily scramble over fences, walls, even roofs. Deadheading faded flowers will prolong bloom.

Rose rules

Buy big. Look for plump, healthy bare-root plants in winter (or order bare-root from mail-order sources in late winter for delivery at planting time in your region). Look for roses numbered 1 or 1½, with three living canes on each plant. During the growing season, container-grown plants allow for a better selection, because you can evaluate bloom color and fragrance.

Perfect planting. Although some experts advise letting roses adapt to your soil, it's generally recommended to loosen the soil to a depth of 2 feet and amend with rich organic matter, such as compost. Add lime if the soil is acidic.

Shine on. Roses need at least 6 hours of full sun during their growing season. Don't plant in shade or canes will grow spindly and weak.

Fresh air. Good air circulation is crucial for warding off diseases such as mildew, black spot, and rust. Set out bushes so they'll be at least 1 foot apart when mature.

Mulch is a must. Maintain a 1–3-inch circle of mulch around roses, leaving a 3-inch circle of open soil around each plant's trunk.

Pest prevention. To stave off pests such as scale, spray stems with horticultural oil during the dormant season. Include a fungicide to help prevent diseases.

Cut to size. Prune roses according to your zone when new leaf buds begin to swell in late winter or early spring. Shear them to a lower height or prune arching shrubs by thinning out old, grayish canes, crossing stems, and any dead branches. Some roses need only light, occasional pruning.

Not too wet. Water roses deeply during the first year and directly after the first bloom. Set drip emitters on '1 gph' or 'high' for one hour, twice a week—three times a week during hot weather. But water well-established roses only once a week.

Pest patrol. It's wise to inspect roses for pests once a week. Look for aphids, ants crawling on stems, leaves sticky with aphid honeydew, or webbing near leaf stems (caused by spider mites or leaf-chewing caterpillars).

Growing hips. Stop snipping blooms by Halloween in mild-winter areas, mid-August in cold-winter areas, to allow roses to form their fruits (called hips). This helps them enter their dormant phase for a healthy winter rest. Rake away fallen leaves and debris, which may harbor overwintering insects and diseases.

Rough and ready rugosas

Rugosa roses are easily identified by their pleated, or leathery, leaves, which help protect them from insect damage and foliage diseases. Harsh conditions, such as sub-zero temperatures, drying winds, and salt spray do not diminish their deep green foliage, abundant blooms, and ample fall hips.

These roses are not for the formal garden, for their bloom is intermittent and they grow in a sprawling fashion more suited to hillsides and casual terraces. Wild at heart, rugosas are at their best in full sun and well-drained soils. They rarely need spraying with chemicals or feeding with fertilizer.

A riot of roses billowing from a profusion of perennials is opulent testament to the value of proper siting and good care.

A special rose garden

Most gardeners have brought home a rosebush or two that attracted every insect on the block and caught every disease on the afternoon breeze. Many believe that it's impossible to grow roses without inviting plagues that require pesticides. However, a special Southern California public rose garden is proving this isn't so.

The Victorian Rose Garden at the Arboretum of Los Angeles County is jampacked with visitors from March through November. Yet this gorgeous rose garden requires no pesticides. Prevention is key. For one thing, copious amounts of organic material were worked into the soil before the roses were planted, and additional organic mulches and fertilizers are added throughout the year. Another preventive measure is found in the roses themselves—all strong, disease-resistant varieties. They include the popular David Austin types, the old garden roses, and early hybrid teas. By eliminating susceptible roses from the garden, its managers have gone a long way toward reducing the need for disease and pest control.

How the garden stays healthy

In the spring and early summer, gardeners control aphids by knocking them off the roses with streams of water. Hosing is done often to keep this insect population under control (100% of aphid offspring are female, and they are born pregnant). Later, naturally occurring ladybugs keep the aphid population in check. In late summer, water is also used to knock off spider mites. The grasshoppers are caught by hand—not hard to do, volunteers say, once you get the hang of it.

Overhead watering early in the day keeps most mildew under control; hand-spraying with a water-and-baking-soda mixture handles severe problems. If a rose is attacked by black spot or rust, its leaves are stripped off, diseased leaves are carefully picked up, old mulch is replaced, and the plant is sprayed with a summer-oil-and-water mixture to prevent recurrence.

Thrips—difficult to control even with a pesticide—are few, and their damage is slight, so no attempt is made to eradicate them. The lack of thrips is attributed to the choice of roses and to the soil, fertilizer, and mulches that keep them in good health.

If you look at individual bushes, you will find some rust, mildew, and evidence of insects. But you have to look closely. Step back just a few steps, and what you see is a healthy and beautifully blooming garden.

'Desprez à Fleur Jaune' (climbing Noisette rose, France, c. 1830) at the Victorian Rose Garden.

Planting Bare-root Stock

The difference between bare-root and container-grown nursery plants has little to do with plant quality. Bare-root roses, deciduous trees, and shrubs are usually sold from autumn to late winter when they are dormant and less bulky to handle. (Mail-order plants are usually shipped this way.) Bare-root specimens get an early start in your garden when they awaken and leaf out as the weather warms. Roses, citrus, Japanese maples, and some other plants are sometimes grafted (also called "budded") onto a hardy or more vigorous rootstock. Typically, own-root plants are a little smaller when purchased. Not all plants are available bare-root. Conifers, broad-leaf evergreens, and shrubs with delicate root systems (such as *Bougainvillea),* are typically sold in containers.

1. *Remove packing material from the roots and soak the plant in a bucket of water. Dig a hole at least 2 feet wide and 1½ feet deep. Shovel some loosened soil back into the hole to make a cone-shaped mound. If the soil is sandy or heavy, add some additional organic material such as compost to your backfill mix.*

2. *Spread the roots of the plant over the soil cone. Trim any long roots with sharp shears so they will fit into the hole without bending. Prune off any torn or damaged roots as well. If you are planting a large tree, have a helper hold the trunk as you arrange the roots around the cone of soil.*

Top: Bare-root plants may be grafted onto a rootstock (left) or grown on the plant's own roots (right). Own-root plants usually start out smaller. Bottom: Plants in nursery containers are actively growing in 1-gallon, 5-gallon, or larger plastic or wooden containers. At this stage, you can evaluate leaf and flower color, fragrance, and other qualities.

3. *Lay your shovel handle across the hole to determine the soil level. Add or remove soil on the cone to set the plant so that the crown or bud union (the bump on the lower stem at the point of a graft) is just above the soil level. Where winter temperatures drop below 10°F, place the bud union just below soil level.*

4. *Gently shovel backfill soil into the hole, firming it over the roots to stabilize the plant. Fill the rest of the hole with water to soak and settle the soil. After the water drains, finish backfilling with more soil. Tamp the earth firmly and then water the planted area gently until it is well soaked.*

Garden-friendly Roses

Be bold with roses and you can create a spectacularly colorful landscape. But first, you may have to change the way you think about these familiar plants. Many gardeners grew up in the heyday of hybrid teas—long-stemmed beauties with perfectly formed buds that make wonderful cut flowers but so-so landscape plants. But lately, western gardeners are trying floribundas, grandifloras, and English roses, as well as rediscovering old roses for hedges and borders.

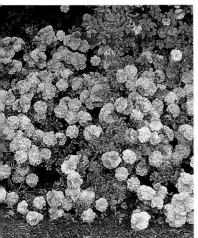

'Mary Rose'

The best roses for landscape use are repeat bloomers—attractive, compact plants with clean-looking foliage and strong resistance to pests. While many roses meet these criteria, some stand out for particular uses.

Small hedges, borders. As a group, floribundas are probably the finest landscape roses. They bear large clusters of flowers atop compact 3- to 6-foot-tall plants that are covered with glossy green leaves. Spaced 18 to 24 inches apart, they make excellent hedges, borders, or edgings along garden paths. Dependable varieties include white 'Iceberg', pink 'Simplicity', yellow 'Sun Flare', and red 'Europeana'. The polyantha rose, a parent of many modern floribundas, carries abundant small flowers in big clusters, making it an excellent hedge as well. Particularly attractive are 'The Fairy' and 'China Doll'.

Ground covers. For low raised beds, banks, and sunny parking strips, roses that grow no taller than 2 feet and spread their canes widely are perfect. Choose vigorous, disease-resistant growers such as 'Flower Carpet', with its bright pink flowers.

Fence drapes. Some climbers (leaners, really, that do not cling to surfaces on their own) are particularly beautiful against weathered split-rail fences. Easy-care types include red 'Blaze', 'White Dawn', coral 'Cl. Mrs. Sam McGredy', and multicolored 'Joseph's Coat'.

Mixed borders. Some roses combine handsomely with perennials in mixed borders. 'Graham Thomas' (a yellow English rose), 'Sally Holmes' (a pale pink to white shrub rose), and 'Dainty Bess' (a rose pink hybrid tea) pair well with perennials like catmint, cranesbill, lavender, and *Salvia superba* 'East Friesland'.

Trellises, arbors. Some climbing roses are quite vigorous and are at their best when supported on sturdy trellises or redwood arches. Two climbers to consider are 'Cl. Cécile Brunner', a polyantha with pale pink flowers that has a romantic old-fashioned look (especially when trained against white lattice), and the evergreen 'Lady Banks' rose, with large clusters of small yellow or white flowers that are stunning against a sun-splashed adobe wall.

Rosa banksiae

Cottage gardens. For a soft, romantic look, try old roses—notably the mounding, shrubby types with long, graceful canes, such as hybrid perpetuals and some Bourbons. In cold mountain areas, rugosa roses are good choices.

The stiff, fleshy leaves of Aloe polyphylla *spiral outward—either clockwise or counterclockwise—from a central rosette.*

March

Pacific Northwest Checklist

SHOPPING & PLANTING

☑ **PLANT BULBS, CORMS, AND TUBERS. Zones 4–7:** Plant summer-blooming bulbs (acidanthera, callas, crocosmia, gladiolus, ranunculus, and tigridia) from mid-month on. If a hard frost is predicted, cover bulb beds with 1 inch of organic mulch.

☑ SHOP FOR CAMELLIAS. **Zones 4–7:** Nurseries have a supply of plants in bloom. Buy now and slip them into decorative containers near a window or on a deck while in flower. When blooms fade, get the plants in the ground.

☑ **LAWNS.** Throughout the Northwest, now is the ideal time to start a new lawn. First, spade and rake the top 6 to 12 inches of soil to a fine consistency and amend it with organic matter. Next, lay sod or rake in a seed mix of bent, blue, fescue, and ryegrasses. In Zones 4–7, bluegrass should be the predominant seed. Water the newly planted lawn regularly.

☑ **MOW GROUND COVERS AND MEADOWS.** To encourage ground covers such as creeping lilyturf and St. Johnswort to produce strong new growth, mow them to the ground. Mow and fertilize meadow grasses.

☑ **SOW COOL-SEASON CROPS. Zones 4–7:** Sow seeds of beets, carrots, chard, lettuce, peas, radishes, spinach, and most members of the cabbage family.

☑ **START WARM-SEASON CROPS. Zones 1–7:** Start seeds for tomatoes, peppers, and other heat-loving crops indoors—on windowsills or in greenhouses. When the weather warms, transplant the seedlings outdoors.

MAINTENANCE

☑ **CLEAN BEDS.** Follow up on your fall cleanup efforts by going over beds again this month. Rake up and dispose of wind-downed debris. Cut back perennials that you may have left standing to provide winter interest. Pull weeds that have sprouted. Give beds a top dressing with fresh compost or soil. You may want to blast moss and slime off paving with a pressure washer.

☑ **DIVIDE PERENNIALS. Zones 4–7:** Dig, divide, and replant overcrowded summer- and fall-blooming perennials early this month. In Zones 1–3, wait until April to do this job. Wherever you garden, wait until autumn to divide spring-flowering perennials. If you divide them now, you'll miss a year of bloom.

☑ **FERTILIZE LAWNS. Zones 1–7:** Start your lawn feeding program this month. Use a fertilizer with a 3-1-2 ratio of nitrogen, phosphorus, and potassium. Apply ½ pound of actual nitrogen per 1,000 square feet of turf. Water it in thoroughly.

☑ **FEED ORNAMENTALS.** Fertilize spring-blooming trees and shrubs with a complete fertilizer. Feed azaleas and camellias after flowering; use an acid-type fertilizer. Feed roses with a commercial rose food every 4–6 weeks until October.

☑ **PRUNE CLEMATIS. Zones 4–7:** Cut back summer-flowering clematis now. After pruning, scatter a handful of fertilizer at the base of plants (10-10-10 is a good choice). In Zones 1–3, do this job after danger of a hard frost has passed. In all zones, prune back spring-flowering varieties as soon as they finish blooming.

PEST CONTROL

☑ **SLUGS.** Whatever your method (hand-picking, beer traps, or poison bait), go after slugs now.

Northern California Checklist

PLANTING

☑ PLANT CITRUS. Zones 7–9, 14–17: For fast establishment, purchase young trees in 5-gallon cans. Try 'Washington' orange, 'Eureka' or 'Meyer' lemon, 'Oroblanco' grapefruit-pummelo hybrid, or 'Moro' blood orange. In Zones 15–17, try 'Trovita' orange, which not only sweetens better than other oranges in cool temperatures, but also does well in heat. In Zones 7–9, wait until the end of the month to plant.

☑ PLANT STRAWBERRIES. Zones 7–9, 14–17: Select a site in full sun with well-drained soil. Set plants in the ground so the base of the crown (the area from which the leaves rise) is level with the soil; roots should barely be covered. Mulch the soil, water regularly, and keep the bed free of weeds.

☑ PLANT SUMMER BULBS. Zones 7–9, 14–17: Calla, canna, dahlia, gladiolus, and tigridia bulbs are available at nurseries this month. Plant in well-drained soil or containers (use only dwarf varieties of cannas in containers); mix a balanced fertilizer into the soil before planting.

☑ START VEGETABLES. Zones 7–9, 14–17: Make successive sowings of these spring vegetables right in the ground: beets, carrots, lettuce, peas, radishes, spinach, Swiss chard, and turnips. Set out broccoli, cauliflower, and cabbage seedlings. Plant potato tubers. If the last frost has passed, you can also start planting the first warm-season crops when they appear in nurseries. Most need warm (at least 60°F) soil to thrive. To give plants a boost, plant through black plastic and use floating row covers.

Sunset
CLIMATE ZONES
- ☐ Mountain (1-2)
- ☐ Valley (7-9)
- ☐ Inland (14)
- ☐ Coastal (15-17)

MAINTENANCE

☑ CARE FOR HERBS. Zones 7–9, 14–17: To rejuvenate perennial herbs such as mint and sage, cut back old or dead growth on established plants, then fertilize and water the plants to stimulate new growth. Also set out fresh plants of herbs, such as mint, oregano, parsley, rosemary, sage, and thyme, in loose, well-drained soil. You'll find them at nurseries this month in cell-packs and 2- to 4-inch pots.

☑ FERTILIZE. Feed spring-bloomers with a complete fertilizer. Feed azaleas and camellias with an acid-type plant food after they bloom.

☑ ROSES. Zones 1–2: Prune roses unless temperatures dip below freezing at night.

☑ CHECK DRIP SYSTEMS. Zones 7–9, 14–17: Flush out sediment from filters and check screens for algae (clean the screens with a toothbrush if necessary). Turn on the water and check to make sure all emitters are dripping. Clean or replace clogged ones. (If you can't get an emitter out, install a new one next to it.) Check for leaks in the lines and repair them if necessary.

PEST CONTROL

☑ WASH APHIDS OFF ROSES. Zones 7–9, 14–17: As the weather warms, aphids start appearing on succulent new growth and rosebuds. To control them in the least toxic way possible, blast aphids off with a strong blast of water from a hose. If water doesn't control them, spray with insecticidal soap (you can also use a more toxic control, such as malathion).

☑ CONTROL MOSQUITOES. Zones 7–9, 14–17: Mosquitoes breed in standing water left in birdbaths, buckets, old pots, and ponds. Dump out or drain the water from pots or saucers. Clean birdbaths regularly. In ponds, float donut-shaped briquettes on the water (one per 100 square feet of surface area), which release *Bacillus thuringiensis israeliensis* for more than 30 days.

Southern California Checklist

PLANTING

☑ PLANT AZALEAS AND CAMELLIAS. Select plants while they're still in flower and plant them as soon as possible. Plants are dormant while in bloom, but they begin growing again soon after flowering. Amend the soil well with organic material and a soil acidifier such as oak leaf mold or peat moss. Plant both azaleas and camellias a bit high so that the tops of the root balls are an inch or so above-ground after the soil settles.

☑ PLANT PERENNIALS. Nurseries are well stocked with blooming perennials. And, next to fall, early spring is the best time to get them started in the garden.

☑ REPLACE WINTER ANNUALS. As the weather warms, replace fading winter/spring annuals with summer bedding plants. Choices include ageratum, amaranth, begonia, coleus, impatiens, lobelia, marigolds, nasturtium, nicotiana, petunias, phlox, and verbena, among others. In the high desert (Zone 11), set out warmth-lovers such as marigolds, petunias, and zinnias late this month.

☑ SOW FLOWER SEEDS. Coastal gardeners (Zones 22–24) can sow seeds of aster, cleome, lobelia, lunaria, marigold, nasturtium, nicotiana, sunflower, and zinnia in flats or directly in the garden. Inland gardeners (Zones 18–21) should wait until at least mid-month. In colder areas, sow seeds of alyssum, calendula, candytuft, clarkia, and larkspur.

Sunset
CLIMATE ZONES

1-3 7-9 11 13 14-24

MAINTENANCE

☑ FEED PERMANENT PLANTS. Ground covers, shrubs, perennials, and ornamental and fruit trees are putting out new growth now and will benefit from the application of an all-purpose balanced fertilizer. Wait until flowering ends to feed azaleas and camellias; they are dormant while in bloom. California natives and drought-tolerant Mediterranean plants are also exceptions. Don't feed them; they're slowing down prior to their summer dormancy.

☑ FEED LAWNS. Apply high-nitrogen fertilizer to warm- and cool-season turf-grasses. Mow and fertilize meadows.

PEST CONTROL

☑ CONTROL APHIDS. Tender new plant growth attracts these sucking pests. Dislodge aphids with a strong blast of water from a hose or, if blossoms are delicate, mist plants with insecticidal soap. You can also strip aphids from plants by hand, but this is tedious work.

☑ PREPARE FOR WHITEFLIES. Set out yellow sticky cards (available in most nurseries) around abutilon, fuchsia, and other plants that are susceptible to these pests.

☑ MANAGE SNAILS. Control now to reduce their numbers for the rest of the year. Hand-pick—you'll often find them hiding under strap-leafed plants like agapanthus and clivia. Trap them by allowing them to collect on the underside of a slightly elevated board. Or set out commercial snail bait. Surround trunks of citrus trees and tender seedlings with copper barriers. The snails receive a mild shock when they come in contact with the copper, and don't proceed further.

Mountain Checklist

PLANTING

☑ **BARE-ROOT STOCK. Early this** month, set out bare-root plants of small fruits like grapes, raspberries, and strawberries; vegetables like asparagus and horseradish; and all kinds of fruit and shade trees. Bare-root plants cost less than those sold in containers and adapt more quickly to native garden soil. It's essential to bring home nursery plants with their bare roots wrapped in damp cloth or sawdust: If they dry out, they die.

☑ LAWNS. You can overseed an old lawn or plant a new one this month. To overseed, first rough up the soil and sow it with the same kind of grass that was already growing there. Otherwise the texture and color of the new grass will contrast with the old. For a new lawn, till 2 inches of organic matter into the top 8 inches of soil before you sow. Keep all newly sown areas well watered until the grass is tall enough to mow.

MAINTENANCE

☑ FEED BERRIES. Established blackberries, blueberries, and raspberries can all use a dose of high-nitrogen fertilizer or well-aged manure this month. But hold off feeding new plantings until their roots have taken hold.

☑ FEED EVERGREENS AND SHRUBS. Sprinkle high-nitrogen fertilizer over the root zones around plants and water it in thoroughly. Feed early-blooming shrubs with a high-nitrogen fertilizer as soon as they have finished blooming. Do this on a mild day when temperatures are well above freezing.

Sunset
CLIMATE ZONES
☐ 1-3 ▨ 10-11

☑ FEED ROSES. Pick a day when nighttime temperatures are forecast to remain above freezing. Water established plants, let the soil drain, apply a complete fertilizer, and then water again.

☑ TRIM PERENNIALS. Cut last year's growth off perennials when you see strong new growth at the base of the plant.

☑ BULBS. If foliage of snowdrops and daffodils is hidden by debris, clear debris away so shoots can emerge easily. Buy daffodils (but not paper whites) or croci blooming in containers for planting next month.

☑ INSTALL IRRIGATION SYSTEMS. Install drip-type irrigation systems or lay ooze-type soaker hoses in beds before plants leaf out.

☑ PREPARE BEDS. Once the soil has thawed, dig compost or well-aged manure into planting beds. If you have really bad soil, till 4 to 6 inches of organic matter into the top foot of soil. Rake amended beds, water them, and let them settle for a week before planting.

☑ START COMPOSTING. As you get the garden in shape for planting, use the weeds you pull to start a compost pile. Layer green leaves with dry leaves, straw, or sawdust. Keep the pile damp and turn it weekly with a pitchfork. The compost should be ready in a few weeks.

PEST AND WEED CONTROL

☑ APHIDS. In small numbers, these sucking insects do relatively little damage to plants. But when populations build up, they can do great harm. Watch tender new growth carefully. When you see a population develop, blast them off with hose water or spray with insecticidal soap.

☑ WEEDS. Hoe them now while they're young and shallow-rooted. If you wait until they form deep taproots, they'll sprout—and you'll weed again. If weeds germinate between the time you prepare a flower bed and plant, hoe them lightly without disturbing more than the top ½ inch of soil. If you hoe any deeper, or till more, you'll just bring up a fresh batch of weed seeds.

Southwest Checklist

PLANTING

☑ **ANNUALS.** Zones 10–11: Plant cool-season annuals such as calendula and cornflower. Zones 12–13: Set out warm-season flowers such as black-foot daisies *(Melampodium),* cosmos, celosia, gomphrena, lisianthus, Madagascar periwinkle, marigolds, portulaca, and salvia.

☑ **CITRUS TREES.** Zone 12 (Tucson): Set out mandarins such as 'Fairchild', 'Fortune', and 'Fremont'. Zone 13 (Phoenix, Yuma): Plant grapefruits, grapefruit-pummelo hybrids ('Oroblanco', 'Melogold'), lemons, and sweet oranges ('Marrs', 'Trovita', 'Valencia').

☑ **GROUND COVERS.** Zones 12–13: Set out aptenia, calylophus, dwarf rosemary, lantana, Mexican evening primrose, verbena, and vinca.

☑ **PERENNIALS.** Zones 10–13: Aster, autumn sage *(Salvia greggii),* chrysanthemums, coreopsis, feverfew, gerbera, helianthus, hollyhock, penstemon, Shasta daisies, and statice can all go in the ground now.

☑ **SUMMER BULBS.** Zones 10–13: Shop for caladium, canna, and crinum this month, but wait until the soil warms to 65°F before planting. Set out dahlia and gladiolus after danger of frost is past.

☑ **VINES.** Zones 10–13: Plant hardy vines like Boston ivy, Carolina jessamine, Japanese honeysuckle, Lady Banks' rose, silver lace vine, trumpet creeper *(Campsis radicans),* Virginia creeper, and wisteria.

☑ **VEGETABLES.** Zones 10–11: Plant cool-season crops such as broccoli, cabbage, carrots, cauliflower, kohlrabi, lettuce, potatoes, radishes, and spinach right away. Zones 12–13: Sow asparagus beans, black-eyed peas, bush and lima beans, cucumbers, melons, soybeans, summer squash, and sweet corn. Set out plants of peppers and tomatoes now.

MAINTENANCE

☑ **GROUND COVERS AND MEADOWS.** Mow ground covers such as creeping lilyturf and St. Johnswort to the ground to encourage strong new growth. Mow and fertilize meadow grasses.

☑ **DIVIDE PERENNIALS.** Zones 10–13: Dig and divide clumping perennials such as bearded iris, chrysanthemums, and daylilies.

☑ **MAINTAIN DRIP SYSTEMS.** Clean algae and sediment from drip tubing and emitters (a solution of water and either bleach or vinegar will help clear them out), replace any clogged emitters you can't clear, and clean all filters.

☑ **MULCH PLANTS.** Zones 12–13: After soil has warmed, spread 3 to 4 inches of organic mulch around roses, shrubs, and trees, and in rows between flowers and cool-season vegetables. Mulch warm-season vegetables next month.

☑ **TRIM ORNAMENTAL GRASSES.** When new growth appears, cut back the old grass to keep clumps from looking ratty.

☑ **FERTILIZE.** Zones 10–13: Feed roses, trees, and spring- and summer-blooming shrubs as well as cool-season vegetables and citrus. Use high-nitrogen fertilizer.

Preparing a Garden Bed

When you're getting ready to dig a new garden bed, the soil should be neither too wet nor too dry: a handful squeezed in your fist should form a ball that crumbles apart, yet still feels moist. If you dig into soil that's too wet, you'll compact it (making it difficult for air to penetrate throughout the soil once it dries) and destroy beneficial microorganisms. You can't work amendments evenly into wet soil, either.

Garden beds are of two basic types. Some are dug directly in the ground, while others (raised beds) are located in frames that sit on the soil surface.

Digging a planting bed in the ground

When making new in-ground beds, some gardeners always raise them, even if just by a few inches, using decorative stones, bricks, or bender board as an edging. They'll tell you that by the time they amend the bed's soil, it's "fluffed up" higher than its original boundaries anyway. The raised soil gives plant roots a few more inches of growing room, and the edging keeps the soil in place.

Other gardeners make mounds as they dig. In this case, the bed's edges are close to the original soil surface, while the center is elevated; plants can grow both on top of the mound and on its sides. You may want to create several mounds, adding large decorative stones for accents; in this case, the mounding forms part of the landscaping. As is true for the slightly raised beds just described, the mounded soil ensures plenty of depth for root growth as well as excellent drainage.

In the vegetable garden, such mounds are convenient for scrambling, vining plants such as melons and squash. You'll also see various types of raised or mounded rows in vegetable gardens; in most, the seedlings are planted at the top to maximize root growth and drainage.

When you dig, start by clearing most of the debris from the soil. Then use a sharp, square-bladed spade or a spading fork to break up the soil to a spade's depth—typically 8 to 12 inches. Don't turn each spadeful completely over; if you do, roots and debris remaining on the soil surface may form a one-spade-deep barrier that cuts off air and water. Instead, turn the loosened spadefuls of soil only onto their sides. Once you've broken up the soil, change to a round-point shovel for mixing in amendments and evening the surface.

If you're digging a large bed, consider using a power-driven rototiller. If the soil hasn't been worked in a long time, go over it first with the blades set to a shallow level. Spread amendments over the surface, then rototill again with the blades set deeper into the soil.

Once a bed is ready for planting, don't walk on it. Following this rule will be simpler if you can easily reach all parts of the bed from its borders; if it must be wide, add board paths or steppingstones to control foot traffic.

A slightly mounded bed shows off blooming perennials to best advantage—and guarantees good drainage, too.

In hot, dry climates, gardeners sometimes favor sunken beds over raised ones; a sunken planting area holds water more efficiently during irrigation.

Building a Raised Bed

Raising your garden above the ground can solve some of the most frustrating problems gardeners face. An easy-to-build bed makes it possible for plants to thrive where soil is poor, wildlife is hungry, or the growing season is short. And if you need easy access to your plants—due to a disability or simply to eliminate back-bending labor—you can sit on the edge of the bed and garden in comfort.

Fill the bed with the best soil you can. Good soil means that plants can be placed closer together, making a small area more productive. Line the bottom of the bed with wire screening to keep out pests, or fit it with a PVC framework for bird netting.

A raised bed can be any size, but if it is more than 4 feet wide it will be difficult to reach the middle from either side. If the sides will double as benches, build the frame 18 to 24 inches high.

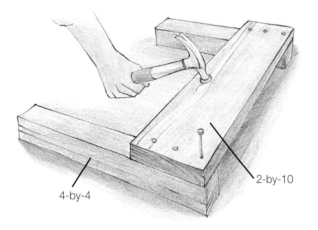

4-by-4

2-by-10

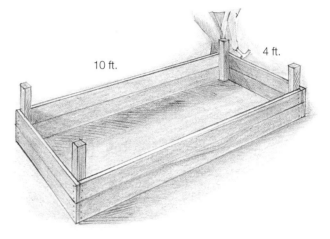

10 ft.

4 ft.

1. *Orient a rectangular bed from north to south. For a 4-by-10-foot bed, first nail short sides of 2-by-10s to 3-foot-high 4-by-4 corner posts. Use rot-resistant lumber and galvanized nails.*

2. *Flip structure over and nail 10-foot lengths to corner posts. For added strength, install wooden bracing or metal L-straps. Work on level ground so that the bed is as square as possible.*

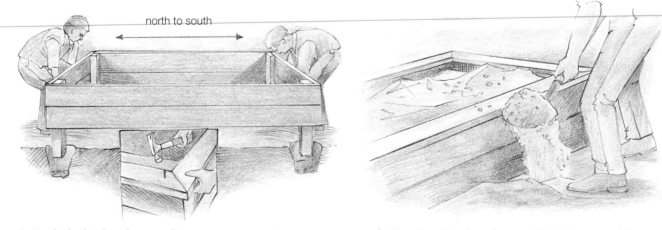

north to south

3. *Set the bed right side up and insert corner posts into pre-dug foot-deep holes. Level if necessary. Cap the top with surfaced redwood 2-by-6s, with ends cut at a 45° angle (inset).*

4. *Place 3 to 4 inches of new soil in the bottom of the bed and mix it into the ground to aid drainage. This 20-inch-deep bed holds about 2½ cubic yards of soil.*

An ornamental grass sampler

NAME	LIGHT	BLOOMS	DESCRIPTION/LANDSCAPE USES
Arrhenatherum elatius bulbosum 'Variegatum' Bulbous oat grass	Sun or partial shade	Summer	White-striped foliage. Showy, erect, oatlike flower spike. Short-lived in hot inland areas. Dormant in summer. Effective as accent in perennial borders and large rock gardens.
Briza media Quaking grass	Sun or partial shade	Spring	Heart-shaped florets resemble rattlesnake rattles; good for cutting. Green foliage. Evergreen. Use as accent or in groups in shrub and perennial borders.
Calamagrostis acutifolia 'Stricta' Feather reed grass	Sun	Late spring to fall	Bright green foliage. Tall, erect flower spikes, but bloom varies, depending on climate. Good for cutting. Deciduous in colder areas; semi-evergreen in mild areas. Makes strong vertical accent plant; in groups, plant at rear of a border.
Carex buchananii Leather leaf sedge	Sun or partial shade		Coppery red-brown foliage with curled leaf tips. May be short-lived. Evergreen. Use as accent, in groups, or combined with blue, gray, or dark green foliage.
C. morrowii 'Goldband' 'Goldband' Japanese sedge	Shade or partial shade		Lustrous, bright yellow-striped foliage. May be short-lived. Evergreen. Use as accent, alone or in groups, in borders, or spilling over rocks or walls.
Festuca amethystina, F. cinerea Blue fescue	Sun or partial shade	Spring	Foliage may be green, blue, or gray. *F. amethystina* 'Superba', with blue-green weeping foliage and pink flowers, is best bloomer. Evergreen. Use as ground cover, in groups, or as a single accent. Makes good edging for borders.
Imperata cylindrica 'Rubra' Japanese blood grass	Sun; partial shade in heat		Leaves are bright green with blood red tips; turn reddish brown in fall. Spreads slowly.
Stipa tenuissima Mexican feather grass	Sun or partial shade	Summer	Tall, fine-textured green foliage clumps. Tan in winter. Flowers fine-textured, filmy, green turning tan. Can become invasive.
Helictotrichon sempervirens Blue oat grass	Sun	Late summer to fall	Blue-gray foliage with sharply pointed tips. Showy flowers; blooms best in cool areas. In hot areas, and in wet, heavy soil, root rot may occur. Evergreen. Makes good accent alone or in groups, in borders and rock gardens.
Miscanthus sinensis 'Gracillimus' Maiden grass	Sun or shade	All year	Narrow, green foliage. Showy beige flowers; good for cutting. Evergreen. Use as a specimen or plant at back of a border.
Pennisetum setaceum 'Rubrum' Purple fountain grass	Sun	Summer to fall	Purple foliage topped by red-purple plumes; good for cutting. Evergreen to deciduous. Cold-hardiness varies greatly. Noninvasive type. Effective as accent or in groups in perennial or shrub borders. Striking with blue and gray plants.
Stipa gigantea Giant feather grass	Sun	Summer	Gray-green foliage. Golden flower spikes dangle from stems; good for cutting. Evergreen. Use as a specimen or in groups, particularly in perennial borders.
Cortaderia selloana 'Gold Band' or 'Sun Stripe' Yellow pampas grass	Sun	Late summer to fall	Yellow-green leaves with yellow stripes. Erect, creamy white flower spikes; good for cutting. Noninvasive type. Evergreen. Use as dramatic accent with shrubs or in background plantings.
Miscanthus sinensis Eulalia grass	Sun or shade	Summer to fall	Green foliage, some with white or yellow. Cultivars differ greatly. Showy plumes; good for cutting. Deciduous. Use as specimen or in groups.

Side labels: ▼ UNDER 2 FEET | ▼ 2 TO 4 FEET | ▼ OVER 4 FEET

Molinia caerulea 'Variegata'

Imperata cylindrica 'Rubra'

Stipa tenuissima

Helictotrichon sempervirens

Lawns and Turfgrasses

Traditional turfgrasses provide a perfect soft surface for children's play, sports activities, and simply lounging around. But not every garden needs a lawn. Although there's an attractive simplicity to maintaining a single crop plant such as lawn grass, weigh this against the amount of fertilizing, irrigating, mowing, weeding, and raking that the lawn requires. In fact, if the only person who ever walks on the lawn is the person who mows it, consider substituting a ground cover plant or an area of interesting paving.

Your climate plays a critical role in determining which grass species will be the easiest to care for. Cool-season grasses are those that grow best between 60° and 75°F (generally spring and fall) and tolerate winter freezes—in hot weather, they will grow slowly but remain green if well watered. Warm-season grasses prefer high temperatures and mild winters but turn brown during winter months. Although cool-season grasses such as bluegrass are well-adapted to parts of the country with abundant summer rainfall, they are not the best low-maintenance choice in arid areas.

Recommendations for fertilizing lawns vary, but you can adjust the frequency of application according to how lush you wish your lawn to appear.

Feeding your lawn

A lawn needs nitrogen for healthy growth and to outcompete weeds. The amount of nitrogen depends on your climate and which grass you're growing.

As a rule of thumb, fertilize as little as you can to achieve the quality you want. You don't need to apply excessive amounts of nitrogen to keep a lawn green.

Which fertilizer? Bagged lawn fertilizers take the guesswork out of feeding; recommended application rates are shown on the labels. Most contain nitrogen in both fast- and slow-acting forms as well as phosphorus, potassium, and micronutrients such as iron. Fast-acting nitrogen gives the lawn an instant boost; the slow-acting form is released over a period of time. Always spread fertilizer evenly and water immediately to prevent burning.

Organic lawn foods are now readily available. Organic nitrogen is released slowly so there's no danger of it burning the grass. It isn't readily leached out of the soil, which makes it environmentally friendly. But organic nitrogen sources break down into usable forms only during mild weather. Organic lawn food is expensive, and you need to apply more of it to get the same amount of nitrogen.

When to feed? It depends on whether you have cool- or warm-season grass. Cool-season grasses grow vigorously in spring and fall, so that's when they need fertilizer. Make two applications in spring and two in fall. Warm-season grasses such as Bermuda grow actively in the warm months, so apply fertilizer from March to October. Feed Bermuda lightly in summer to restrain aggressive growth.

Patching a lawn

If you need to repair parts of the lawn that are dead or worn out, start by preparing the soil. Rake out dead grass, then rough up the top inch of soil with a bow rake or a cultivator. Scatter a light dose of lawn fertilizer over the area, then sow seeds to match the existing grass, as shown. Lightly rake the seeds into the soil, and cover with a thin layer (¼ inch) of organic mulch such as peat moss. Keep the seeded area well watered (perhaps twice a day in hot weather) until the grass is tall enough to mow.

USING A DROP SPREADER

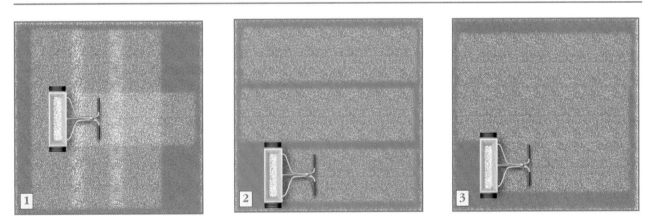

1. Don't go over the same area twice when you apply lawn fertilizer. Double doses burn or kill grass. **2.** Don't include wheels when you calculate width of swath; unfertilized wheel tracks will appear later as light green stripes. **3.** Do overlap wheel tracks so that swaths just touch. The result will be an evenly green lawn.

Match the grass to your climate

Your garden's climate is the key factor in choosing a cool- or warm-season grass.

Cool-season grasses, including bent, bluegrass, fescue, and ryegrass, grow best when temperatures are between 60° and 75°F. When it gets warmer, most of them go into summer dormancy, turning a straw color and even dying if they don't get water. Spring, late summer, and early fall are the best times to plant these.

Warm-season grasses, including Bermuda, blue grama, buffalo, St. Augustine, and zoysia, thrive in hot weather (80° to 95°F is optimal), but they turn brown in winter. These are best planted in late spring and early summer.

Wherever you live, you'll want to select a grass with a reliable record of performance.

■ *In the coastal Pacific Northwest,* blends of perennial ryegrass, fescue, and bent or Kentucky bluegrass are the lawns of choice. Although tall fescue is available, it has trouble competing with the other grasses during wet, chilly winters.

■ *In the intermountain West,* Kentucky bluegrass is a favorite, though buffalo grass (sometimes blended with blue grama) is making inroads with gardeners who want to save water. Tall fescue is another good choice: It needs less water than Kentucky bluegrass and is greener than buffalo grass (but not as cold-tolerant).

■ *In mild areas of California,* dwarf tall fescue has become popular because it needs less water and tolerates summer heat better than most other cool-season grasses. New, slower-growing varieties stay acceptably green all year.

■ *In hot-summer areas of California and the Southwest's low and intermediate deserts,* Bermuda grass is still the favorite. It makes a fine-textured turf that tolerates drought and wears well. In autumn, common Bermuda grass can be overseeded with perennial ryegrass for a good-looking winter lawn. Zoysia is also coming into its own. This cold-hardy grass takes some shade and doesn't demand much water or fertilizer.

Seed

Hulled Bermuda grass seed

Unhulled Bermuda grass seed

Fescue seed coated with fungicide

Uncoated tall fescue grass seed

Grass seed is sold uncoated, or coated with fungicide or fertilizer. Bermuda grass seed is sold hulled or unhulled; hulled seed has a higher germination rate. **1.** After preparing the site, scatter seed and lawn fertilizer if seeds are uncoated. **2.** Lightly rake seed into soil. **3.** Spread ¼ inch of mulch; then roll with an empty roller to press seed into soil.

■ *Along the Southern California coast,* St. Augustine grass is popular. It holds its color in winter if you give it a pound of fertilizer per 1,000 square feet of turf every 6 weeks. St. Augustine also grows well in the low desert, but it needs plenty of water.

Seed, sod, sprigs, or plugs?

Lawn grass is sold in several forms. All except sod require diligent weed control after planting. Seed is widely available at garden centers and nurseries. Sod, sprigs, and plugs can all be or-

dered from sod farms, usually through nurseries or landscape designers.

Seed is the cheapest way to start a lawn. Before you buy, read the seed package label as much for what it doesn't say as for what it does. Look for names on the bag: for instance, you want a named variety such as 'Bonsai 2000', 'Finelawn', or 'Jaguar II', not a generic tall fescue. Also, if the label bears the notation VNS (variety not stated) or UCT (uncertified), the seeds may be from old or inferior stock; they might be cheaper but not as good. Look for current seed test and expiration dates; plant within a year of the

Installing sod

To install sod, moisten prepared soil. 1. Unroll strips and lay them in brick-bond fashion, pressing the edges together firmly. **2.** Use a knife to trim sod to fit snugly around paving and obstacles. **3.** Roll the lawn with a roller half-filled with water to press roots firmly into the soil. Water every day (more often in hot weather) for 6 weeks.

test date for best germination.

Seed rates run from 1½ pounds (for Kentucky bluegrass) to cover 1,000 square feet up to 10 pounds (for tall fescue) to cover the same area.

Sod is the most expensive way to go but gives you instant coverage with almost no weed problems. When you order, try to time delivery for a dry day (if you stack sod during rainy weather, the grass can develop mildew and die). Make sure the soil is moist before you put the sod down.

Ask your sod supplier for the names and proportions of the grass varieties your sod contains so that when you wear holes in the sod, you can re-seed the area with the same grass.

Plugs give spreading grasses a well-rooted start on life. Plant 2-by-2-inch plugs at 8- to 16-inch intervals and water well.

Sprigs, or shredded stolons, of spreading warm-season grasses give faster coverage than seeds. Plant sprigs 2 to 3 inches deep at 4-inch intervals in rows 6 to 12 inches apart. One end of each sprig should barely poke out of the ground.

Another way to plant sprigs is called stolonizing: Spread 5 to 10 bushels of sprigs over 1,000 square feet of ground, then barely cover them with topsoil. Do this in 1-yard-square patches, watering each patch as you go. Don't let the sprigs dry out or they'll be history.

Site preparation

When you plant a new lawn, whether you use seed, sod, sprigs, or plugs, it's best to start with a clean slate. Remove existing sod with a lawn stripper or kill the grass with an herbicide. When the old grass is gone, till the site to a depth of about 8 inches. (If the soil contains too much clay or sand, spread 3 to 4 inches of organic amendment before you till.) Pick out rocks and roots, level the site, water well, and wait 2 days for the soil to settle. Then rake seed, lay sod, or plant sprigs or plugs. Cover seeds or sprigs with a ¼-inch layer of mulch. Water to keep the top ½ inch of soil (or sod) moist until the grass takes hold and winter rains take over.

Plugs and sprigs

Buffalo grass plug

Bermuda grass sprig

Two-inch plugs of buffalo grass (above) and some other spreading, warm-season grasses are sold in trays. Planted at 8-inch intervals, these plugs will grow together in a year. Torn to pieces by machines, sprigs of hybrid Bermuda grass (right) will root and spread quickly in well-prepared soil. Water plugs or sprigs frequently until their roots take hold.

Garden Grass Guide

Cool-season grasses

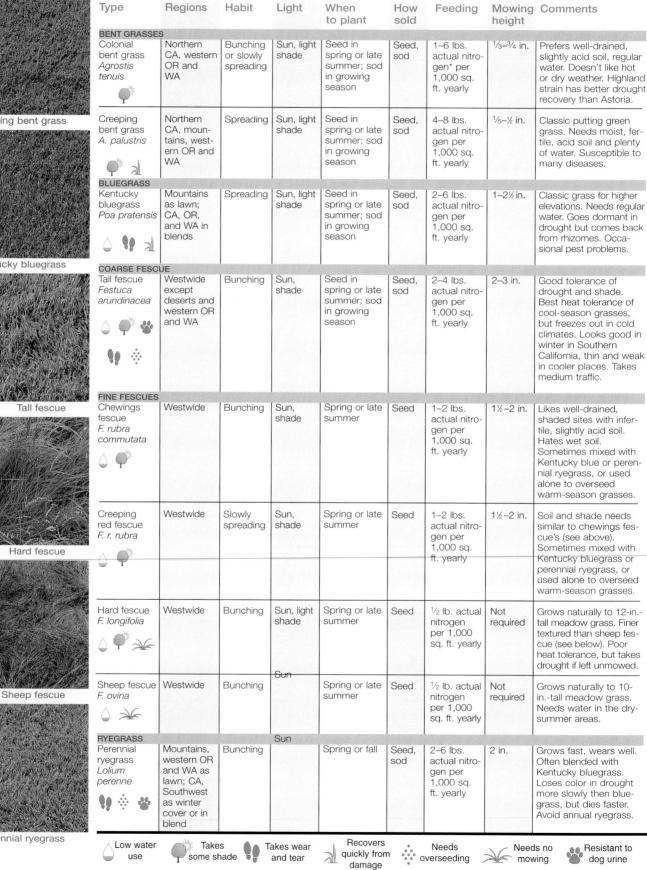

Type	Regions	Habit	Light	When to plant	How sold	Feeding	Mowing height	Comments
BENT GRASSES								
Colonial bent grass *Agrostis tenuis*	Northern CA, western OR and WA	Bunching or slowly spreading	Sun, light shade	Seed in spring or late summer; sod in growing season	Seed, sod	1–6 lbs. actual nitrogen* per 1,000 sq. ft. yearly	⅓–¾ in.	Prefers well-drained, slightly acid soil, regular water. Doesn't like hot or dry weather. Highland strain has better drought recovery than Astoria.
Creeping bent grass *A. palustris*	Northern CA, mountains, western OR and WA	Spreading	Sun, light shade	Seed in spring or late summer; sod in growing season	Seed, sod	4–8 lbs. actual nitrogen per 1,000 sq. ft. yearly	⅕–½ in.	Classic putting green grass. Needs moist, fertile, acid soil and plenty of water. Susceptible to many diseases.
BLUEGRASS								
Kentucky bluegrass *Poa pratensis*	Mountains as lawn; CA, OR, and WA in blends	Spreading	Sun, light shade	Seed in spring or late summer; sod in growing season	Seed, sod	2–6 lbs. actual nitrogen per 1,000 sq. ft. yearly	1–2½ in.	Classic grass for higher elevations. Needs regular water. Goes dormant in drought but comes back from rhizomes. Occasional pest problems.
COARSE FESCUE								
Tall fescue *Festuca arundinacea*	Westwide except deserts and western OR and WA	Bunching	Sun, shade	Seed in spring or late summer; sod in growing season	Seed, sod	2–4 lbs. actual nitrogen per 1,000 sq. ft. yearly	2–3 in.	Good tolerance of drought and shade. Best heat tolerance of cool-season grasses, but freezes out in cold climates. Looks good in winter in Southern California, thin and weak in cooler places. Takes medium traffic.
FINE FESCUES								
Chewings fescue *F. rubra commutata*	Westwide	Bunching	Sun, shade	Spring or late summer	Seed	1–2 lbs. actual nitrogen per 1,000 sq. ft. yearly	1½–2 in.	Likes well-drained, shaded sites with infertile, slightly acid soil. Hates wet soil. Sometimes mixed with Kentucky blue or perennial ryegrass, or used alone to overseed warm-season grasses.
Creeping red fescue *F. r. rubra*	Westwide	Slowly spreading	Sun, shade	Spring or late summer	Seed	1–2 lbs. actual nitrogen per 1,000 sq. ft. yearly	1½–2 in.	Soil and shade needs similar to chewings fescue's (see above). Sometimes mixed with Kentucky bluegrass or perennial ryegrass, or used alone to overseed warm-season grasses.
Hard fescue *F. longifolia*	Westwide	Bunching	Sun, light shade	Spring or late summer	Seed	½ lb. actual nitrogen per 1,000 sq. ft. yearly	Not required	Grows naturally to 12-in.-tall meadow grass. Finer textured than sheep fescue (see below). Poor heat tolerance, but takes drought if left unmowed.
Sheep fescue *F. ovina*	Westwide	Bunching	Sun	Spring or late summer	Seed	½ lb. actual nitrogen per 1,000 sq. ft. yearly	Not required	Grows naturally to 10-in.-tall meadow grass. Needs water in the dry-summer areas.
RYEGRASS								
Perennial ryegrass *Lolium perenne*	Mountains, western OR and WA as lawn; CA, Southwest as winter cover or in blend	Bunching	Sun	Spring or fall	Seed, sod	2–6 lbs. actual nitrogen per 1,000 sq. ft. yearly	2 in.	Grows fast, wears well. Often blended with Kentucky bluegrass. Loses color in drought more slowly then bluegrass, but dies faster. Avoid annual ryegrass.

Key:
- Low water use
- Takes some shade
- Takes wear and tear
- Recovers quickly from damage
- Needs overseeding
- Needs no mowing
- Resistant to dog urine

Creeping bent grass

Kentucky bluegrass

Tall fescue

Hard fescue

Sheep fescue

Perennial ryegrass

Blue grama makes an informal, drought-tolerant lawn in Santa Fe. You can mow this grass or let it grow into a 12-inch-tall meadow.

Warm-season grasses

Type	Regions	Habit	Light	When to plant	How sold	Feeding	Mowing height	Comments
Blue grama *Bouteloua gracilis*	Mountains, Southwest	Bunching	Sun	Early summer	Seed	½–2 lbs. actual nitrogen* per 1,000 sq. ft. yearly	2–3 in.	Tolerates drought, temperature extremes, and wide range of soils, even alkaline ones. Goes brown in winter. Low-quality turf when it's used alone; better when blended with buffalo grass.
Buffalo grass *Buchloe dactyloides*	CA, mountains, Southwest	Spreading	Sun	Early summer	Seed, sod, plugs	½–2 lbs. actual nitrogen per 1,000 sq. ft. yearly	3 in.	Lowest water need of any warm-season grass. Takes drought, heat; doesn't like humidity. Goes brown in winter.
Common Bermuda grass *Cynodon dactylon*	CA, low and intermediate deserts	Spreading	Sun	Early summer when evening temperatures are above 65°F	Seed	2–4 lbs. actual nitrogen per 1,000 sq. ft. yearly	1 in.	Great tolerance of wear, drought, and a wide range of soils, but not cold. Goes brown in winter; greens up when soil reaches 60°F in spring. No serious pest problems.
Hybrid Bermuda grass *Cynodon*	CA, low and intermediate deserts	Spreading	Sun	Early summer when evening temperatures are above 65°F	Sod, sprigs, plugs	4–6 lbs. actual nitrogen per 1,000 sq. ft. yearly	½–¾ in.	Similar to common Bermuda grass (see above), but doesn't self-sow.
St. Augustine grass *Stenotaphrum secundatum*	Southern CA, low and intermediate deserts	Spreading	Sun, shade	Early summer	Sod, sprigs, plugs	3–6 lbs. actual nitrogen per 1,000 sq. ft. yearly	¾–3 in.	Widely adapted to soils, but does best along coast. Needs regular water. Poor frost tolerance. Goes brown in winter. Susceptible to chinch bug.
Zoysia species	CA, low and intermediate deserts	Spreading	Sun, shade	When evening temperatures are above 65°F	Sod, sprigs, plugs	1½–4 lbs. actual nitrogen per 1,000 sq. ft. yearly	½–1 in.	Excellent tolerance of wear, drought, heat, and cold. Goes brown in winter. Slow to establish. No significant pest problems. DeAnza, El Toro, and Victoria varieties hold winter color best, especially on coast.

Buffalo grass

Hybrid Bermuda grass

St. Augustine grass

Zoysia

*Actual nitrogen is the amount of unadulterated nitrogen (N) in a bag of fertilizer. For example, if a 50-pound bag is labeled with a 20-27-5 N-P-K formula, it contains 20 percent, or 10 pounds, of actual nitrogen, plus phosphorus (P) and potassium (K).

Pots of colorful gerberas (also called South African daisies) appear in nurseries around the West this month.
They bloom in six-week cycles from late April until fall.

Mountain Checklist

PLANTING

✔**PLANT BARE-ROOT STOCK.** Set out bare-root berries, grapes, roses, and both fruit and ornamental trees this month. Bare-root plants are less expensive than container-grown stock, and they adapt to garden soil more easily.

✔**PLANT FLOWERS.** Nurseries are full of cool-season annual seedlings. You can set out annuals such as calendulas, English daisies, pansies, primroses, snapdragons, stock, and violas and a host of flowering perennials, including bergenia, bleeding hearts, and forget-me-nots.

✔**PLANT HARDY VEGETABLES.** Early in the month, plant bare-root asparagus, horseradish, and rhubarb. As soon as you can work the soil, sow beets, carrots, endive, kohlrabi, lettuce, onion, parsley, parsnips, peas, radishes, spinach, Swiss chard, and turnips. Set out transplants of broccoli, Brussels sprouts, cabbage, cauliflower, and green onions. Plant seed potatoes. Use floating row covers or hot caps to protect seedlings from late frosts and to hold warmth around plants so they get off to a fast start.

✔**PLANT SPRING-BLOOMING TREES AND SHRUBS.** You can buy and plant flowering shrubs in containers, including flowering quinces, forsythias, magnolias, and redbuds.

MONTANA
Helena

Boise
IDAHO   WYOMING
Cheyenne

NEVADA
Reno   Salt Lake City   Denver

UTAH   COLORADO

Las Vegas

Sunset
CLIMATE ZONES
☐ 1-3   ☐ 10-11

MAINTENANCE

✔**FEED LAWNS.** Apply 1 to 2 pounds of high-nitrogen fertilizer per 1,000 square feet of turf (put more on heavily used lawns and those growing in poor soil). Spread the fertilizer evenly over the lawn, then water it in thoroughly.

✔**MULCH.** A 2- to 3-inch layer of organic mulch suppresses weeds, holds in moisture, and—when the weather heats up—keep roots cool. Spread mulch around annuals, perennials, trees, and shrubs. But keep mulch a few inches away from warm season vegetables since their roots need the warmest soil possible until hot weather sets in.

✔**PRUNE.** Early in the month, before new growth emerges, finish pruning grapes, roses, vines, and deciduous fruit and ornamental trees. Wait until after flowering to prune spring-blooming trees and shrubs such as forsythia and spiraea; or prune them lightly after buds swell, and bring the cuttings indoors to display in vases.

✔**MOW.** Begin to mow when turf-grass is dry. Mow and fertilize meadow grasses.

PEST AND WEED CONTROL

✔**APPLY DORMANT SPRAY.** After pruning but before leaves and flowers appear, spray fruit trees with a mixture of dormant oil and lime sulfur or oil and copper. If rain washes it off within 48 hours, reapply. If you use oil and copper, keep sprays off walls, fences, and walks that might become stained.

✔**DIG OR HOE WEEDS.** When weeds are small, wait until soil is dry, then hoe early in the day. Sun and dryness will kill tiny roots by day's end. For larger weeds, water them thoroughly, then pop them out with a hand weeder, roots and all. Let whole weeds dry in the sun before you compost them. Remove weeds near emerging bulb shoots. If needed, spot-treat with glyphosate, but protect the bulb foliage with cardboard.

✔**ROTATE VEGETABLE BEDS.** To avoid soil-borne diseases, never plant the same kinds of crops in the same beds two years in a row. For example, if you planted cabbage family members in a bed last year, switch to a completely different crop (such as tomatoes) this year.

Southwest Checklist

PLANTING

☑ ANNUALS. Zones 10–13: Try ageratum, calliopsis, celosia, cosmos, four o'clock, globe amaranth, gloriosa daisies, kochia, lisianthus, marigolds, Mexican sunflowers, portulaca, strawflowers, vinca rosea, and zinnias.

☑ CITRUS. Zones 12–13: Plant 5- to 7-gallon citrus trees in full sun in holes dug as deep as the root balls and 2 to 3 times as wide. Water 2 or 3 times per week at first; by summer's end, you'll need to water only every 5 to 7 days. Wrap trunks in white cloth or paint with white latex to prevent sunburn.

☑ LAWNS. Zones 1–2, 10 (Albuquerque and El Paso): Sow or reseed cool-season lawns with bluegrass, fine or tall fescue, and perennial ryegrass. Zone 11 (Las Vegas): You can grow hybrid or common Bermuda, but tall fescue and perennial ryegrass are the lawns of choice. Sow them this month. Zones 12–13: When average nighttime temperatures top 70°F, plant hybrid Bermuda grass.

☑ PERENNIALS. Start chrysanthemums, columbine, coreopsis, gaillardia, gazania, geraniums, gerbera, hollyhock, salvia, and Shasta daisies.

☑ SUMMER BULBS. After danger of frost is past, plant caladium, canna, crinum, dahlias, daylilies, gladiolus, irises, and montbretia. You can also buy container-grown agapanthus, society garlic (*Tulbaghia violacea*), and zephyranthes.

☑ VEGETABLES. Zones 10–11: Sow cucumbers, melons, okra, pumpkins, soybeans, squash, and watermelons; set out eggplant, peppers, sweet potatoes, and tomatoes. Zones 12–13: Sow beans and cucumbers by mid-April; set out eggplant, okra, peanuts, squash, and sweet potatoes any time this month.

☑ VINES. Zones 12–13: Plant tender vines such as bougainvillea, cape honeysuckle, and pink trumpet vine. Put them in a warm spot that gets good winter protection.

MAINTENANCE

☑ FEED GARDEN PLANTS. Almost everything in the garden can use a dose of fertilizer now. Apply about 1 pound of a complete fertilizer (10-10-10) per 100 square feet. Water the day before you spread the fertilizer and immediately afterward.

☑ FEED LAWNS. To give Bermuda grass a push for the summer, apply 3 to 4 pounds of high-nitrogen fertilizer per 1,000 square feet about 2 weeks after the grass greens up. Water thoroughly.

☑ MULCH SOIL. A 2- to 3-inch layer of organic mulch suppresses weeds, holds in moisture, and keeps roots cool. Spread it around all annuals, perennials, trees, shrubs, and vegetables, especially where summers are hot and dry.

☑ STAKE TREES. If spring winds are a problem where you live (especially in west Texas), stake new trees and thin them so wind will pass through.

PEST CONTROL

☑ CONTROL APHIDS. Check tender new growth on plants for aphid infestations. Spray them off with a jet of water, then follow up with insecticidal soap.

Cold-tolerant Rhododendrons

Rhododendron aficionados in cold parts of the Northwest owe much to the late Ernest H. Wilson, curator of Boston's Arnold Arboretum. From 1891 into the early 1900s, a string of brutally cold winters stung New England. As a plant explorer, Wilson carefully noted which rhododendrons survived the frigid weather. His findings helped the Northwest's frontier gardeners get off to a good start.

Today, this hardy group of rhododendrons is known as the Ironclad hybrids, and they provide gardeners in Zones 1 through 3 with a fine selection of cold-tolerant plants in a wide range of flower colors. Several varieties on Wilson's original list—including 'Catawbiense Album', 'Purpureum Grandiflorum', and 'Roseum Elegans'—are still treasured by gardeners today, but the ranks of Ironclad hybrids have grown extensively, thanks to breeders in the Northwest. Now, there are dozens of plants that will survive prolonged exposure to temperatures below -20°F (see the list of Ironclad hybrids below right).

This month, nurseries will be selling rhododendrons in containers. Set in the ground now, a plant has three seasons to get established before winter puts it to the test.

Choose a site where plants will be protected from intense sun and drying winds, such as in the shade of a north-facing or east-facing wall or under tall trees. Rhodies require acid soil and good drainage. In areas with alkaline soil, you'll need to supplement it with acid amendments. Dig a large planting hole (4 feet square by 2 feet deep is not too big) and replace existing soil with a blend of humus and finished compost mixed with an ample amount of peat moss or well-rotted manure (use a combination of some or all of these additives). The top of the root ball should be level with the existing soil grade. Water plants frequently through summer and fall.

Early-blooming 'PJM' rhododendron bears inch-wide blossoms among leaves that take on a mahogany cast in winter.

A dozen choice plants

Here are 12 of the hardiest and most popular Ironclad hybrids.

'Catawbiense Album'. White flowers with yellow blotches; plants grow 4 to 6 feet tall.

'Catawbiense Boursault'. Rose-lilac flowers with a yellow blotch; 6 feet or taller.

'English Roseum'. Rosy pink flowers; 6 feet or taller.

'Ken Janeck'. White flowers with pink shading; 3 to 4 feet.

'Lee's Dark Purple'. Royal purple flowers; 6 feet or taller.

'Minnetonka'. Lavender-pink flowers with a chartreuse blotch; 3 to 4 feet.

'Nova Zembla'. Red flowers with black spotting on the top petal; 4 to 6 feet.

'Olga Mezitt'. Deep-pink flowers; mature leaves are bronzy green; 4 to 6 feet.

'PJM'. Lavender-pink flowers (shown above); to 4 feet.

'Purpureum Elegans'. Purple flowers with brown spots; 4 to 6 feet.

'Purpureum Grandiflorum'. Violet flowers with green flecks; 4 to 6 feet.

'Roseum Elegans'. Rose-lilac flowers; 6 feet or taller.

Ponds and Fountains

It doesn't take much water to soothe the soul—even the smallest pond can have a cooling effect on a garden. The size of your pond will be restricted by the space available, but its shape and style are only limited by your imagination. If you wish to start small, consider the portable decorative pools available at garden centers and statuary stores, or create your own tub version.

Large traditional ponds of brick, concrete, fitted stone, or tile can blend as easily into contemporary gardens as formal ones. They present the opportunity to introduce color and texture to the garden with aquatic plants such as water lilies and floating hyacinths. A raised pond with brick walls provides a classic home for goldfish and koi.

Water features fall into one of three categories: spray fountains, waterfalls, or spill fountains. Spray fountains are most suitable for formal ponds and are made versatile by assorted heads that shoot water in massive columns or lacy mists. Waterfalls send a cascade toward the pond from a simple outlet pipe. Spill or wall fountains flow from the outlet into a pool or series of tiered pans or shelves. They're good choices for smaller gardens and can even stand alone, independent of ponds.

Placing the pond

The obvious spot for a pond is where everyone can enjoy it. But because children find ponds irresistible, the safest locations are in fenced backyards. Check with your local building

Spray fountains add life to any pond; they are available with jets, pumps, and accessories.

department about any requirements for fencing with self-latching gates, as well as setbacks from property lines, electrical circuits for pumps and lights, and pond depth. Generally, ponds less than 24 inches deep do not need a building permit.

If you are planning to add plants or fish to your pond, first consider the climate in your garden. The pond must be protected from wind and situated away from deciduous trees that shed a steady supply of leaves and twigs into the water. Proper drainage is also important: Don't choose a low-lying (or "bottom") area that will con-

stantly overflow in wet weather. And remember that the backyard needn't be the only place for a pond. The addition of moving water to a front patio or entryway both cools the air and blocks the noise of passing traffic.

Often it's the border that harmonizes the pond with the surrounding landscape. The choices are many: a grass lawn; an adjoining bog garden or rock garden (often piled against a partially raised pond or used at one end of a sloping site); native stones and boulders; flagstones laid in mortar; a wide concrete lip (especially useful as a mowing strip if grass adjoins the area); brick laid in sand or mortar; redwood or other rot-resistant wood laid as rounds or upright columns; terracotta tiles; or railroad ties.

Flexible pond liners are made from a variety of materials and can be found at home-and-garden centers or through mail-order catalogs. Although PVC plastic is the standard material, it becomes brittle with exposure to the sun. More UV-resistant—but twice the price—are industrial-grade PVC and butyl-rubber liners. Some pool builders prefer EPDM, a roofing material, available in 10- to 40-foot-wide rolls. Most liners can be cut and solvent-welded to fit odd-shaped ponds.

Another option is a preformed fiberglass pool shell. A number of shapes and sizes are available, but many are too shallow to accommodate fish. Although these cost more than PVC-lined pools, they can be expected to last longer—up to 20 years.

---

1. *Look to the landscape for guidance on edgings, shape, and scale. Boulders and plants interspersed around an edging of irregular flagstone help this pond blend into its surroundings.*

2. *Tucked into a corner of a redwood deck, this angular tub garden is fed by a built-in spill fountain. A mossy ground cover and surrounding planters piled high with impatiens and lobelia add lushness.*

3. *Contemporary masonry is featured in this edging of interlocking pavers that match the patio floor. A compact pond mirrors a colorful border filled with foxgloves, lilies, poppies, and roses.*

A simple pond

Outlet is 120 volts and powers pump

Plant shelf

Sand bed, 2 inches thick, cushions liner

Submersible pump circulates water to waterfall or fountain jet

Prefilter helps keep pump free of debris

Flexible liner follows shape of hole and tucks under flagstone edgings

Depth of 24 inches is best for plants and fish

Water features

Garden ponds range from complicated formal reflecting pools and deep, plant-filled koi ponds with sophisticated pumps and filters to simple ornamental styles with just a couple of water plants and a few goldfish. A do-it-yourselfer can easily build a pond such as the one shown above—much of the work lies in excavating the hole and adding a sand bed for cushioning.

The sound and sight of water tumbling down a small stream and over a waterfall can add to the pleasure of a pond. To create a stream, mound up soil collected during the pond excava-tion, then form a waterway in the mound and cover it with a length of liner material. Stack broad, flat rocks like steps, overlapping and slanting down from one level to the next. Look to nature for design guidance so your construction doesn't look artificial.

A submersible pump will circulate water from the pond to the head of the waterfall or stream. You can find a variety of pump sizes at home-and-garden centers or through mail-order pond suppliers. (The volume of water and the height of its lift determine the size of the pump required.)

A built-in flow-reducing valve on the pump's outlet side will reduce the flow of water in the falls. Most pumps come with a small strainer on the intake side, but this can easily become clogged with debris. It's best to add a large prefilter, available from the same sources.

To power the waterfall or fountain pump, or any adjacent lighting, you'll need a 120-volt outdoor outlet with a ground fault circuit interrupter (GFCI) near the pond. You must get an electrical permit before installing a new outdoor outlet.

Installing a Garden Pond

With either a flexible plastic or rubber pond liner and a bit of elbow grease, even a beginner can fashion an average-size garden pond in a single weekend, though plantings and borders will take somewhat longer to establish.

Even a pond with an unusual shape should not present a problem. A liner can take almost any shape, accommodating curves and undulations. It's also possible to weld two pieces of liner together with solvent cement, or have the supplier do it for you.

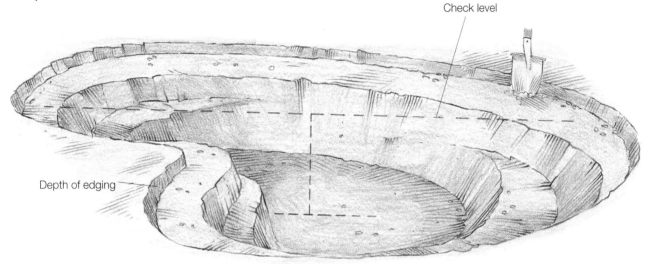

Check level

Depth of edging

1. *Mark the pond's outline with a hose or a length of rope. Dig all around the outline with a sharp spade; remove any sod and keep it in a shady spot for later patching. Excavate the hole to the desired depth and width, plus 2 inches all around for a layer of sand. Dig down to the thickness of any edging material. Check level carefully, using a straight board to bridge the rim.*

Liner

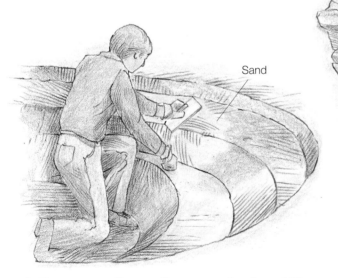

Sand

3. *Open up the liner and let it soften in the sun. Then spread it over the hole, evening up the overlap all around. Place heavy stones or bricks around the perimeter to weigh it down, then slowly begin to fill the pond with water.* (Continued on next page.)

2. *Next, remove all protruding roots and rocks and fill any holes with soil. Pack a 2-inch layer of clean, damp sand into the excavation. Smooth the sand with a board or a concrete float.*

Installing a Garden Pond, *continued*

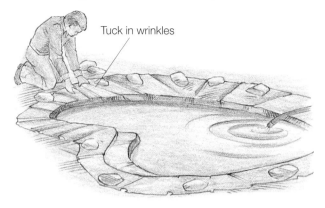

Tuck in wrinkles

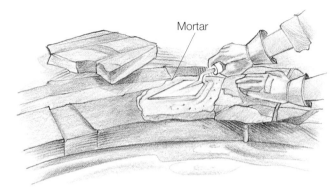

Mortar

4. *Continue filling, tucking in wrinkles all around; as required, fold pleats at hard corners (they won't be visible when the pool is filled). You can wade into the pool to tuck in the lining, but the water's weight will make it fit the contours of the hole.*

5. *When the pond is full, add overhanging edging. Lay flagstones or brick in a thin bed of mortar. Bring the liner up behind the edging, then trim the liner. Drain the pool and refill it with fresh water.*

Water hyacinths (Eichhornia crassipes) *can be plopped in the pond and—even if chewed by raccoons—will quickly multipy. Duckweed is considered an unwelcome addition to most ponds as it chokes other plants and blocks sunlight, but just skim off the excess with a wooden board. This bubbling mask keeps the water moving.*

A pond in a pot

A glazed ceramic pot at least 30 inches in diameter, without a drain hole, makes a simple, handsome water feature. Fill it about two-thirds full with water, then add plants—each in its own pot (set plants on inverted pots to raise them). Choice plants include water lilies and water irises. The size of the container dictates the number of plants you need. Once they're in place, fill the rest of the tub with water.

To control mosquito larvae, add mosquito fish *(Gambusia)* or goldfish. The fish will also feed on algae in the tub. To acclimate the fish before releasing, place them, still in their plastic bag, in the tub garden for about 20 minutes. A 30-inch-diameter tub can accommodate about six fish.

Once a year, without emptying the water, scrub the plant pots and the inside of the tub with a stiff brush. Remove loose algae. Drain when 2 inches of decomposed matter accumulates on the bottom (every few years). Scrub the inside surfaces and divide plants.

How to Shop Smart

"When I go nursery shopping, I'm like a kid in a candy store. Everything's so beautiful that I want to buy one of each!" says one eager spring shopper. The colorful promise of a nursery in April is irresistible, with literally thousands of annuals and perennials to choose from. But impulse buying is a sure way to run up a major tab, and it all but guarantees a mishmash in the landscape.

The best advice for great performance and the most value for your dollar? Be a smart shopper.

Before you leave home, have an idea of your needs based on space, sun exposure, and soil conditions. And think about potential plant combinations with an eye toward compatible bloom times, colors, heights, and frequency of watering and fertilizing. Also, estimate how many plants you'll need, allowing for growth. (Whether you plant a coreopsis from a jumbo pack or a 1-gallon container, the ultimate size is the same.)

These details, plus the smart-shopping guidelines on the following pages, will help you navigate nursery aisles with ease.

Let the season be your guide

How do you choose from among so many plant possibilities? It depends upon whether you're searching for summer-long bloom, a splash of instant color, or both. The following tips will help you choose the right annuals and perennials for what you wish to accomplish.

Annuals are plants that complete the life cycle in one growing season. Some annuals grow during the warm season, while others are cool-season plants. In March and April, you'll find a relatively small selection of cool-season annuals but an abundance of warm-season annuals.

Cool-season annuals (listed at right) look good now in nurseries and are great when you want a burst of color for a party or special occasion. But in inland areas, they'll bloom themselves out as summer sets in, and plants will die. (In mild coastal areas, they may flower into summer.) These annuals are better planted in the fall in mild-winter regions.

Warm-season annuals (listed at right) are a better buy at this time of year. You can expect a full summer of bloom from young, healthy seedlings. Plants will fade at summer's end.

Perennials grow and bloom each year, usually for at least three years. Longevity distinguishes perennials from annuals. Each perennial variety has its own bloom season.

Spring bloomers (which include columbine, coral bells, foxglove, and rockcress) are often near peak bloom in nurseries in March and April, but once you transplant them in the garden they may be on their way out of flower. It's best to plant these perennials in fall for bloom from early spring into summer.

Perennials that bloom through the summer (coreopsis, gaillardia, penstemon, rudbeckia, salvia, Shasta daisy, verbena, and yarrow) are a better bet. Although fall is the best time to plant most of these perennials, if you buy and plant these soon, you can expect excellent results.

COOL-SEASON ANNUALS

The following plants grow in the cool season. You'll find some or all of these in nurseries now, with a bigger selection in the Northwest and mountain regions. Though they provide instant color, they'll bloom out by summer. You'll get the longest bloom if they're planted earlier (in fall in mild-winter climates, in early spring in colder regions).

- *Annual phlox (Southern California and desert only)*
- *Bachelor's button*
- *Chrysanthemum multicaule*
- *C. paludosum*
- *Dianthus (Southern California and desert only)*
- *Forget-me-not*
- *Nemesia*
- *Pansy*
- *Poppy*
- *Sweet alyssum*

WARM-SEASON ANNUALS

These annuals grow during the warm season and provide summer bloom. Depending on where you live, they start appearing in nurseries in February (Southern California, desert areas), March (Northern California), April (the Northwest and warmer parts of the mountain region), or May (mountain region).

- *Ageratum*
- *Annual phlox*
- *Celosia*
- *Cosmos*
- *Dianthus*
- *Impatiens*
- *Lobelia*
- *Marigold*
- *Nasturtium*
- *Nicotiana*
- *Petunia*
- *Portulaca*
- *Salvia*
- *Sunflower*
- *Sweet alyssum*
- *Verbena*
- *Zinnia*

NORMAN A. PLATE

Dianthus (usually grown as an annual) comes in a variety of container sizes. Not shown: jumbo pack, with six 2½-inch cells.

8-inch pulp pot

1 gallon

4-inch pot

Sixpack with 1-inch cells

Plants come in all sizes, but small is usually best

Nurseries now carry plants in different sizes of containers. Choices can be overwhelming.

Annuals are readily available in sixpacks (also called pony packs and cell-packs), with six 1-inch-wide cells; jumbo packs (or color packs), with six 2½-inch-wide cells; 4-inch pots; 1-gallon containers; and 8-inch-wide pulp pots. And in Southern California, annuals are sometimes sold in undivided flats, as shown at right.

In the past, perennials were sold primarily in 1-gallon containers. Then a few years ago, nurseries started carrying plants in 4-inch pots. Over the past couple of years in California, more and more perennials have become available in sixpacks or jumbo packs.

Which should you buy?

If cost is a concern, small plants are typically a better value. But even if cost isn't a consideration, healthy plants in small containers, if they're not rootbound, generally offer major advantages. They usually go through less transplant shock and get established faster than larger plants. In most cases, they catch up to their larger counterparts within a few weeks and they also bloom for a longer period of time.

Also, most horticulturists agree that for a long season of bloom it's best to buy plants before they flower. (In some areas, it may be difficult to find even the smallest plants without bloom.) That doesn't mean you never should buy blooming plants in 4-inch or 1-gallon containers. If you're having a party and want instant color, go ahead and splurge. Or, if it's late in the season and you don't want to wait the few extra weeks for flowers, indulge yourself.

Annual plants are commonly sold in flats of 64 or 81 annuals. Sometimes quarter- or half-flats are sold.

Perennials like this coreopsis often come in three sizes: sixpacks, 4-inch pots, and 1-gallon containers

Effects of container size on growth

Here is how three kinds of perennials—perennial statice *(Limonium perezii)*, delphinium (not shown below), and erodium—in sixpacks, 4-inch pots, and 1-gallon containers, performed in a growth test.

Within six weeks, growth of the 4-inch statice, delphinium, and erodium caught up to the 1-gallon plants. It's interesting to note that there were more blooms on the 4-inch statice and erodium (although the statice flowers weren't open completely). About three weeks after the photograph below, the sixpack sizes of statice and delphinium caught up. Only the sixpack of the slower-growing erodium remained smaller during the first season of growth than the plants from the 4-inch and 1-gallon containers. For slower-growing perennials such as armeria, coral bells, and erodium, you may want to buy plants in 4-inch containers so they fill in faster. Otherwise, sixpacks are your best buy and give the best performance for the money. Bear in mind, however, that many perennials—especially the more uncommon varieties—are still available only in gallon containers.

Before planting: Sixpack, 4-inch, and 1-gallon sizes of statice, delphinium, and erodium line up.

Erodium six weeks after planting

1-gallon   *4-inch*   *Sixpack*

Statice six weeks after planting

1-gallon

4-inch

Sixpack

Choosing healthy plants

Annuals and perennials planted now for summer bloom need to grow vigorously. By choosing healthy seedlings and caring for them properly, you won't be disappointed. As a general rule, nurseries tend to take better care of plants than discount stores that sell everything from clothing to plumbing supplies.

No matter where you shop, look for compact plants with good leaf color. Leaves should be perky, not limp or wilted. Straggly or stretching seedlings may indicate crowding or insufficient light. If plants are rootbound, pass them by.

Occasionally you'll find seedlings that were recently planted into their cell-pack or 4-inch containers and aren't yet ready for the garden. If the leaves of the plant extend to the edge of the container, then the root system is probably developed enough for transplanting into your garden.

Healthy flowers like these cleome (spider plant) start from healthy plants.

Right: When you shop for plants, knowing what not to buy is as important as knowing what to buy. The snapdragon at left is pale and wilty because of dry soil; delphiniums (center) are too wet, and are rotting; and campanula is young and too small for the pot.

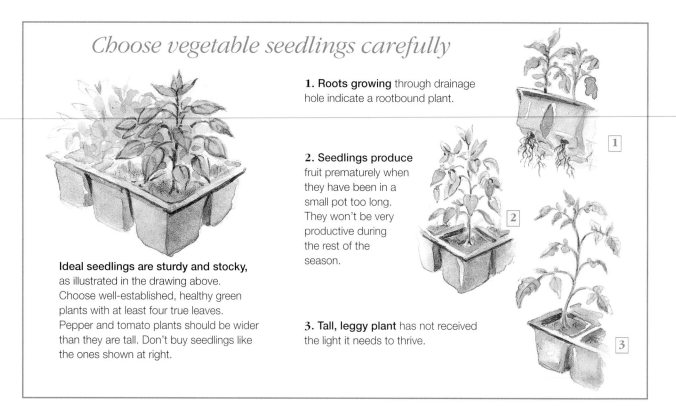

Choose vegetable seedlings carefully

Ideal seedlings are sturdy and stocky, as illustrated in the drawing above. Choose well-established, healthy green plants with at least four true leaves. Pepper and tomato plants should be wider than they are tall. Don't buy seedlings like the ones shown at right.

1. Roots growing through drainage hole indicate a rootbound plant.

2. Seedlings produce fruit prematurely when they have been in a small pot too long. They won't be very productive during the rest of the season.

3. Tall, leggy plant has not received the light it needs to thrive.

Weed Control

Weeds are wild plants (and some invasive cultivated plants) that compete with your garden plants for water, nutrients, and space. They're inevitable, but you can control them. Prevention—mulches, landscape fabrics, and blanket-like ground covers—is the first line of defense. Hand-weeding before weeds set seed is also critical. If you're vigilant for a few years, you'll be rewarded with a sharp decline in your weed population.

Because they develop extensive root systems, perennial weeds are more difficult to manage once they've grown past the seedling stage—to get rid of the plant, you have to dig out the roots. Hasten their demise by repeatedly cutting back the tops, which stresses the plants, but it may take several seasons to eradicate them. Annual weed seeds can be windborne or delivered by birds, arrive in nursery containers, or be present in certain mulches (only use mulches that are certified weed-free).

Herbicides are powerful chemicals that can damage desirable plants and contaminate water and soil. Before buying a herbicide, always read the label to ensure you have the correct product for the weeds in your garden.

Some ornamental plants can become invasive in good growing conditions and may eventually overpower your garden or invade wild areas. Below is a list of some of the worst offenders in Western gardens.

Types of herbicides

There are two main types of herbicide, or weed-killer: Pre-emergents prevent seeds from germinating; post-emergent "contact" types kill weeds on contact; slower-acting 'translocated' post-emergents interfere with the weed's metabolism (they are best for perennial weed control). Most herbicides are further specified as selective or nonselective; the latter kill any plant with which they come in contact. Brand names vary from place to place; look for the "active ingredient" to determine which chemicals an herbicide contains, and how it should be applied.

For lawns, common pre-emergents contain one or more of the following ingredients: atrazine, dithiopyr, isoxaben, oryzalin, pendimethalin, and trifluralin. Post-emergents for control of broadleaf weeds include dicamba, MCPP, and 2,4-D. For crabgrass, use MSMA or DSMA. For nutsedge in lawns, use bentazon.

In ornamental plantings, long-lasting pre-emergent products include dichlobenil (Casoron) and trifluralin (Preen) granules, and oryzalin spray (Casoron for woody ornamentals only). For established weeds, first try glyphosate (Roundup) or herbicidal soap; both must be sprayed directly—and only—on the target weed. Selective chemicals for grassy weeds include fluazifop-butyl and sethoxydim. For brush control, try glyphosate, triclopyr, 2,4-D or glufosinate.

Too much of a good thing

Bamboo, golden and black
Phyllostachys aurea and P. nigra

Bellflower, creeping and Siberian
Campanula

Calla lilies
Zantedeschia

Dame's rocket
Hesperis matronalis

English ivy
Hedera helix

Fountain grass
Pennisetum setaceum

Four o'clocks (Pacific Northwest)
Mirabilis jalapa

Giant Burmese honeysuckle
Lonicera hildebrandiana

Horsetail
Equisetum hyemale

Japanese anemone
Anemone hybrida

Jubata grass
Cortaderia jubata

Mint
Mentha

Morning glory
Ipomoea tricolor

Pampas grass
Cortaderia selloana

Purple loosestrife (Northwest and mountain states)
Lythrum virgatum

Sweet violet
Viola odorata

Trumpet vine
Campsis radicans

Bindweed

Blackberry

Nutsedge

Mallow

Purslane

Thistle

Groundsel

Creeping bellflower

Oxalis

THE WORST WEEDS

THICKET- AND GROVE-FORMING WEEDS

Blackberry. Perennial; spreads by underground stems; canes can grow 20–30 ft. in one season.

DEEP-ROOTED WEEDS

Bindweed. Perennial; spreads by rhizomes, but seeds can lie dormant for 50 years before sprouting. Roots can penetrate 10 ft. into soil.

Dandelion. Perennial; reproduces by seed and roots; forms deep taproot.

Mallow. Annual or biennial; reproduces by seed; forms deep taproot.

Nutsedge. Perennial; spreads on tubers as deep as 18 in.

Thistle. Annual, biennial, and perennial; reproduces by seed; grows from deep, wide-spreading roots.

SHALLOW-ROOTED WEEDS

Purslane. Annual; spreads by seed or reroots from stem fragments. Easy to pull or hoe.

Spurge. Annual; spreads by seed. Easy to pull or hoe.

RAMPANT RESEEDERS

Creeping bellflower. Spreads by seed and deep-seated creeping rhizomes.

Groundsel. Annual; spreads by seed; often several generations in a year.

Yellow oxalis. Perennial; reproduces by above ground runners and seeds. Seed capsules can shoot seeds as far as 10 ft. away.

ANNUAL GRASSES

Bluegrass. Annual (some perennial); sets seed rapidly in cool weather, often before plants can be pulled.

Crabgrass. Annual; spreads by seeds and rooting along the stems.

PERENNIAL GRASSES

Bermuda grass. Perennial; spreads by rhizomes, aboveground runners, and seed.

Kikuyu grass. Perennial; spreads by rhizomes, aboveground runners, and seed. Few chemical controls effective.

Preventing and controlling weeds

Space fast-growing annuals and ground covers closely together and they will eventually shade out weeds as they grow. Staggered, intensive planting is most natural looking; set plants an equal distance from one another in all directions. But restricted air flow and trapped moisture can invite insects and disease.

Fabric weed barriers trap perennial weeds underneath, but seeds of annual weeds can sprout and grow in the mulch above. Use landscape fabric in permanent plantings around perennials and shrubs, or in pathway construction. Cover the fabric with 2 or 3 inches of mulch to disguise it.

Pre-emergent herbicides are available in granular form, and as soluble liquids that can be applied with a hose-end sprayer. Apply them to the soil or lawn early in the season before weeds germinate. Read the label to learn which weeds the herbicide controls best and whether it can be used on a lawn.

Spot sprays kill weeds that have already sprouted. But because they don't distinguish between valued plants and weeds, you must apply these products carefully. In close quarters, use a paintbrush rather than a spray applicator.

Long-handled weeding hoes let you remove weeds without bending. Pincer-type tools have a forked blade that makes it easy to pop the long root out of moist soil with minimal disturbance to the surrounding area.

Sweep a propane-powered flamer a few inches above weeds in pathways or along curbs. Rather than burning up, the cells of the weed actually burst and it quickly dies. Take care with the flamer in dry, fire-prone areas.

Mulch

There's probably no single weed-prevention technique better than applying a thick mulch over all exposed areas in your garden. It smothers emerging weed seeds as they germinate and makes it easier to pull out those that persevere through the mulch layer. If a plant is susceptible to a soilborne disease, mulching around its base will keep disease-bearing soil from splashing up onto leaves during rain or watering.

In addition to weed and disease prevention, mulch serves many other useful purposes. It keeps the soil's surface temperature down—especially important in areas of the West with long, hot summers, when roots near the surface will wither and die in the heat. It also helps keep the top of the soil from crusting over and taking on cementlike characteristics, particularly a problem if the soil is clayey. If the soil surface crusts over, it's harder for air needed by the plant to penetrate the surface, and irrigation water may just run off.

In colder-winter areas, mulch can also help some plants survive. For example, a thick mulch may keep soil from freezing (when soil is frozen, its water isn't available to plants).

Finally, mulch makes a garden look tidy and more attractive. If you've gone on any local garden tours, you'll notice that the beds are often covered with a fresh layer of thick mulch—it unites the garden visually and gives it a more professional look.

Some of the materials described as amendments, such as ground bark, sawdust, compost, and soil conditioners, also work well as mulches. Bark chips of various sizes are frequently used in the West, as is straw, especially in vegetable gardens. Other mulches are available through organic gardening suppliers. A popular one is cocoa bean hulls. While expensive for large areas, it is very attractive for small beds. It gives off a faint chocolate fragrance as a bonus.

If you're using a mulch made from wood products—such as bark chips, wood chips, or fresh sawdust—you need to add nitrogen to the soil as you lay down the mulch. These products are low in nitrogen and will rob existing nitrogen from the soil as they decay. Add 1 pound of nitrogen to each 15 pounds of wood product. To determine nitrogen weight, multiply the percentage of nitrogen listed on the product's label by the product's weight.

How to use mulch

Mulch is applied in different thicknesses, depending on its type. In all cases, take care to avoid mounding any mulch up around a plant's trunk, because the trunk could draw moisture from the mulch and rot.

If you use organic mulch, add 1–6 inches each season (1 inch is the minimum for getting any benefit). A standard amount is 2–3 inches. In some circumstances, 6 inches may be a good choice—for example, in a warm-

Above: Organic mulches such as pine needles should be renewed annually; 2–3 inches is the minimum, but you can lay it thicker if you like. Purchase only guaranteed weed-free material— straw, hay, and many manures, for instance, may contain weed seeds. Right: A mulch of flagstone rubble keeps weeds under control while providing a river-bed effect.

climate vegetable garden. One other note: If you're vegetable gardening in a cool area, you may want to start the season with a clear plastic mulch that will help warm the soil. As the season progresses, you can remove the plastic and replace it with an organic mulch to preserve water and keep the soil cool during any hot spells.

For purposes of pest and disease prevention, dispose of garden mulch as you go about your fall cleanup tasks. If the mulch is compost or some other organic material, work it into the ground. Otherwise, remove it. If you live in a cold-winter area, wait until spring to apply mulch again. If your area is mild and rainy, apply new mulch after removing all old and diseased leaves, stems, or plants from your garden. An application of fresh mulch before winter rains will help keep your garden free of any weeds that grow in winter and early spring.

Above: Black plastic sheeting used as mulch helps to warm soil, conserve moisture, and suppress weeds. It's particularly good for heat-loving plants such as melons. Below: Gravel and stone mulches are suitable for desert gardens. They also help eliminate muddy strolls in rainy regions.

Laying landscape fabric

Landscape fabric allows water and air to penetrate. Fabric mulches should be covered with a more attractive (and weed-free) mulch. Unroll the fabric, then cut x-shaped slits for plants with scissors. Then tuck the flaps around the plant's base.

*Roses brought West by pioneers—such as this hybrid China 'Paul Ricault' (1845)—
are still thriving, thanks to the efforts of dedicated rosarians.*

May

Pacific Northwest Checklist

PLANTING

☑ **ANNUAL FLOWERS.** Zones 4–7: Set out ageratum, globe amaranth, cosmos, impatiens, lobelia, marigolds, nicotiana, petunias, salvia, sunflowers, sweet alyssum, and zinnias. Zones 1–3: Plant these warm-season annuals after the last frost. Cold-hardy calendula, pansies, and sweet peas can go into the ground immediately.

☑ **BULBS.** In Zones 1–3, plant summer-blooming bulbs such as ornamental onion and montbretia.

☑ **HERBS AND VEGETABLES.** Zones 4–7: When the soil warms up, plant herbs (basil, dill, fennel, rosemary, sage, and thyme) and vegetables (beans, corn, eggplant, melons, okra, peppers, pumpkins, squash, and tomatoes). In Zones 1–3, choose short-season vegetables and plant through black plastic mulch. Use hot caps, row covers, or even old tires to hold warmth around the plants.

☑ **DAHLIAS AND BEGONIAS.** Planted now, both will reward you with blooms from summer into fall. Stake or cage tall dahlias at planting time to avoid puncturing tubers later in the season.

☑ **FUCHSIAS AND GERANIUMS.** Zones 4–7: Early in the month, plants can go into the ground or in outdoor containers. Put plants in rich, loose soil and water well. Begin a feeding program 2 weeks after you set them out. In Zones 1–3, wait until month's end to set plants out.

☑ **PERENNIALS.** Throughout the Northwest, nurseries will be well stocked with plants in 4-inch pots and 1-gallon containers. Buy now and plant immediately.

MAINTENANCE

☑ **FERTILIZE.** As soon as annuals get established, start feeding them. Liquid plant food such as fish emulsion works well because the nutrients go directly to the roots. For perennials, use liquid or granular fertilizer. For shrubs, scatter a granular fertilizer around the base of each plant. For lawns, apply a high-nitrogen fertilizer evenly over the grass to keep it growing thick and green.

☑ **PRUNE SHRUBS.** If you prune spring-flowering shrubs such as lilacs and rhododendrons while they are in bloom, you can use cut blossoms for indoor bouquets. Remove damaged and crossing branches first, then prune for shape, working up from the bottom of the plant and from the inside out.

☑ **TRIM HEDGES.** If you prune hedges twice each year, shear or clip them between now and early June. A good rule of thumb is to shear coniferous hedges and clip broad-leafed ones. Trim hedges so that the bottom is wider than the top; this allows sunlight and rain to reach the foliage.

☑ **REMOVE FADED BLOOMS.** Deadheading makes plants look neater and stops faded blooms from turning into seed pods, thus channeling the plant's energy into active growth.

PEST & WEED CONTROL

☑ **SLUGS.** Newly set-out flower and vegetable seedlings are sitting ducks for hungry slugs. Spread a defensive circle of poison bait around plants or set out beer traps.

☑ **BENEFICIAL INSECTS.** To help control aphids, mealybugs, scale, and other soft-bodied insects, buy and release lacewings, a parasitic insect that feeds on a variety of garden pests.

☑ **WEED.** Pull weeds now while they're young and most have not yet formed seeds.

Northern California Checklist

PLANTING

☑ **ANNUALS AND PERENNIALS.** Zones 7–9, 14–17: Set out ageratum, coreopsis, dahlias, gaillardia, globe amaranth, impatiens, lobelia, Madagascar periwinkle (vinca), marigolds, nicotiana, penstemon, perennial statice, petunias, phlox, portulaca, salvia, sanvitalia, sunflowers, sweet alyssum, torenia, verbena, and zinnias. Zones 1–2: Wait to plant warm-season annuals until after the last frost. You can still plant cold-hardy calendula, pansies, and sweet peas.

☑ **DAHLIAS AND BEGONIAS.** Planted now, both will reward you with blooms from summer into fall. Among dahlias, choices run from dwarf varieties to ones that grow 6 feet tall and bear plate-size flowers. Stake or cage tall dahlias at planting time to avoid puncturing tubers later in the season. Among tuberous begonias, choose upright types for beds or cascading types for hanging baskets.

☑ **HERBS AND VEGETABLES.** It's prime time to plant heat-loving herbs and vegetables, including basil, beans, corn, eggplant, melons, okra, peppers, pumpkins, squash, and tomatoes. In Zones 1–2 and 17, choose short-season varieties and plant through black plastic. Use row covers or hot caps to hold warmth around plants and protect them from late spring frosts.

☑ **TOMATOES.** It's late to start plants from seed, so buy nursery-grown seedlings. Select stocky, not leggy, plants with a rich green color. At transplanting time, pull off the lowest leaves and plant up to the next leaf set; roots will form along the buried stem.

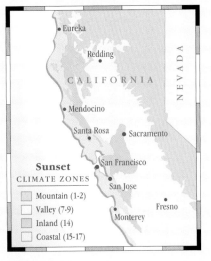

Sunset
CLIMATE ZONES
☐ Mountain (1-2)
☐ Valley (7-9)
☐ Inland (14)
☐ Coastal (15-17)

MAINTENANCE

☑ **TREES.** In windy areas, stake young trees using two stakes, each placed a foot out from the trunk. Tie the tree to the stakes with a flexible loop of plastic tree tie or cord. Tie the tree loosely enough so that the trunk is not rigid. The trunk should be able to move a bit in the wind.

☑ **AERATE LAWNS.** To improve air and water circulation in the soil around roots, aerate the lawn. You can rent an aerator from an equipment supply store (look in the yellow pages under Rental Service Stores and Yards). Rake up the cores and topdress with mulch. If you haven't fed the grass lately, apply a lawn fertilizer and water it in well.

☑ **HARDEN OFF SEEDLINGS.** Zones 1–2: Move seedlings of warm-season flowers and vegetables outdoors to a cold frame or other protected spot and gradually expose them to longer periods of stronger sunlight. As planting time draws near, cut back on water and fertilizer to ease transplant shock.

☑ **MAKE COMPOST.** A well-tended compost pile can break down an amazing amount of garden debris and kitchen waste: annual weeds, coffee grounds, eggshells, evergreen needles, fruit and peels, grass clippings, leaves, prunings, sawdust, small wood chips, and tea leaves. (Do not add any animal or fish residue or pet manure.) Keep the pile evenly moist and occasionally add a handful of nitrogen fertilizer or manure. Turn the pile frequently with a spading fork. When the compost is crumbly and develops an earthy brown color, use it as a soil amendment or as a water-conserving mulch.

☑ **STAKE PERENNIALS.** If you use either hoop or enclosed square stakes, install them when plants are small, so foliage can grow up through the openings. Once plants are bushy, these stakes are almost impossible to install.

☑ **THIN FRUIT.** Zones 7–9, 14–17: On apples, nectarines, peaches, and Asian pears, gently twist off enough immature fruit to leave 4 to 6 inches between remaining fruit. This allows the remaining fruit to grow larger and may also reduce problems with insects (such as codling moth) and diseases (such as apple mildew and apple scab) because there's more room for air circulation around the fruit and they aren't touching each other. Zones 1 and 2: Thinning should be done in early summer.

PEST CONTROL

☑ **BENEFICIAL INSECTS.** To help control aphids, mealybugs, scale, and other soft-bodied insects, buy and release lacewings, a beneficial insect that feeds on a variety of garden pests.

Southern California Checklist

PLANTING

☑ **PLANT SUMMER ANNUALS.** Nurseries carry a huge selection this month. Sturdy standbys such as petunias and vinca are available in refreshing pastel shades. There are rudbeckias compact enough for containers. And some coleus now thrive in the sun. Other options include alyssum, candytuft, bedding dahlias, dianthus, geraniums, lobelia, marigolds, nicotiana, phlox, portulaca, and verbena. Start cleome, cosmos, nasturtiums, sunflowers, and zinnias from seed. They're all easy and rewarding.

☑ **PLANT HERBS.** Nurseries are well stocked with herbs, and it's a good time to plant them. Try basil, chervil, chives, lemon grass, marjoram, mint, oregano, parsley, rosemary, sage, savory, tarragon, and thyme. Cilantro and dill are best started from seed.

☑ **PLANT SUMMER VEGETABLES.** Set out plants of cucumber, eggplant, melon, pepper, squash, and tomato. Sow seeds of corn, cucumbers, lima and snap beans, melon, okra, pumpkin, and summer and winter squash. In the low desert (Zone 13), plant Jerusalem artichoke, okra, peppers, and sweet peppers.

☑ **START LAWNS.** This is a good month to plant subtropical grasses such as St. Augustine, Bermuda, and zoysia. You can lay sod (the simplest method) or plant plugs.

☑ **LATE-BLOOMING PERENNIALS.** Selection at nurseries is at its peak. To extend your bloom period, look for varieties that will continue blooming through the summer into fall. These include aster, chrysanthemum, gaillardia, gayfeather, helianthus, lion's tail, penstemon, pentas, reblooming daylily, salvia, and yarrow.

Sunset
CLIMATE ZONES
1-3 7-9 11 13 14-24

☑ **SUBTROPICALS.** Late spring is the best time to plant subtropicals. They'll have all summer to grow before they slow down and harden off for winter. If appropriate for your zone, plant bougainvillea, gardenia, ginger, hibiscus, and palm. This is also a good time to add subtropical ornamental trees—such as the Hong Kong orchid tree—as well as avocado, banana, citrus, and other subtropical fruit trees.

MAINTENANCE

☑ **STEP UP WATERING.** As temperatures warm, plants need to be watered more often. Check new plantings regularly. Seedlings and transplants need frequent shallow watering for a few weeks to establish new roots. Water established plants—including lawns—less often but more deeply to encourage deep root growth. Use a soil probe to test moisture content, and irrigate as needed. Adjust or override automatic sprinklers to meet water needs.

☑ **PINCH BACK MUMS.** For an ample supply of flowers and an attractive bushy plant, pinch back the growing tips of chrysanthemum plants.

☑ **REPLENISH MULCH.** A 3- to 6-inch layer of mulch around trees, shrubs, and established perennials keeps roots cool and moist and discourages weeds. To prevent diseases, leave a clear area around the base of trunks.

☑ **PREVENT BLOSSOM-END ROT IN TOMATOES.** Overfertilizing and heat waves in late spring and early summer trigger this frustrating disease. To prevent it, be stingy with feeding, mulch deeply around plants, and maintain even soil moisture.

PEST CONTROL

☑ **WATCH FOR TOMATO HORNWORMS.** The green worms will be easier to spot if you sprinkle the tomato foliage lightly with water first. Then shake off the water to make worms more visible. Hand-pick them.

☑ **COMBAT POWDERY MILDEW.** Warm days and cool nights are ideal conditions for powdery mildew in susceptible plants such as roses. Frequently hose off foliage in the early mornings to wash off spores. Or spray with 1 tablespoon each baking soda and summer oil diluted in a gallon of water. (Don't spray when temperatures exceed 85°F.) Neem oil is another good alternative.

Mountain Checklist

PLANTING

☑ **ANNUALS.** Early in the month, set out hardy bachelor's buttons, lobelia, pansies, and violas. At month's end, set out warm-season annuals (marigolds, petunias, sunflowers, and zinnias), but if frost is predicted, cover them with hot caps or row covers.

☑ **LAWNS.** New plantings should go into tilled, raked, fertilized, and relatively rock-free soil. Sow bluegrass, fescue, rye, or—better yet—a mix of those grasses. Consider low-water turfgrasses such as blue gamma grass *(Bouteloua gracilis),* buffalo grass *(Buchloe dactyloides),* and tall fescue *(Festuca arundinacea).*

☑ **PERENNIALS.** Plant bleeding heart, bluebells, blue flax, campanula, columbine, delphiniums, gaillardia, geraniums, hellebore, *Heuchera,* Iceland and Oriental poppies, lady's mantle, lupines, Maltese cross, penstemon, phlox, primroses, purple coneflower, Russian sage, Shasta daisies, sweet woodruff, veronica, and yarrow.

☑ **PERMANENT PLANTS.** Set out container-grown shrubs, trees, vines, and hardy ground covers such as *Lamium maculatum* and woolly thyme. They'll have the summer to get roots established before they have to face fall freezes and winter snows.

☑ **VEGETABLES.** Plant seedlings of cool-season crops such as beets, carrots, lettuce, peas, and Swiss chard. Early in the month, sow seeds indoors for warm-season crops (basil, corn, cucumbers, eggplant, melons, peppers, squash, and tomatoes) to transplant after danger of frost is past. If there's no danger of frost, sow these, and beans, directly into well-prepared soil.

Sunset
CLIMATE ZONES

☐ 1-3   ☐ 10-11

MAINTENANCE

☑ **CARE FOR TOMATOES.** Indeterminate types (vinelike types that keep growing all season), need to be staked or caged early or they'll sprawl all over. Keep soil moisture even (mulch and drip irrigation help) to minimize blossom-end rot.

☑ **FERTILIZE.** Before planting beds of flowers or vegetables, amend the soil by digging in 1 to 2 pounds of a complete fertilizer per 100 square feet. Start a monthly fertilizing program for annuals, long-blooming perennials, and container plants. If you live where hyacinths rebloom, fertilize them this month with superphosphate to build up bulbs for next year's bloom.

☑ **HARDEN OFF TRANSPLANTS.** Before transplanting, move seedlings to a partially shaded patio or cold frame, gradually exposing them to more sun and nighttime cold. After 7 to 10 days, they ought to be tough enough to get into the ground.

☑ **MAKE COMPOST.** Alternate 4-inch-thick layers of green matter, such as grass clippings, with brown matter, such as dead leaves and straw. Keep the pile as moist as a wrung-out sponge and turn it weekly.

☑ **MULCH.** Spread organic mulch around annuals, perennials, and vegetables. Ground bark, compost, grass clippings, and rotted leaves all do a good job of suppressing weeds and conserving soil moisture.

☑ **PINCH BACK FLOWERING PLANTS.** Encourage branching and compact growth by pinching or tip-pruning plants such as azaleas, fuchsias, and geraniums.

☑ **PRUNE FLOWERING SHRUBS.** After spring bloom, prune plants such as lilacs, mock orange, and spiraea.

PEST & WEED CONTROL

☑ **WEED.** Hoe weed seedlings on a warm morning, and the afternoon sun will finish them off. Pull larger weeds out by the roots a few hours after you've watered deeply.

☑ **PROTECT CROPS FROM BIRDS.** Bird netting can protect all kinds of small fruits from hungry birds. Fasten edges shut (clothespins are good for this) so birds can't get in.

Southwest Checklist

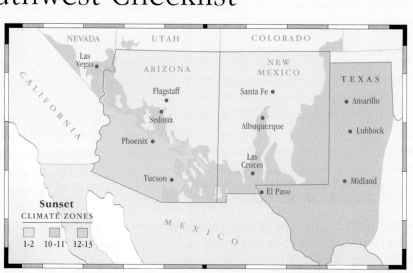

PLANTING

☑ **COLOR IN THE SUN. Zones 10–13:** Set out ageratum, celosia, coreopsis, cosmos, firebush *(Hamelia patens)*, four o'clock, gaillardia, globe amaranth, gloriosa daisies, kochia, lantana, lisianthus, nicotiana, portulaca, salvia, strawflowers, tithonia, vinca rosea *(Catharanthus roseus)*, and zinnias. **Zones 1–2:** Plant any of the above after danger of frost is past.

☑ **COLOR IN THE SHADE.** Good choices include begonias, caladium, chocolate plant *(Pseuderanthemum alatum)*, coleus, gerbera, impatiens, lobelia, oxalis, pentas *(P. lanceolata)*, spider plant, and *Tradescantia fluminensis*.

☑ **LAWNS. Zones 12–13:** Plant Bermuda or improved buffalo grass when nighttime temperatures rise above 70°F. **Zones 1–2, 10–11:** Plant or overseed with bluegrass, fescue, rye, or a combination of these early in the month.

☑ **PERMANENT PLANTS. Zones 1–2, 10–11:** Plant container-grown trees, shrubs, vines, and ground covers.

☑ **SUMMER BULBS.** Plant acidanthera *(Gladiolus callianthus)*, cannas, dahlias, daylilies, gladiolus, montbretia, tiger flower *(Tigridia)*, and zephyranthes (except in Zones 10–11). **Zones 12–13:** Also plant agapanthus, caladium, and crinum. **Zone 13 only:** Plant society garlic *(Tulbaghia violacea)*.

☑ **VEGETABLES. Zones 12–13:** Plant eggplant, Jerusalem artichoke, okra, peanuts, peppers, soybeans, summer squash, and sweet potatoes. **Zones 10–11:** Plant all of the above, plus beans, corn, cucumbers, melons, pumpkins, radishes, southern peas, and tomatoes. (Put most in early in the month; okra, southern peas, and sweet potatoes can be planted through mid-month.) **Zones 1–2:** Plant cool-season crops outside and start seeds indoors for warm-season crops (corn, cucumbers, eggplant, melons, peppers, squash, and tomatoes) to transplant into the garden after danger of frost is past.

MAINTENANCE

☑ **INCREASE WATERING.** When daytime temperatures start hitting 100°F, check plants—especially any new growth—twice a day for wilting. Most plants will need extra water, even cacti and succulents.

☑ **CARE FOR ROSES. Zones 12–13:** When heat starts to take its toll on May's flush of bloom, water plants deeply, mulch, and fertilize. In the Phoenix area, try to give plants afternoon shade.

☑ **FERTILIZE.** Feed flowering shrubs after bloom. Start monthly feedings of annuals, long-blooming perennials, and container plants. For citrus trees, water first, then feed with 1 cup ammonium sulfate per inch of trunk diameter; water again. If citrus foliage still looks yellow, apply chelated iron, magnesium, and zinc.

Laying Out a Vegetable Garden

The best garden starts with a plan you draw on paper and then lay out on the ground using a tape measure and string. Whether your garden is large or small, a thoughtful plan can ensure that you won't waste space and that the vegetables and berries you select will have plenty of room to thrive and to grow successfully to maturity.

To help you visualize how your garden might be laid out, take a look at the sample plans on the next few pages. These plans show a variety of efficient, highly productive gardens that take the greatest advantage of available spaces and growing periods.

Draw your intended garden to scale on graph paper (the examples shown use one square to represent 1 square foot). On the grid, indicate rows or blocks of plants. As you plan, be sure to allow for the proper spacing between plants.

On level ground, plan to run rows north to south; that way the plants will get the maximum amount of sunlight as the sun travels along its east-to-west path. If you'll be planting on a slope, run the rows along the contour of the hill. Be sure to place all tall crops, such as corn and pole beans, on the north side of the garden so that as they mature they won't shade the lower-growing plants.

Put perennial plants, such as asparagus and berries, in their own section of the garden. This way you won't risk disturbing—and harming—their roots each year (or season) when you prepare the soil for other crops.

Consider how you intend to supply water—by overhead sprinkler, by flood irrigation, or by drip irrigation. You won't want, for example, irrigation rows that run downhill or tall or large-leafed plants blocking sprinklers.

Finally, plan how you'll gain access to the plants. Be sure to allow yourself enough room to get in easily when you want to harvest the crops.

This garden plan allows room for climbing plants and successive plantings for long harvests.

Continuous-harvest plan

You can lay out a garden that will produce a continuous supply of crops from spring through autumn and even winter. The plan below shows one way to push a single garden's productive season to the maximum and increase the number and variety of crops you can grow.

This basic 22-by-16-foot garden plot is divided into halves, separated by 4 feet of space to allow access for cultivation. In early spring, plant the left half of the plot with cool-season vegetables—carrots, lettuce, cabbage, peas—that will mature before the heat of summer (see the plan below, left half). One end of the plot is reserved for cane berries, such as raspberries.

In later spring, after all danger of frost is past, plant the right half of the plot with warm-season vegetables such as corn, squash, and tomatoes, which will mature in the late summer and autumn (see the plan below, right half).

In mid- to late summer, when most of the left plot is harvested or "played out," you can rework the soil and replant that plot as shown on the next page, rotating placement of crops such as cabbage to avoid fostering soilborne diseases. At this time, you can add new cool-season vegetables, such as broccoli and cauliflower, for harvest in late summer and autumn.

With this continuous-harvest plan, you can use three special techniques—succession planting, double-cropping, and intercropping—to further increase the amount and variety of your garden's output.

Succession planting. For vegetables that come to maturity all at once, or within a short period of time, you can stretch the harvest period by staggering

SPRING PLANTING

1 square = 1 square foot

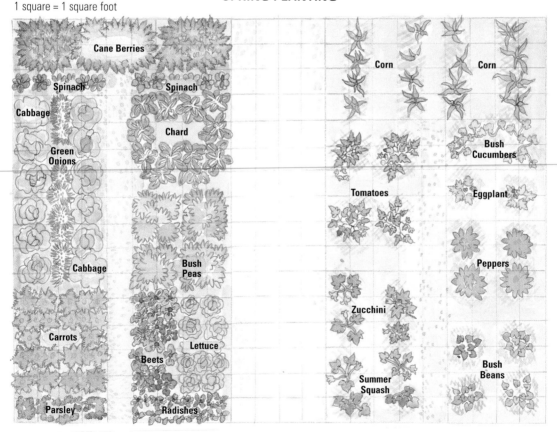

Left side: plant in early spring

Right side: plant in late spring

plantings of seeds or young plants at roughly 2-week intervals. These successive plantings will produce a continuous supply of a given vegetable. In the plan shown, for example, the carrots are planted in two side-by-side plots, one planted 2 weeks after the other. (The plantings of bush beans in the right half of the plot could also be divided into halves for successive sowing.)

In addition, replanting the entire left half of the plot in mid- to late summer enables you to harvest two cool-season crops from the left half while the crops in the right half, planted later, mature through the longer warm season.

Double-cropping. Some vegetables—radishes, lettuce, and green onions (scallions) are classic examples—grow so quickly that you can raise a second crop in the same spot within the same season after the first crop has been completely harvested. The space for carrots on the left side of the plot shown, for example, could be replanted for a second harvest within the spring growing season if your climate permits.

Intercropping. Two vegetables can occupy the same allotted space if one matures quickly before the one that grows more slowly crowds it out. In the left side of the plot shown, the green onions will mature and be pulled before the cabbage plants fill the entire space. Similarly, fast-growing spinach occupies the fringe of the berry area before the berries completely take over.

Spinach, lettuce, green onions, and radishes are good intercrop choices for cool-season gardens. You also can grow them in summer gardens (between tomato plants, for example) and harvest them before the weather heats up.

SUMMER PLANTING

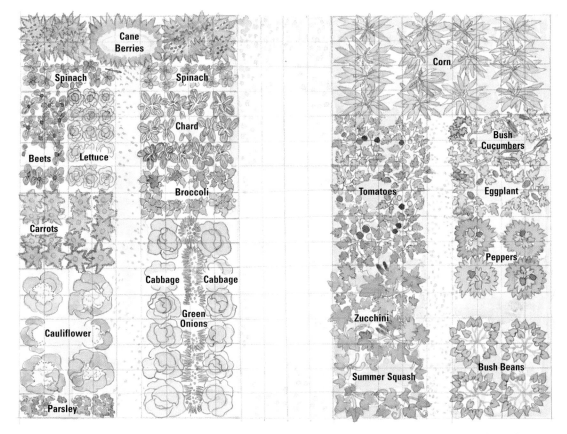

Left side: replant mid- to late summer

Right side: plant these crops in late spring

Space-saver garden plans

Although some gardeners might consider small space a handicap, the small produce garden offers an exciting challenge: how to reap a diverse and bountiful harvest from a limited plot. The examples here show you ways to organize two small plots—one rectangular, the other square—for maximum productivity and variety. The keys to a good harvest are thorough preparation and careful plant selection and placement.

Soil and water. In a small-space garden, you need to spend extra time on soil preparation. Add soil amendments liberally. You might even consider double digging the ground or planting the whole garden as a raised bed. The beauty of raised beds is that they allow you to plant in "perfect" soil.

In addition, you may want to install a drip-irrigation system. A drip system entails a minimal outlay of time and money to ensure that the entire plot is watered evenly and without waste.

What to plant. The small-space garden rules out crops that take a lot of room to produce low yields per square foot, such as corn, all types of melons, and some squashes. For maximum yields, seek out vegetable varieties that are especially productive; some are specifically labeled for small-space gardening. Plant ideas can be found in both nurseries and seed catalogs.

You can also maximize your small-space productivity by planting both early- and late-maturing varieties of the same vegetable.

1 square = 1 square foot

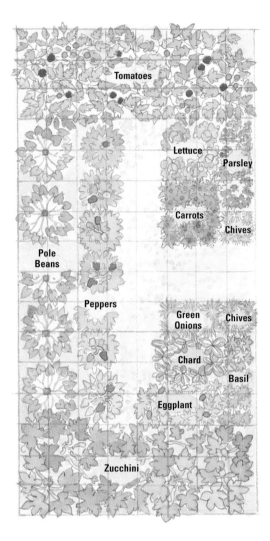

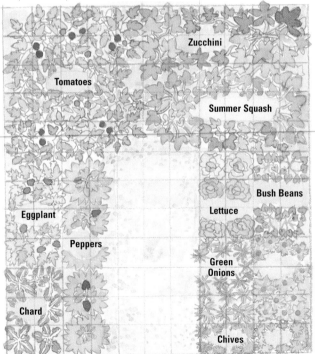

Garden layout. Several techniques make the most of available space. Whenever possible, use vertical supports such as stakes, frames, and trellises to extend your garden up rather than across. Try various modes of continuous-harvest planting. Use any chance to interplant fast-growing crops among slower-growing ones. Spinach, lettuce, green onions (scallions), and radishes are fine intercroppers. Whenever season and climate allow, practice double-cropping as soon as the first crop is harvested. In the plans on this page, lettuce, green onions, carrots, and bush beans might be double-cropped.

Note that the plans show blocks rather than rows of lettuce, carrots, and green onions. These (and other vegetables not shown) could also be planted thickly in French intensive-bed fashion, with the thinned-out vegetables being the first to reach your kitchen.

Staking vegetables

Some vegetables benefit from support: climbing vegetables, such as pole beans and peas, and sprawling vegetables, such as tomatoes, cucumbers, and melons. Not only will you save space by tying or propping up these crops, but you'll also harvest more fruits—keeping fruits such as tomatoes and melons off the ground will avoid a common cause of rotting.

The best time to put up stakes, poles, trellises, and other supports for vegetables is at planting; because roots haven't yet formed, you needn't worry about disturbing them. Train or tie the plants as they grow.

Tepee of bamboo poles tied together at top supports beans planted beside poles.

Cylinder of welded wire and two stakes support tomato plant with minimum of tying. Reach through mesh to harvest.

Strings stretched over A-frame made of 2-by-2s are for beans, peas to climb.

Bamboo poles in ground, tied together at crosspole, will hold up row vegetables tied to them with cloth strips.

Sturdy frame leaning on wall makes trellis for cucumber or squash vines.

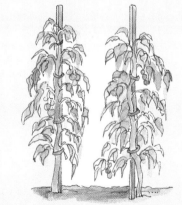

Tall wooden stakes hold up tomato plants. Use soft ties to fasten stems.

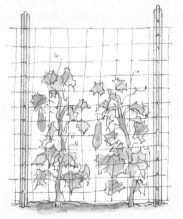

Broad-mesh plastic netting attached to hooks in metal fencing stakes can support cucumbers, squash, beans, peas.

Herbs for Every Garden

A good cook simply can't live without certain herbs. Here are the ones that specialists from across the West consider essential garden and cooking ingredients. These are basic "kitchen herbs," the ones recipes most often call for.

French tarragon

Basil *(Ocimum basilicum)*. This fragrant warm-season herb bears tender green leaves on 2-foot-tall stems. Start with seeds or seedlings. Basil needs full sun and warm nights to grow well.

Pinch plants for bushiness and keep flowers constantly picked off. To harvest for pesto, cut plants back halfway and allow to regrow. Or plant basil seedlings in succession every month or so and harvest entire plants for pesto. Grow four to six plants (if you plan to make pesto). *Annual. All zones.*

'Berggarten' sage *(Salvia officinalis* 'Berggarten*)*. This pungent, musky herb is the first choice of herb professionals for culinary sage. It grows about 2 feet tall, has round, grayish leaves, and doesn't usually blossom like other sages. Grow one or two plants. *Perennial. All zones.*

Chives *(Allium schoenoprasum)*. Plants form 12- to 24-inch-long grasslike spears in clumps. Rose-purple flowers appear on top of thin stems in spring. Harvest chives by snipping the spears to the ground. Otherwise you'll have unsightly brown foliage mixed in with the green. Increase the number of plants by dividing every two years. Grow three or four plants. *Perennial. All zones.*

Cilantro *(Coriandrum sativum)*. Fragrant, bright green leaves grow on foot-tall stems. Cilantro refers to the leaves; the seeds are called coriander.

'Berggarten' sage

When cilantro goes to seed, the flavor of the leaves changes—it becomes more like coriander. Start cilantro from a bolt-resistant variety of seed. It does best in cool weather. Grow two or three plants. *Annual. All zones.*

Common thyme *(Thymus vulgaris*; sometimes also called English thyme*)*. Tiny, sweetly pungent leaves grow on upright stems about 12 inches tall. Plants tend to flop over onto the ground. Harvest before blossoms appear. To harvest, hold the foliage like a ponytail and shear it to about 6 inches tall. Grow three or four plants. *Perennial. All zones.*

Fennel *(Foeniculum vulgare)*. Finely cut green leaves taste like anise. Flower stalks grow to 4 feet tall but fo-

Chives

liage is low. Seeds are also used as a flavoring. To save the seeds, cover the seed heads with brown bags just as the seeds start turning brown. Allow seeds to finish ripening, then shake loose. Grow two plants. *Perennial. All zones.*

French tarragon *(Artemisia dracunculus sativa)*. Shiny, narrow dark green leaves have a spicy anise flavor. Woody stems on the 1- to 2-foot-tall plant should be cut to the ground in June and August to encour-

Culinary uses

BASIL: Marinades, meats, pastas, salads, soups, and stews. This is the best herb to add to tomato, mushroom, and Italian dishes.

CHIVES: Butters, eggs, mayonnaise, potatoes, sauces, seafood, soups, sour cream, stews, and vegetables.

CILANTRO: Beans, curries, fish, fowl, lamb, Mexican dishes, salads, sauces, and stir-frys. Mix it into bean soup, serve it with lime juice as a green salsa, use it in fajitas, and put it in yogurt. Use with restraint, according to taste. Cilantro can easily over power a dish with its distinctive taste.

FENNEL: Use foliage to flavor fish and vegetables, and as a garnish. Use seeds in baked goods, fish, meats, poultry, sauces, sausages, and soups.

MARJORAM: Cheeses, eggs, fish, meats, pastas, poultry, rice, sauces, soups, stews, and vegetables.

MINT: Baked goods, beverages, desserts, fish, fruits, ice cream, jellies, sauces, soups, tea, and vegetables. Mint has a cooling effect on powerful aromatics, such as basil and cilantro, and on chilies and salsas.

OREGANO: Beans, cheeses, meats, pastas, salsas, and vegetables; use sparingly in sauces, soups, and stews.

This two-tiered herb bed contains basil and chives (top), and rosemary, fennel, common thyme, and sage.

age new growth. Divide plants every four years. Grow four plants. *Perennial. All zones.*

Mint *(Mentha)*. Spearmint *(M. spicata)*, with bright green, shiny leaves, is the preferred mint for cooking. It grows 1½ to 2 feet tall. Peppermint *(M. piperita)*, with narrow, dark green leaves, is best for tea. Plant grows to 3 feet tall. Cut back plants to about 2 inches tall twice a year—in late spring and fall—before flowers form. Plant one or two kinds in separate containers to control vigorous underground stems. *Perennial. All zones.*

Oregano. All herb professionals agree that Greek oregano *(Origanum vulgare hirtum)* is one of the best oreganos for cooking. The shrubby plant with slightly fuzzy, pungent leaves grows 3 feet tall. For something milder, an excellent alternative is Italian oregano *(O. majoricum)*, which has bright green foliage and grows 2½ feet tall. The oil is strongest when the plant is in bud but before flowers open. Cut plants back to 4 inches tall in late spring, summer, and fall. Make room to grow two plants of Greek or one of each. *Perennial. All zones.*

Parsley *(Petroselenium)*. Chefs prefer Italian flat-leafed parsley *(P. crispum neapolitanum)*, but curly-leafed types *(P. crispum)* are good for garnishes. Plants grow 6 to 12 inches tall. Set out parsley any time of year (except winter in cold climates). In hot climates, plants may bolt when set out in summer, so plant in partial shade. Grow three plants of each. *Biennial. All zones.*

Rosemary *(Rosmarinus officinalis)*. Short, narrow green leaves with gray undersides grow on woody stems. Varieties have a similar intense,

PARSLEY: *Bouquets garnis,* casseroles, fish, meats, omelets, poultry, sauces, soups, stews, vegetables, and as a garnish. Add parsley to fresh vegetables at the end of cooking to avoid overcooking it.

ROSEMARY: Breads, cheeses, dressings, eggs, fish, game, legumes, marinades, oils, potatoes, poultry, roast game, soups, stews, stuffings, and vegetables. Rosemary sprigs also make attractive decoration.

SAGE: Apples, beans, breads, cheeses, game stuffings, marinades, pork, poultry, soups, and stews. Since sage helps digest fatty foods, it works well with duck.

SWEET BAY: *Bouquets garnis,* breads, fish, fowl, marinades, meats, puddings, and stuffings. Fresh bay leaves have a nutmeg and vanilla quality.

TARRAGON: Chicken, dressings, eggs, fish, meats, pickles, sauces, vegetables, and vinegars.

THYME: *Bouquets garnis,* breads, casseroles, cheeses, eggs, fish, grains, marinades, meats, mushrooms, poultry, soups, stews, tomato-based sauces, and vegetables.

WINTER SAVORY: Beans, marinades, meats, poultry, and vegetables. Strong-flavored winter savory is considered a bean herb—that's its best use.

peppery flavor but different habits (upright or trailing) and flower colors (blue, pink, or white). 'Arp' is hardy to 15°, but it's not as bushy as other types of rosemary. Plants take sun or partial shade. Prune to shape. Grow one or two plants. *Perennial. Zones 4–24.*

Sweet bay *(Laurus nobilis)*. This is the bay (also referred to as Grecian laurel) used for cooking. The evergreen shrub or tree grows 12 to 40 feet tall and is best when used as a background shrub. Leathery, 2- to 4-inch-long dark green leaves are very aromatic. Because it's slow-growing, it does well in containers. *Zones 5–9, 12–24.*

Sweet marjoram *(Origanum majorana)*. Tiny gray-green leaves have a sweet, floral scent and a milder flavor than Greek oregano. Grows 1 to 2 feet tall. Follow harvest suggestions for oregano. Grow three plants. *Perennial in Zones 4–24; annual elsewhere.*

Winter savory *(Satureja montana)*. Low-growing, 12- to 15-inch-tall mounding plant with pungent, peppery-tasting ½- to 1-inch-long dark green leaves that are more intensely flavored than those of summer savory. A good substitute for salt. Harvest leaves as needed before flowers appear, or shear back twice a year. Grow two or three plants. *Perennial. All zones.*

HOW TO GROW AND MAINTAIN HERBS

Herbs are easy to grow if the soil drains well (if not, amend it with plenty of organic matter, or plant in raised beds). Choose a site that gets 6 to 8 hours of full sun.

Water perennial herbs to get them established, then taper off to occasional supplemental irrigations. Annual herbs such as basil and chives prefer evenly moist soil.

To keep foliage fresh and at peak quality for cooking, herbs must be cut back regularly. Follow the pruning guidelines under individual herb descriptions.

In early spring, feed herbs with a nitrogen fertilizer or spread compost around the base of plants. After chopping back basil and chives, feed the plants with fish emulsion.

Nine kinds of traditional and flavored basil grow in this bed at the Elizabeth F. Gamble Garden Center in Palo Alto.

Growing Gourmet Herbs

Once you've grown and experimented with basic kitchen herbs and are familiar with their flavors, try growing herbs with more complex flavors. Gourmet herbs are not more difficult to grow. They challenge the palate instead of your gardening skills.

Bronze fennel *(Foeniculum vulgare purpureum)*. Like green fennel, it has an aniselike taste, but foliage is bronze. *Perennial. All zones.*

Caraway-scented thyme *(Thymus herba-barona)*. Caraway-flavored leaves. Creeping plant to 4 inches tall. *Perennial. All zones.*

Culantro *(Eryngium foetidum)*. Flowers and leaves have the intense flavor of cilantro. Produces all season, even in hot climates. Grows 8 to 12 inches tall. *Tender perennial. All zones.*

Garlic chives *(Allium tuberosum)*. Similar to chives, but leaves are slightly larger, and they have a mild garlic flavor. *Perennial. All zones.*

Lemon grass *(Cymbopogon citratus)*. The blanched white ribs (used in Thai cooking) are spicy and lemony. Use the sweet, lemony leaves at the base of "pups" (young plants) for tea. *Perennial in Zones 16–17, 23–24; elsewhere, overwinter a division in a pot indoors.*

Lemon thyme *(Thymus citriodorus)*. Dark green foliage has lemon flavor. Grows 1 foot tall. *Perennial. All zones.*

Lemon verbena *(Aloysia triphylla)*. Long (3 inches), narrow leaves have intense lemon scent. Use for lemon flavoring or tea. Gangly shrub 3 to 6 feet tall. Perennial. *Zones 9–10, 12–24.*

Mexican tarragon *(Tagetes lucida)*. The narrow, dark green leaves of this 3- to 4-foot-tall marigold species have a sweet licorice flavor similar to tarragon. *Perennial in Zones 8–9, 12–24; annual elsewhere.*

Pine-scented rosemary *(Rosmarinus angustifolia)*. Similar to rosemary, but leaves have a pine fragrance. *Perennial. All zones.*

Sorrel *(Rumex acetosa)*. Tangy, lemony, bright green leaves perk up soups and salads. Harvest during cool weather. *Perennial. All zones.*

Vietnamese cilantro *(Polygonum odoratum)*. A perennial that has the flavor of cilantro, but doesn't go to seed. *Tender perennial. All zones.*

Fertilizers

Fertilizer sections at nurseries, garden centers, and supply stores dazzle the gardener. The shelves are piled with boxes and bottles, the floors covered with bags stacked high. Labels identify the package contents as "rose food" or "vegetable food," "lawn fertilizer" or "general-purpose fertilizer." In some stores, you'll find bins filled with bone meal, blood meal, or hoof-and-horn meal—all labeled "natural fertilizer." Choosing the right products to keep your plants healthy can often be a bit confusing.

Understanding N-P-K

Regardless of its type, any fertilizer you buy will come with information about the nutrients it contains. Prominently featured will be the N-P-K ratio, the percentage the product contains by volume of nitrogen (chemical symbol N), phosphorus (P), and potassium (K). A 16-16-16 fertilizer, for example, contains 16% nitrogen, 16% phosphorus, and 16% potassium. A 25-4-2 formulation contains 25% nitrogen, 4% phosphorus, and 2% potassium. All fertilizers contain at least one of these components; if any is missing, the ratio will show a zero for that nutrient (a 12-0-0 fertilizer contains nitrogen but no phosphorus or potassium, for instance). Boxed, bagged, and bottled products display the N-P-K ratio on the label. For fertilizers sold in bulk from self-serve bins, the ratio is noted on the bin; for future reference, be sure to write the information on the bags you fill and bring home.

The chart at right shows some of the plant nutrient elements you may see listed on fertilizer labels.

Plant nutrients

MACRO-NUTRIENTS	CHEMICAL SYMBOL
Carbon	C
Oxygen	O
Hydrogen	H
Nitrogen	N
Phosphorus	P
Potassium	K
SECONDARY NUTRIENTS	
Calcium	Ca
Magnesium	Mg
Sulfur	S
MICRONUTRIENTS	
Copper	Cu
Iron	Fe
Manganese	Mn
Zinc	a

TWO COMMON FERTILITY PROBLEMS

Without sufficient nitrogen, plant leaves yellow from their tips toward the stem and from the bottom of the plant upward. The growth of the plant is also stunted by nitrogen deficiency.

Iron deficiency causes yellow leaves with green veins and stems. A chelated iron solution sprayed directly onto leaves ("foliar feeding") is usually quicker acting than one added to the soil.

Complete and incomplete fertilizers

A fertilizer containing all three major nutrients is called a complete fertilizer; a product that supplies only one or two of them is an incomplete fertilizer. Using a complete fertilizer for every garden purpose seems sensible, but in fact it isn't always the best choice. If the soil contains sufficient phosphorus and potassium and is deficient only in nitrogen (as is often the case), you can save money by using an incomplete fertilizer that provides nitrogen alone (ammonium sulfate, for example). In some instances, complete fertilizers can even harm a plant. Exotic, bright-blossomed proteas, for example, will not tolerate excess phosphorus: They "glut" themselves on it and then die.

The inexpensive soil test kits sold at garden centers can give you a rough idea of the nutrients available in various parts of your garden; for a more detailed evaluation, you may want to pay for a professional analysis. By revealing which nutrients may be lacking, such tests can help you choose an appropriate fertilizer.

Available dry fertilizers include (clockwise from top left): granules (synthetic), fish meal (organic), and controlled-release granules (synthetic).

General- and special-purpose fertilizers

The various products labeled "general-purpose fertilizers" contain either equal amounts of each major nutrient (N-P-K ratio 12-12-12, for example) or a slightly higher percentage of nitrogen than of phosphorus and potassium (such as a 12-8-6 product). Such fertilizers are intended to meet most plants' general requirements throughout the growing season.

Special-purpose fertilizers, on the other hand, are formulated for specific needs. They're aimed at the gardener who wants a particular combination of nitrogen, phosphorus, and potassium for certain plants or garden situations. These fertilizers are of three general types.

One type, used during the period of active growth, contains largely nitrogen. Such products, with N-P-K ratios such as 16-6-4, are often used in spring, when you want to encourage lush growth or green up your lawn.

Another type is meant to stimulate root growth, stem vigor, and flower and fruit production. Fertilizers of this sort contain little nitrogen and higher levels of phosphorus and potassium; the N-P-K ratio may be 3-20-20, for example. These products are applied at different times and in different ways, depending on what you want to achieve. When you prepare a new planting area, for instance, you'll work a dry granular fertilizer of this sort deeply into the soil, putting the phosphorus and potassium where roots can absorb them. The nutrients help strengthen the new plants' developing stems and encourage the growth of a dense network of roots.

To promote flower production and increase the yields of fruit or vegetable crops, you apply the same sort of fertilizer to established plants after they've completed their first flush of growth. You can use either dry granules, scratching them lightly into the soil, or apply a liquid formula with a watering can or a hose-end applicator.

A third group of fertilizers is designed for use on specific plants. These feature the N-P-K ratios determined to elicit the best performance from the particular plant, as well as other elements proven valuable to that plant. Such fertilizers are named according to

When you shop for fertilizer, check the N-P-K ratio on the label to see if the fertilizer is complete or incomplete and to determine the percentage of each major nutrient it contains.

the plant they're intended to nourish. Especially useful are formulas for citrus trees and acid-loving plants such as camellias and rhododendrons.

Recently, other such plant-specific fertilizers have appeared on nursery shelves, each claiming to be the best choice for a certain plant or group of plants; you may see several sorts of "tomato food" or "flower fertilizer," for example. The jury is still out on the benefit of many of these products, and you will often do just as well to use a general-purpose type. The main distinction is often the price: The "special" formulas are usually costlier than general-purpose kinds.

Rhododendron
'Formosa'

Synthetic and organic fertilizers

Some fertilizers are manufactured in the laboratory, while others are derived from natural sources. Each has certain advantages.

Synthetic fertilizers. These products are derived from the chemical sources listed on the product label. They're faster acting than organic kinds and provide nutrients to plants quickly, making them a good choice for aiding plants in severe distress from nutrient deficiencies. Synthetic fertilizers are sold both as dry granules to be applied to the soil and as dry or liquid concentrates to be diluted in water before application. In dry form, they're usually less expensive than their organic counterparts. In some of the dry granular types (those known as controlled-release fertilizers), the fertilizer granules are coated with a permeable substance; with each watering, a bit of fertilizer diffuses through the coating and into the soil. Depending on the particular product, the nutrient release may last anywhere from 3 to 8 months.

Some synthetic products are packaged for special purposes; you'll find spikes and tabs for container plants, for example.

Note that synthetic fertilizers usually do not contain any of the secondary nutrients or micronutrients—but in most cases, they are already present in the soil. If a test indicates that some are missing, look for a fertilizer that provides them.

Organic fertilizers. Organic fertilizers are derived from the remains of living organisms; blood meal, bone meal, cottonseed meal, and fish emulsion are just a few of the many available types. Organic fertilizers release their nutrients slowly: rather than dissolving in water, they're broken down by bacteria in the soil, providing nutrients as they decompose. Because these fertilizers act slowly, it's almost impossible to kill lawns or plants by applying too much (overdosing with synthetics, in contrast, can have potentially fatal results). Some manufacturers combine a variety of organic products in one package, then offer them for general-purpose or specialized use.

Two commonly used soil amendments—compost and manure—have some nutritive value and can be used as part of an organic fertilizing program. The N-P-K ratio of compost varies from 1.5-.5-1 to 3.5-1-2. Chicken manure's N-P-K ratio ranges from 3-2.5-1.5 to 6-4-3; that of steer manure is usually a little less than 1-1-1.

FERTILIZING WITH SEAWEED

Fertilizers containing seaweed are gaining favor with many gardeners. Besides providing nutrients in a form immediately available to plants, seaweed contains mannitol, a compound that enhances absorption of nutrients already in the soil, and various hormones that stimulate plant growth. And the carbohydrates in seaweed break down rapidly, nourishing soil-dwelling bacteria that fix nitrogen and make it available to plant roots.

Mixed with water and sprayed directly on foliage, seaweed-containing fertilizers can have dramatic effects in a matter of days. Plants green up and begin to produce new growth, and those that are weak stemmed and straggly straighten up and become stronger.

Increasingly popular as a fertilizer, seaweed is also an excellent mulch. Here, it blankets the soil of a potato patch. Nutrients gradually move from seaweed to soil during irrigation; after harvest, any remaining mulch can be worked into the bed.

When to fertilize

To get your plants off to a good start, fertilize when the spring growing season begins. Many gardeners use a general-purpose fertilizer at this time (either an evenly balanced formulation or one slightly higher in nitrogen); others add only nitrogen. How often you fertilize later in the year depends on the plant. Nutritional needs differ, so it's important to check the particular requirements of the plants you buy. Some are heavy feeders and benefit from regular applications of general-purpose fertilizers and extra nitrogen throughout the growing season. Others—often those that evolved in nutrient-poor environments—may need only one annual feeding with a general-purpose fertilizer (or they may flourish with no feeding at all).

Avoid root burn

Don't apply liquid fertilizer at the same time you plant. No matter how carefully you remove plants from their containers and place them in the ground, some root hairs will break. The fertilizer will reach the roots immediately and enter them at the broken points, "burning" them and causing further dieback. Wait 2 to 3 weeks after planting before you fertilize; by then, the newly set-out plants should have recovered from any root damage.

Too much of a good thing? In its native environment, wild lilac (Ceanothus) survives with minimal water and grows on rocky slopes. Given rich soil and liberal fertilizer, it responds with fast, lush growth and bloom—but its life cycle speeds up as well, so that it dies at an early age (10 years or younger), leaving you with a hole in your garden.

Applying fertilizers

Use a spading fork to work a dry granular fertilizer into a new garden bed. This technique puts phosphorus and potassium at the level where they can best be absorbed by plant roots. Water the planting bed thoroughly after incorporating the fertilizer.

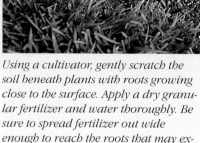

Using a cultivator, gently scratch the soil beneath plants with roots growing close to the surface. Apply a dry granular fertilizer and water thoroughly. Be sure to spread fertilizer out wide enough to reach the roots that may extend several feet beyond the drip line.

Liquid fertilizers can be applied with a watering can. You can also use an injector device to run the fertilizer through your watering system. A simple siphon attachment (above) draws a measured amount of fertilizer into a hose from concentrate in a pail.

Lilacs for Mild Climates

Flowers as pretty as party dresses, with a gently sweet fragrance reminiscent of Grandma's dressing table, make lilacs sentimental favorites. In a world that swirls around us too fast, lilacs spark nostalgia—possibly for a place where they once flourished, or perhaps for another era.

But this nostalgia isn't easy to create everywhere. In mild-winter climates, you can't pop just any lilac *(Syringa vulgaris)* into the ground and expect an exuberant show of blooms come midspring. You'll need to buy low-chill varieties.

Why? Because most lilacs prefer the kind of winter chill that sends us scrambling for heavy wool coats. Not so the low-chill varieties.

The first low-chill lilac, called 'Lavender Lady', was developed in Southern California 30 years ago by Walter Lammerts, a researcher and hybridizer with Rancho del Descanso—a former wholesale nursery that's now the site of Descanso Gardens, a botanical garden open to the public. Although many varieties of lilacs are sometimes attributed to Lammerts,

'Lavender Lady' bears 6-inch-long clusters of blooms starting in early spring.

'Lavender Lady' and 'Angel White' were his only direct creations.

But other descendants from the original plantings have been introduced through the years by Descanso's staff. The lilacs—often referred to as Descanso Hybrids—now number a dozen or so, and many of them can still be seen growing at the gardens.

How to grow the best flowers

Like roses, lilacs are a bit greedy. To flower, they need plenty of sun and space; crowding reduces air circulation and makes them prone to powdery mildew. In Southern California, don't plant them near lawns; year-round watering can prohibit dormancy and flowering.

Unlike many plants that thrive in rainy eastern climates, lilacs prefer the arid West's alkaline soil. It's generally not necessary to add soil amendments at planting time unless the soil is very sandy or heavy clay.

After planting and until plants are established, water regularly to keep the soil moist but not soggy. In Southern California, after the third season of growth, hold off watering starting in late September to induce winter dormancy (colder winter temperatures throughout most of Northern California induce dormancy naturally, so it's not necessary to cut off water). If winter rains are sporadic, begin watering again when the buds start to swell (around late February).

Fertilize lilacs in late winter with an organic fertilizer or with a commercial product.

After lilacs bloom, remove the spent flowers where the leaves join the stems just above the points where next year's flowers are forming; leaving spent flowers on the plants can inhibit next year's bloom. Don't prune lilacs heavily (or later than June) or you'll cut off developing flower buds. To control growth and shape the plants, pinch back new shoots.

Low-chill lilacs

If you can't find the variety you want, your nusery may be able to special-order it.

DESCANSO HYBRIDS

'Angel White': Mildly fragrant white flowers develop on the upper branches of a thick, bushy shrub that grows 8 to 10 feet tall. Selected and introduced from Lammerts' original plants by Monrovia Nursery. The idea was to name it after the baseball team and call it Los Angeles Angels, but it didn't get registered that way.

'California Rose': Mildly fragrant medium pink flowers appear in profusion on a vigorous shrub that grows 8 to 10 feet tall.

'Lavender Lady': Lavender flowers with good fragrance develop on a shrub about 8 to 10 feet tall. 'F. K. Smith' and 'Sylvan Beauty' are similar, but the flowers on 'F. K. Smith' are a bit lighter on an 8- to 10-foot-tall plant, and 'Sylvan Beauty' has pinker, more open blooms on a 10- to 12-foot-tall plant.

OTHER LOW-CHILL LILACS

'Blue Skies': Very fragrant lavender flowers appear on an 8-foot-tall plant. Heavy bloomer. No need to adjust water to induce dormancy. Developed by rose hybridizer Ralph Moore in Visalia, California.

'Esther Staley' *(Syringa hyacinthiflora)*: Very showy, pure pink flowers with good fragrance develop on rounded shrubs that grow to about 8 feet tall.

'Excel' *(S. hyacinthiflora)*: Light lavender flowers with good fragrance appear on rounded shrubs 8 feet or taller. Massive bloomer. Blooms earlier than the others listed (late February or early March).

Along the walkway of this Albuquerque courtyard, drought-tolerant and native plants form a dense tapestry of foliage and flowers.

June

Pacific Northwest Checklist

PLANTING

☑ ANNUALS. Zones 1–7: All annuals, from ageratum to zinnias, can go into the garden now. Before you plant, soak plants overnight in their nursery containers so they take up as much water as possible before going into the ground.

☑ DAHLIAS. Zones 1–7: Get tubers into the ground pronto for bloom from summer to early autumn.

☑ FUCHSIAS. Zones 1–7: Set out newly bought fuchsias in pots or hanging baskets; repot overwintered plants in rich, quick-draining soil. Pinch back growth to encourage bushier plants.

☑ PERENNIALS. Zones 1–7: Blooming plants are available in 1-gallon cans. Soak overnight before planting to reduce transplant shock. Don't fertilize newly set out plants until flowers fade.

☑ VEGETABLES. Zones 1–7: Sow bush beans, rutabagas, and turnips. Set out seedlings of basil, cucumber, eggplant, peppers, and squash.

MAINTENANCE

☑ CUT ROSES. Harvest roses so the cut is just above a leaflet with 5, not 3, leaves. New growth will emerge just below the cut.

☑ DIVIDE PERENNIALS. Dig and divide plants right after blooms fade, to cause as little disruption as possible in their flowering cycle. Circle each overgrown plant, slicing down with a sharp spade or shovel. Pop the plant out of the ground and cut it into chunks; a dinner plate-size clump will make four new plants. Remove hard, old roots and any pieces of the crown that have died out. Replant the divisions immediately in rich soil amended with organic matter; water thoroughly. Do not fertilize them until early next spring.

☑ THIN FRUITS. Once trees have dropped their immature fruit naturally, thin clusters so the remaining fruit develops to full size. On trees with heavy crops, thin doubles and triples to one or two, respectively, then thin remaining fruit to 6-inch intervals along the branch. You'll get fewer, but larger, fruits, and you'll ease the strain on tree limbs.

☑ CLIP HEDGES. Twice-a-year hedge trimmers should get busy early this month, then again in late summer or early fall. Once-a-year trimmers can do the work in early to mid-July. Trim so that the hedge is slightly wider at the base than at the top, allowing sunlight and rain to reach the entire foliage surface.

PEST & WEED CONTROL

☑ BATTLE SLUGS. Set out traps or bait in the late afternoon before a string of dry days. Slugs are most active between dusk and dawn. Keep children and pets away from poison bait.

☑ WEED. Hoe or pull weeds young, before they can set seed.

☑ BEFRIEND GARTER SNAKES. These docile, nonvenomous snakes serve as pest police in the vegetable patch. On the west side of the Cascades, encourage them by putting a pile of rocks or a 4-by-8-foot piece of plywood at the sunny end of the garden. From this hideout, they'll slither out to gobble up bothersome bugs and slugs. (Warning: If you try this on the east side of the Cascades, you'll attract rattlesnakes as well.)

Northern California Checklist

PLANTING

☑ **PLANT SUMMER BLOOMERS.** For annuals, try garden verbena, gentian sage, globe amaranth, Madagascar periwinkle *(Vinca),* portulaca, scarlet sage, sunflower, 'Victoria' mealy-cup sage, and zinnias. For perennials, look for coreopsis, gaillardia, 'Homestead Purple' verbena, penstemon, rudbeckia, Russian sage, salvia, statice, and summer phlox. Good foliage plants for fillers are low-growing artemesias, dusty miller, and golden or purple sage.

☑ **PLANT VEGETABLES.** June is prime planting time for warm-season vegetables. Start beans, carrots, and corn from seed. You can also plant cucumber, pumpkins, and squash from seed, but be sure to get them in the ground as soon as possible.

☑ **SOW HERBS.** To make sure you have plenty of basil and cilantro for cooking through the summer and fall, plant successive crops of seeds every 6 to 8 weeks. For basil try 'Anise', purple 'Red Rubin', Thai lemon, or one of the Italian types, such as 'Genova Profumatissima'. Grow a slow-bolting variety of cilantro.

MAINTENANCE

☑ **REMOVE FIRE HAZARDS.** In fire-prone areas, clean up brush and debris to reduce the fuel volume. When grasses turn brown, mow them down to about 4 inches. Prune dead and diseased wood from trees and shrubs. Prune tree limbs lower than 20 feet off the ground. Cut branches back at least 15 feet from the house. Clean off any plant debris that may have accumulated on the roof.

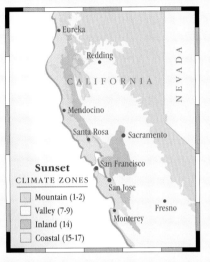

Sunset
CLIMATE ZONES

- ☐ Mountain (1-2)
- ☐ Valley (7-9)
- ☐ Inland (14)
- ☐ Coastal (15-17)

☑ **STAKE TALL, FLOPPY FLOWERS.** To hold up sprawlers like bachelor's buttons, carnations, and yarrow, insert four stakes at least 2 feet tall (depending on the height of the flowers) into the soil around the plant; wrap the outside with two layers of twine, one toward the top and one toward the bottom of the stakes.

☑ **FEED AND GROOM ROSES.** To encourage growth and new flowers on repeat bloomers, remove faded flowers and feed plants with a complete fertilizer and, if necessary, iron chelate. Mulch to conserve soil moisture. On hybrid teas and grandifloras, nip off faded blooms ¼ inch above the first (top) leaf with five leaflets.

PEST CONTROL

☑ **SPRAY ROSES.** Aphids, black spot, powdery mildew, rust, and whiteflies can all cause severe damage to roses. Now they can all be controlled with one biodegradable, organic pesticide derived from neem-tree seed. Spray according to label directions when pests build up to damaging numbers or when diseases first appear.

☑ **CHECK ROSES FOR RUST.** Cool, moist springs promote rust—a fungus that causes rust-colored pustules on the undersides of leaves. Hand-pick and dispose of diseased leaves. Spray with a sulfur-based fungicide. Water early in the morning and avoid wetting foliage.

☑ **CONTROL BUDWORMS.** If your geraniums, nicotiana, penstemons, and petunias appear healthy but have no flowers, budworms are probably eating the flower buds before they open (look for holes in the buds). Spray every 7 to 10 days with *Bacillus thuringiensis* (Bt).

☑ **CONTROL LAWN MOTHS.** Sod webworm moths appear in late spring or early summer to lay eggs in lawns. The adults fly at night just above the grass, dropping their eggs, and then hide during the day. Damage is caused by the worms, which hatch from the eggs and feed on grass blades. Saucer-size brown patches appear on the lawn surface. You may also find areas of lawn ripped up by raccoons scavenging for the worms. Control the worms with microscopic, environmentally safe nematodes (available at nurseries). Do not spray lawns with pesticides afterward or you will kill the nematodes. Getting rid of the worms should also control raccoons.

Southern California Checklist

PLANTING

☑ **ADD FRAGRANCE.** Summer evenings and sweet flowers were made for each other. Double your sundown pleasure by adding Arabian jasmine *(Jasminum sambac)*, common heliotrope, gardenia, Madagascar jasmine *(Stephanotis floribunda)*, night jessamine *(Cestrum nocturnum)*, sweet olive *(Osmanthus fragrans)*, or tuberose.

☑ **PLANT SUBTROPICALS.** They're widely available in nurseries now and grow quickly in warm weather. Many will provide garden color well into winter. Choices include banana, bird of paradise, cestrum, ginger, hibiscus, palms, philodendron, and tree ferns. And don't forget flowering vines. Look for bougainvillea, bower vine *(Pandorea jasminoides)*, mandevilla, stephanotis, thunbergia, and trumpet vine *(Distictis)*.

☑ **PLANT IN SHADY SPOTS.** The soil in northern and eastern exposures near walls is finally warming up. It's a good time to add ornamentals to these cool spots. Good choices include abutilon, *Brunfelsia pauciflora* 'Floribunda' (yesterday-today-and-tomorrow), clivia, coral bells, hydrangea, Japanese anemone, and shrubby fuchsias.

☑ **PLANT SUMMER VEGETABLES.** Set out transplants of cucumbers, eggplant, melons, peppers, and tomatoes. Sow seeds of beans, corn, cucumbers, New Zealand spinach, okra, pumpkins, and summer and winter squash. Coastal gardeners can squeeze in another harvest of leaf lettuce. High-desert gardeners (Zone 11) can plant short-season varieties of beans, corn, cucumbers, melons, pumpkins, squash, and tomatoes.

Bishop

NEVADA

CALIFORNIA

San Luis Obispo

Bakersfield

Santa Barbara

Tehachapi

Lancaster

Los Angeles

Palm Springs

San Diego

Sunset
CLIMATE ZONES

1-3   7-9   11   13   14-24

MEXICO

☑ **PLANT SUMMER ANNUALS.** Fill empty spots in the garden with heat lovers such as ageratum, portulaca, verbena, vinca, and zinnias.

MAINTENANCE

☑ **SPREAD MULCH.** To conserve water, suppress weeds, and enrich the soil, spread a 2- to 3-inch layer of compost, ground bark, or dry grass clippings around vegetables, trees, shrubs, and flowers.

☑ **FEED ACTIVELY GROWING PLANTS.** Roses, lawns, annual flowers and vegetables, container plants, and just about anything actively growing in the garden will benefit from fertilizing now. Don't feed (or water) natives or drought-tolerant Mediterraneans, unless they are new plantings.

☑ **RESET MOWER HEIGHTS.** Let tall fescues grow taller to shade roots and conserve soil moisture. Set blades to cut at 2 to 3 inches. Cut Bermuda shorter: Set blades to trim at 1 inch. Zoysia, St. Augustine, and kikuyu grass can be cut even shorter.

☑ **DIVIDE IRISES.** Crowded or poorly performing clumps of bearded irises can be divided now. Discard woody centers, rotted portions, and rhizomes without leaves and divide remainder. Each division should have one fan of leaves, a young rhizome, and developed roots. If you garden in the high or low desert (Zones 11 and 13, respectively), wait until October to divide.

☑ **TREAT IRON DEFICIENCIES.** If gardenias, citrus, and other susceptible plants exhibit yellowish leaves with green veins, they may not be getting enough iron. Apply iron chelate as a soil drench or foliar spray.

☑ **STAKE TOMATOES.** For easy picking and to prevent fruit rot, support tomatoes with a cage, stakes, or trellis. Provide the support when you plant. As plants grow, tie vines to supports with plastic ties.

PEST CONTROL

☑ **WATCH FOR PESTS.** Spray or dust plants that have pest caterpillars (such as cabbageworm, corn earworm, geranium budworm, and tomato hornworm) with *Bacillus thuringiensis* (Bt). Apply sparingly, starting when caterpillars are small.

☑ **WASH AWAY PESTS.** Keep aphids, mites, thrips, whiteflies, and other small insect pests to manageable levels by blasting them off plant leaves with water.

☑ **COMBAT ROSE PESTS.** Along the coast, "June gloom" creates ideal conditions for powdery mildew. Combat by hosing spores off foliage frequently in the early morning. Or spray with 1 tablespoon each baking soda and fine-grade horticultural oil diluted in a gallon of water. Avoid spraying when temperatures exceed 85°F. Inland, start watching for spider mites.

Mountain Checklist

PLANTING

☑ ANNUALS. Scatter seed of cosmos, marigold, portulaca, sunflower, and zinnia. Or plant seedlings of any of the above, plus African daisies, bachelor's button, calendula, clarkia, forget-me-nots, globe amaranth, lobelia, pansies, snapdragons, spider flowers, sweet alyssum, sweet William, and violas. After last frost, set out coleus, geraniums, impatiens, Madagascar periwinkle, marigolds, nasturtiums, and petunias.

☑ BULBS. For late-summer color, plant canna, dahlias, gladiolus, montbretia, tigridia, and tuberous begonias. Stake tall varieties of dahlias and glads at planting time.

☑ LANDSCAPE PLANTS. Plant trees, shrubs, ground covers, and vines now. After planting, check soil moisture frequently; water as needed.

☑ PERENNIALS. Sow perennial seeds or set out seedlings. For foliage fillers, plug in artemesia, dusty miller, and golden or purple sage.

☑ STRAWBERRIES. Plant strawberries from nursery sixpacks or pots. Choose a sunny place and provide a coarse soil mix with lots of organic matter.

☑ VEGETABLES. Sow seeds of cucumber and squash, plus successive crops of beets, bush beans, carrots, lettuce, onions, parsnips, peas, radishes, spinach, Swiss chard, and turnips. If the season is long and warm enough in your area, sow corn, melons, and pumpkins, and set out nursery seedlings of eggplant, peppers, and tomatoes.

Sunset
CLIMATE ZONES
☐ 1-3 ☐ 10-11

MAINTENANCE

☑ THIN FRUITS. For larger fruit, thin apples, apricots, peaches, pears, and plums. Space apricots, peaches, and most plums 4 to 5 inches apart, apples and pears 6 to 8 inches apart.

☑ GROOM FLOWERS. Deadhead annuals except for those that form beautiful seed pods, such as love-in-a-mist; keep those dried pods for flower arrangements.

☑ GROOM VEGETABLE GARDENS. Pull up spent cool-season crops in lower elevations and replenish mulch.

☑ CARE FOR ROSES. Cut off faded flowers, fertilize, then build a basin around each plant to concentrate water around the root zone.

☑ FERTILIZE. Feed lawns now with nitrogen fertilizer; repeat in 4 to 6 weeks. If you haven't already done so, apply fertilizer to flower beds and vegetable gardens.

☑ MOW LAWNS. Cut bluegrass, fescue, and ryegrass to about 2 inches, bent grass to 1 inch or less.

☑ PRUNE SPRING-FLOWERING SHRUBS. After forsythia, flowering quince, lilac, spiraea, *Rosa bugonis,* and weigela have bloomed, remove dead, injured, diseased, crossing, and closely parallel branches. Remove stems at base; cut out about a third of the old growth.

☑ TREAT CHLOROSIS. When leaves turn yellow while veins remain green, they're showing the telltale signs of chlorosis—lack of iron. Correct it by applying an iron chelate compound to the soil over the root zone.

☑ WATER. Beyond periodic deep watering for permanent plants, focus your watering efforts on seed beds, new plantings, containerized plants, and anything sheltered from the rain.

PEST AND WEED CONTROL

☑ PROTECT FRUIT CROPS. Cover strawberries and ripening cherries with bird netting or row covers until fruit is ready to pick.

☑ WEED. Remove weeds now, while they're small and haven't set seed.

☑ CONTROL SOD WEBWORMS. If brown spots appear in lawns and leaf blades pull out easily, suspect webworms (look for them feeding on grass blades at night). Treat the infested area and the perimeter with a specific insecticide.

Southwest Checklist

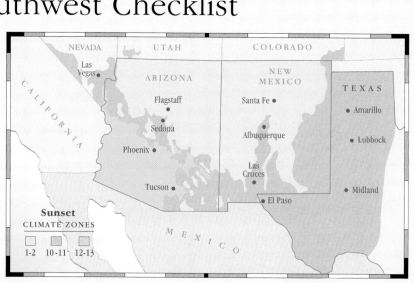

PLANTING

☑ PLANT PALMS. Zones 12–13: Plant or transplant palms into holes as deep as the root balls and twice as wide. Tie the fronds up over the center "bud" or heart to protect it. After new growth begins, cut the twine.

☑ SUMMER COLOR. Zones 10–12: Plant cockscomb, globe amaranth, Madagascar periwinkle, portulaca, purslane, salvia, and zinnia early in the month in a place that gets only filtered sun in the hottest part of the day.

☑ PLANT SUMMER CROPS. Zones 10–11: Plant cucumbers, melons, and summer squash by mid-month, and corn early in the month. Zones 12–13: You can still plant black-eyed peas, corn, melons, okra, peanuts, sweet potatoes, and yard-long beans.

☑ SOW FALL CROPS. Zones 10–11: Sow Brussels sprouts, cabbage, and carrots any time this month; wait until mid-month to sow broccoli and cauliflower. Zones 12–13: Sow tomato seeds indoors for transplanting into the garden in late July. Some good varieties include 'Champion', 'Early Girl', 'Heatwave', 'Solar Set', 'Sunmaster', and 'Surefire'.

☑ HARVEST CROPS. Pick cantaloupe when the skin is well netted and fruit slips from the vine with little pressure; corn after tassels turn brown and milk comes from nicked kernels; eggplant when the skin turns glossy; peppers after they turn color; new potatoes just after plants flower and full-size spuds when tops start to die; and watermelon when the tendrils closest to the fruit begin to brown.

MAINTENANCE

☑ CARE FOR ROSES. Cut off faded flowers, then build a basin around each plant to concentrate water around the root zone. Mulch each plant well. Finally, wet the soil, fertilize, and immediately water again.

☑ MOW. Cut Bermuda, St. Augustine, and zoysia grass 1 to 1½ inches high. Keep hybrid Bermuda at about 1 inch.

☑ MULCH TREES AND SHRUBS. Zones 10–13: Spread a 2- to 4-inch layer of organic or gravel mulch over the root zones of trees, shrubs, vines, flowers, and vegetables.

☑ TREAT CHLOROSIS. When leaves turn yellow while veins remain green, they're showing a sign of iron deficiency (chlorosis). Apply iron chelate.

☑ WATER. Deep-water by flooding or drip irrigation. If you use a drip system, flood-irrigate monthly to wash salts down out of the root zone.

PEST CONTROL

☑ BEET LEAFHOPPERS. These greenish yellow, 1-inch-long insects spread curly top virus to cucumber, melon, and tomato plants. Protect crops by covering them with shadecloth. Remove infested plants.

☑ SPIDER MITES. If you see stippled leaves and fine webs, blast mites off with a strong jet from the hose, or treat with a miticide.

☑ SQUASH VINE BORERS. Look for tiny eggs on squash vines. Rub them off before borers hatch out, drill into the vine, and weaken the plant.

☑ PROTECT GRAPES. Cover ripening grapes with bird netting.

Plumed celosia in three fiery shades sets a bed aflame.

Hot-colored Flowers for Summer Gardens

In 1888, the Dutch painter Vincent van Gogh left Paris for southern France in search of inspiration. He found it in Provence—under the Mediterranean sun. Dazzled by the scenery, van Gogh wrote to his brother Theo: "What intensity of color, what pure air, what vibrant serenity." His paintings of flowers and fields from that period are rendered in intense shades of yellow, orange, and red. These warm hues that so inspired van Gogh are the flower colors that are once again brightening our gardens.

That's a refreshing change, since for the last decade, horticultural fashion has leaned toward cooler pastels such as lavender and mauve. Admittedly, the warmer shades are not as easy to work into the landscape; unless you combine them thoughtfully in just the right places, they can turn a garden into a kaleidoscopic jumble. But use them right and you'll have beds that shimmer like van Gogh's swirling brush strokes.

All the plants you need to paint a summer bed or border are only a nursery stop away. You can't miss such vivid beauties as cannas, celosias, and dahlias; the palette following offers many more choices of annuals, perennials, and bulbs and tubers, including some of the most reliable named varieties. Follow the design guidelines on the next page to blend them on your canvas.

How to paint with hot colors

Pair shades of a single color. Fire-engine red dahlias paired with a matching skirt of red pelargoniums, for example, might spill into a mound of silver *Artemisia* 'Powis Castle'. A similar scene could be composed of yellow daylilies or yarrow and one of the yellow forms of poker plant.

Play warm colors off each other. Try red against yellow, for instance—or be daring and try hot pinks against oranges. Celosias, cannas, and dahlias lend themselves to this approach.

Follow the color wheel. Start a planting with one color, then go to the next shade on the color wheel. For example, plant yellow (maybe *Potentilla fruticosa* 'Jackman's Variety') at one end of a bed, changing to orange *(Kniphofia ritualis)*, then burnt orange, perhaps with a hint of yellow (gloriosa daisies), and finish off with red (cannas).

Contrast cool and hot. Choose a cool color—blue, purple, or white—and use it sparingly to lower the temperature in a feverish bed. A puff of white baby's breath, impatiens, or petunias is great for this. Blues, from tall delphiniums to low-growing lobelias, can take the jitters out of a pulsating combination of reds, oranges, or yellows. Orange lion's tail *(Leonotis leonurus)* sizzles by itself, but when it's placed near deep blue globe thistle *(Echinops exaltatus)* or purple salvia, the heat goes down.

Unify and frame with foliage. Silver or gray foliage is great for visually unifying a bed and separating hot colors. Try dusty miller between two shades of red, for example. Green foliage is equally useful in framing a composition of colorful flowers.

Top: Brilliant dwarf cannas include 'Pfitzer Salmon' (far left), 'Picasso' (yellow petals with red flecks), and 'Lucifer' (red petals with yellow edges). Above: Crocosmia 'Lucifer'. Right: Tithonia 'Goldfinger'.

Flaming reds

Pulsating pinks

Vibrant flower palette for western gardens

Scorching oranges

Sunny yellows

Annuals

CELOSIA ● ● ● ●

CLEOME HASSLERANA ●
(spider flower)

COSMOS ● ● ● ●

GAILLARDIA ● ●
G. pulchella

IMPATIENS ● ●
I. balsamina, New
Guinea hybrids

MARIGOLD ● ●

MEXICAN SUNFLOWER ●
Tithonia rotundifolia
'Goldfinger', 'Torch'

PETUNIA ● ● ●

SUNFLOWER ● ●
Helianthus annuus 'Big
Smile', 'Sunrich Orange',
'Orange Sun'

ZINNIA ● ● ● ●

Perennials

ALSTROEMERIA ● ● ● ●
'Lutea' (yellow), 'Orange
King', 'Florist's Red'

ASTER NOVAE-ANGLIAE ●
'Honeysong Pink'

COREOPSIS ●
'Early Sunrise', 'Robin',
'Sunray'

DAYLILY ● ● ●
'Pardon Me' (dwarf red)

GAILLARDIA ● ● ●
G. grandiflora 'Golden
Goblin' (yellow)

GERANIUM ●
(some species) *G. mad-
erense, G. psilostemon*

GERBERA ● ● ● ●
(Transvaal daisy)

GLORIOSA DAISY ●
Rudbeckia hirta
'Indian Summer'

LIATRIS SPICATA ●
'Kobold'

LION'S TAIL ●
Leonotis leonurus

LOBELIA ●
'Queen Victoria'

MALTESE CROSS ●
Lychnis chalcedonica

ORIENTAL POPPY ●

PELARGONIUM ● ●

PENSTEMON ● ●
'Firebird' (red), 'Apple
Blossom' (pink),
'Huntington Pink'

POKER PLANT ● ● ●
Kniphofia uvaria 'Shining
Sceptre' (yellow-gold),
K. ritualis (orange),
K. northiae (red-orange)

POTENTILLA ● ● ●
P. fruticosa 'Jackman's
Variety' (yellow),
'Klondike' (yellow),
'Sutter's Gold',
'Tangerine', 'Red Ace'

SALVIA (species) ●
S. coccinea 'Lady in Red',
S. elegans, S. splendens

SUMMER PHLOX ● ●
P. paniculata
'Miss Candy' (hot pink),
'Miss Pepper' (pink with
red eye)

SUNFLOWER ●
Helianthus multiflorus
'Loddon Gold' (double
flowers)

YARROW ● ● ●
Achillea filipendulina
'Coronation Gold', 'Gold
Plate'; *A. millefolium*
'Cerise Queen', 'Fire King'

Bulbs, Tubers, and Corms

ASIATIC LILY ● ● ●
'Yellow Gold', 'Juanita'
(orange), 'Hello
Dolly' (red)

BEGONIA ● ● ● ●
(tuberous types)

CANNA ● ● ● ●
'Phasion' (orange)

CROCOSMIA ● ● ●
'Citronella' (yellow),
'Solfatare' (golden
yellow), 'Queen
Alexandra' (orange),
'Lucifer' (red)

DAHLIA ● ● ● ●

ORIENTAL LILY ● ●
'Acapulco', 'Pink Icicles'

Shrub

HELIANTHEMUM ● ●
'Henfield Brilliant'
(orange), 'Supreme' (red)

Common Garden Pests

When you choose the right plants, water and feed them on a regular schedule, and give your garden an annual cleanup in fall, you'll find that few plants will be lost to insect and animal pests. But every garden is subject to attack by creatures that find your plants as attractive as you do. Where you live, and your climate, will determine your worst pest problems. Gardeners on the borders of wild land may find that deer and gophers are a constant menace; in foggy coastal climates, snails and slugs are likely to be everpresent. Many pests multiply during the onset of warm weather, only to recede as nature's balance readjusts and beneficial predators reduce the harmful pests' population. Some pests are happy to feast on a single plant type; certainly most have favorites—but even this varies from place to place. Your local Cooperative Extension agent or a good nursery can tell you the most prevalent pest problems and solutions in your area.

Not only is the pest population diverse, but some pests cause different kinds of damage at different stages of their lives. Many pests are nocturnal, so a weekly check during the evening hours can often help you determine the culprit of a particular kind of damage. Before you treat a pest, identify it correctly. Again, your Cooperative Extension service and local garden center can help, especially if you bring them an example of the pest or the damage it has caused.

Oakmoth caterpillars eat the leaves of oak trees—they can defoliate entire trees. Healthy trees usually bounce back from infestation. In summer, if you see more than 2 dozen caterpillars at a time, hand pick them or spray with carbaryl or acephate. Bacillus thuringiensis (Bt) may control smaller larvae. Large trees should be treated by an arborist.

Mealybugs mass in powdery colonies on the leaves or stems of many ornamental plants. Although mealybugs are related to aphids, their waxy coating protects them from most pesticides. Natural predators—green lacewings and ladybugs—are the best defense. If badly infested, spray ornamentals with acephate.

Snails and slugs eat the leaves and stems of all plants. They feed at night and on overcast or rainy days. Trails of silvery slime between plants signal slugs—stop them with barriers of copper edging, wood ashes, or diatomaceous earth (from a garden center, not the pool-filter type). Hand pick at night, when the pests are active—after 10 p.m. is best. For chemical control, use bait or liquid containing metaldehyde.

Aphids are soft-bodied sucking insects that reproduce quickly and attack a variety of garden plants, particularly feeding on new growth. Control them with regular washings with strong bursts of water from a hose and by spraying with insecticidal soap. Control ants, which feed on the aphids' sticky honeydew. Spray badly infested plants with an insecticide containing pyrethrin, diazinon, malathion, or acephate.

Weevils feed on roots as larvae and on leaves, flowers, and bark as adults. Shrubs, trees, and flowers are all targets. Adults can be trapped or deterred with sticky traps, or treated with rotenone, neem, pyrethrum, or acephate. Beneficial nematodes, applied in fall, can kill larvae. Diazinon or chlorpyrifos kill other types of beetle "grub" in lawns.

You may be able to keep tunneling moles, gophers, and ground squirrels out of your garden by surrounding it with underground fencing 3–4 feet deep. Or, use barriers for raised beds and plant bulbs in baskets. A noisy dog can be a good deterrent. As a last resort, try traps or poison baits, carefully following the manufacturer's instructions.

Cutworms chew leaves and can sever the stems of seedlings or recently transplanted vegetables and flowers. Protect seedlings with paper collars or diatomaceous earth (the type for gardens, not pools) sprinkled in a ring around each plant. Treat infested lawns with a lawn-specific insecticide containing diazinon or chlorpyrifos.

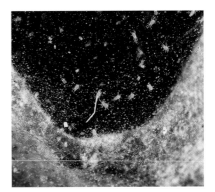

Gypsy moths attack—and kill—many landscape trees, including coniferous evergreens. To prevent adult females from climbing up a tree to lay eggs (and to keep larvae from traveling down), wrap the trunk with a sticky barrier. Hand-pick and destroy egg masses and caterpillars; severe infestations call for an insecticide containing neem, carbaryl, or acephate.

Scales cling to evergreen and deciduous landscape trees like barnacles, protected by a crusty, fuzzy, or bubbly exterior that resembles disease more than insect infestation. Pesticides are more likely to kill the beneficial insects that feast on scales. Instead, scrape scales off leaves and bark with a plastic scouring pad. Control ants, which can cultivate scales for their honeydew.

Mites attack a variety of flowers, vegetables, shrubs, trees, and house plants. They're nearly invisible, except when they cluster together to suck juices from leaves, stems, and flower buds. You can blast mites off plants with a stiff jet of water or use an insecticidal soap formulated for mite control. Most insecticides don't kill mites—buy a miticide formulated for use on the infested plant instead.

Biological controls

Using living organisms such as beneficial insects to destroy common garden pests is called biological control. It is a most effective way to reduce plant damage without using strong chemicals or sprays. Here are beneficial insects that are either common in western gardens or can be released in the garden to reduce pest populations. Also described are other organisms that kill insect pests and a natural hormone product that hopelessly confuses them.

Scale parasites
One tiny parasitic wasp *(Aphytis melinus)* attacks and kills red scale and other types of hard scale. *Metaphycus helvolus* attacks black scale and other hemispherical scales.

Cryptolaemus beetle
The larvae and adults of the *Cryptolaemus* beetle, a ladybird-beetle relative, feed on mealybugs.

Lacewings
Commonly found in gardens, both lacewing larvae and adults feed on a variety of insects and mites.

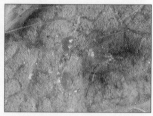

Predator mites
Various species of mites feed on spider mites and sometimes thrips, but do no damage to plants.

Fly parasites
Tiny wasps (many species) that lay their eggs in the pupae of several types of flies, including houseflies, are very effective and most useful in controlling flies on ranches and farms.

Ladybird beetle
The ladybird beetle (or ladybug, as most people know it) occurs naturally in gardens. Larvae (left) and adults feed on aphids, mealybugs, small worms, spider mites, and similar soft-bodied insects. Releasing ladybird beetles in your garden is usually not effective because they fly away. They also migrate annually. If you do release them, do so in the evening because daylight encourages flight.

Whitefly parasite
Several species of small wasps attack immature stages of whiteflies. Control of the greenhouse whitefly using *Encarsia formosa* requires average temperatures above 75°F. The wasps are most effective in greenhouses. A related species that is not commercially available has been released in California to control ash whitefly.

Trichogramma wasps
Larvae of the tiny trichogramma wasp develop within the eggs of caterpillars and eat their way out, destroying the eggs. Adult wasps fly off to find new eggs to parasitize. Repeated releases are usually necessary to reduce a caterpillar infestation.

Semiochemicals
Insects use semiochemicals to communicate. Two general groups are commercially available: pheromones, which affect communications between insects, and kairomones, which affect feeding behavior. Both can be used to attract insects: sometimes to trap (possibly to monitor pest levels for precise timing of sprays) or confuse an insect pest; at other times, to lure beneficials into the garden. Semiochemicals are very target-specific and are available for several common pests.

Parasitic nematodes
Parasitic nematodes include several species of microscopic worms that seek out and eat their way into more than 250 soil-dwelling pests, such as grubs, weevils, sod webworms, and carpenter worms. Read directions carefully. Soil conditions and release techniques must be right for effectiveness.

Bacillus thuringiensis (Bt)
The bacteria Bt controls caterpillars (including worms like budworms). After eating Bt-treated leaves, caterpillars die within 2 to 3 days. Bt can be used on all food crops up to harvest. Mixing it in alkaline water (pH 8 or higher) reduces its effectiveness. Apply it when caterpillars are small; reapply in 3 to 14 days. The strain for most caterpillars is *Bt kurstaki*. Other available strains include *Bt israeliensis* for mosquitoes and *Bt* 'San Diego' for Colorado potato beetle and elm-leaf beetle. Bt is sold under several trade names.

Solving pest problems

When prevention and simple pest-management techniques don't work, pesticides are the obvious choice. But shop carefully—try to pick a product that will solve the problem with the least risk to beneficial creatures, people, and the environment. Insecticidal soaps and dormant and summer oils, for example, kill a variety of insects but are relatively nontoxic. When buying a stronger insecticide, choose single-purpose, rather than broad-spectrum, products to protect the beneficial insects that inhabit your garden. (An easy way to distinguish between products is to count the number of insects the product claims to kill. Shorter lists are more likely to be found on single-purpose pesticides.) When possible, avoid broad-spectrum systemic pesticides. Since systemic pesticides are absorbed by the plant's living tissue, they won't wash off or dissipate into the air. Therefore, every insect that ingests part of the plant could be affected. Before spraying vegetables, check the product label to be sure the pesticide is safe to use on edibles.

Oils smother insects, larvae, and eggs, and help prevent diseases. Light oils, called summer oils, can be used year round. Heavy oils, called dormant oils, should be used when plants are dormant. For large areas, use a pressure-pump applicator.

If the problem is limited to one or several plants, use a hand sprayer to direct an oil mixture or a pesticide right where you want it. Many manufacturers offer premixed pesticides in convenient small-size containers.

Beneficial nematodes are effective against some grubs, including weevils and Japanese beetles. Mix with water and apply in fall, according to the manufacturer's directions. Most can be applied from a simple watering can or a hose-end sprayer.

To protect your tastiest plants from slugs and snails, encircle them with a liquid barrier. But don't use this type of product —or snail and slug baits—where it will be accessible to children and pets.

Combating pests

Active Ingredient	Brand Names/ Manufacturers	Controls	Comments
acephate	Orthene	aphids (large infestations), mealybugs, adult weevils, thrips, oakmoth caterpillars	for ornamental flowers and woody plants, including oak trees; not for edibles
Bacillus thuringiensis (Bt)	many	caterpillars, budworms, gypsy moth caterpillars	for ornamental flowers and woody plants; edible crops
carbaryl	Sevin	aphids, beetles, moths, cutworms, mites, ticks, gypsy moth caterpillars	for woody ornamentals including roses and rhododendrons; lawns
carbaryl/metaldehyde	many; available as granules and bait	slugs, snails, ground-dwelling insects	for ornamental flowers and woody plants; lawns
chlorpyrifos	Dursban; available as spray and granules	ants, fleas, grubs, cranefly larvae, weevils, caterpillars, wasps, mites, ticks, cutworms	for woody ornamentals; lawns; some edibles
diatomaceous earth	many	ants, fleas, earwigs	for ornamentals and edible plants
diazinon	many; available as spray and granules	aphids, cutworms, fleas, beetles, grubs, mites, cranefly larvae	for ornamental flowers and woody plants; some edibles
diphacinone	Green Light gopher killer	pocket gophers	for burrow entrances; soil beneath affected plants
fatty acid soap (repellent)	Hinder	mammals, rodents	for ornamental and edible plants
insecticidal soap	many; concentrated or pre-mixed liquid	aphids, thrips, whitefly, scale, mites, ticks	for many ornamental and edible plants
malathion	many	whitefly, scale, aphids, weevils, caterpillars, mites, ticks	for ornamental flowers and woody plants; lawns; some edibles
metaldehyde	many; available as liquid, granules, and bait	slugs and snails	for ornamental flowers and woody plants; lawns; edibles
methyl nonyl ketone	Dexol Dog & Cat Repellent	mammals	for soil beneath affected plants
neem oil	many	aphids, whitefly, scale, weevils, moths, mites, ticks, thrips	for ornamental flowers and woody plants; some edibles
potassium nitrate/sulfur	Dexol Gopher Gasser	gophers, moles, ground squirrels	for animal burrows; soil beneath affected plants
pyrethrin	many; available as spray and powder	mealybugs, whitefly, scale, weevils, caterpillars, mites, ticks, beetles, spider mites, ants, budworms	for ornamental and edible plants
resmethrin	many	aphids, whitefly, scale, mites, ticks	for many ornamental plants
rotenone	several; available as spray and powder	aphids, ants, scale, mites, weevils	for many ornamental and edible plants

Safety tips

Under lock and key. Store chemicals in locked cabinets or on high shelves to keep away from kids and pets.

For good measure. Mix pesticides exactly as specified on the label, never stronger. Keep a magnifying glass with your chemicals to make it easier to read the label. To ensure accuracy, store a set of measuring spoons with your applicators.

Protect yourself. Wear long sleeves, long pants, closed shoes, a hat, and gloves when mixing and applying pesticides. If your pesticide carries a "warning" rather than a "caution," add goggles and a face mask.

Make a label. Label spray bottles with the product name and the date. Mix only small amounts at a time, so you know the product is fresh.

No dumping. Never pour a liquid pesticide—even if it's diluted—onto the ground or into a drain of any kind (including a sink). Don't use up leftover pesticide by spraying healthy parts of the garden. And never throw pesticide powder or granules into the trash. Instead, call your local recycling center, garbage company, or water agency and find out where you can drop off pesticides.

Pieris japonica *'Mountain Fire' sports vivid red new growth.*

P. *japonica* 'Valley Rose' has upright clusters of rosy pink flowers; P. *japonica* 'Valley Valentine' has deep red flower buds and blooms. P. *japonica* 'Variegata' has white flowers and green leaves with white margins; the foliage has a pink tinge in spring. P. *japonica* 'Spring Snow' bears cream-colored flowers in clusters.

P. *japonica* is hardy in Zones 1 through 9 and 14 through 17. Provide plants with light shade and shelter from drying winds. They also need rich, loose soil with ample water. Fertilize these plants as you do other flowering broad-leafed evergreens, such as azaleas and rhododendrons.

Because P. *japonica* has a penchant for producing lots of side growth, you'll need to keep the suckers clipped off to develop handsome upright trunks and a graceful branch structure. Young plants should be selectively pruned so that trunks grow in the form you want the adult shrubs to take. If you have a big, overgrown bush in your garden, judicious pruning can often restore the plant's naturally elegant form. Working from the bottom up and from the inside out, prune off the small twiggy growth, opening up the trunk and major branches.

You'll Love Pieris in the Springtime

Like movie stars, certain plants suffer from public overexposure or from being cast in the wrong part too often. Among landscape plants, few stars have shone brighter than *Pieris japonica (Andromeda japonica)*, lily-of-the-valley shrub. From the 1940s to the '60s, hardly a garden was without this evergreen. And year after year, the plant turned in a respectable performance, demonstrating its stage presence most vividly each spring by showing off flashy new foliage and clusters of lily-of-the-valley-like flowers. Then the spotlight went out.

This plant's fall from horticultural favor can be attributed to both its ubiquitous presence and overzealous pruning. Early on, gardeners tended to use P. *japonica* as a foundation planting around the base of a house, often pruning plants into rectangles or balls and shearing them back after bloom. This only encouraged the plants to send up vigorous new growth, so that over the years they grew into a snarl of twigs.

In recent years, however, P. *japonica* has made a comeback, as a new generation of garden designers has discovered its virtues—statuesque form, rugged bark, and a crown of dense branches growing in tiers. The species eventually reaches 10 feet tall; compact forms grow to 3 to 6 feet.

There are dozens of named varieties. Probably the most widely sold is P. *japonica* 'Mountain Fire', whose leaves—vivid red when new—turn lustrous dark green when mature.

Pieris japonica *'Valley Valentine' bears clusters of tiny blossoms.*

Making Compost

A garden generates large amounts of organic waste—material you can easily turn into rich compost and return to the soil. The simplest composting method is the familiar backyard pile, but you can also use various bins.

A simple compost pile

For this method, you'll need a space about 10 feet square. Divide the area roughly in half. On one side, alternate 6-inch-thick layers of "green" and "brown" material. Green material includes grass clippings, soft shrub cuttings (chop up any large pieces), kitchen scraps (except meat, fat, and bones), pulled weeds, and the like; brown material includes dry leaves, used potting soil, wood chips, and sawdust. This 50-50 green-brown mixture helps maintain the carbon-nitrogen ratio optimal for decomposition. Aim for a pile that's about knee-high. If you're short on green material, add alfalfa pellets; if you're short on brown, add straw (not hay, which contains weed seeds). Both are available at feed stores.

Once a week, mix and turn the pile, moving it to the other side of the space. In about a month, you'll have coarse compost. If you want a finer texture, continue mixing and turning for another month or two. In dry weather, hose the pile down when you turn it; it should be kept as moist as a squeezed-out sponge. During heavy rainfall, cover the pile with a plastic sheet or tarp.

Note that this method requires you to have sufficient material for the entire pile at one time; you can't add new material until the current batch is finished.

Straw and alfalfa pellets are added to garden debris in this simple compost pile.

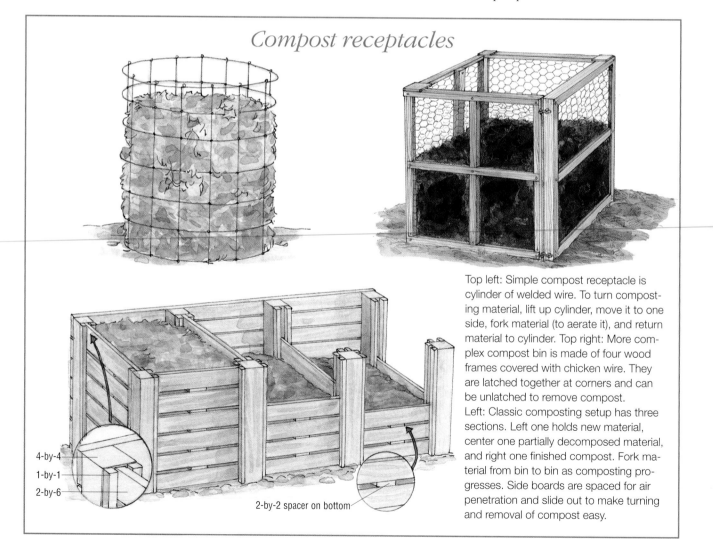

Compost receptacles

Top left: Simple compost receptacle is cylinder of welded wire. To turn composting material, lift up cylinder, move it to one side, fork material (to aerate it), and return material to cylinder. Top right: More complex compost bin is made of four wood frames covered with chicken wire. They are latched together at corners and can be unlatched to remove compost.

Left: Classic composting setup has three sections. Left one holds new material, center one partially decomposed material, and right one finished compost. Fork material from bin to bin as composting progresses. Side boards are spaced for air penetration and slide out to make turning and removal of compost easy.

4-by-4
1-by-1
2-by-6

2-by-2 spacer on bottom

Compost bins

Let's face it—not every gardener likes the idea of tending a compost pile. But home composting can be efficient and time-saving. It eliminates kitchen and yard waste and provides a ready source of amendments for the garden. With the advent of commercial compost bins that are neat and self-contained, the old days of turning, "sweetening," and defending the pile from invaders have passed. All such bins make different claims to fame. Stackable plastic bins let you "turn" the compost by moving the top sections to the bottom on a regular basis. By channeling just the right amount of rainwater into the pile, self-watering plastic bins keep compost at the optimal moisture content to promote rapid, efficient decomposition. Tumbling compost bins, which sit atop a stand, mix and aerate compost while spinning in place; some can be activated by means of a foot pedal built into the side of the bin. For small piles of compost, worm composters are a good option. Throw in your kitchen scraps at the beginning of the week, and, by the end, your red wiggler worms will have turned them into rich compost.

These commercial composters keep compost out of sight. Mix dry brown matter (leaves, wood chips, prunings) and green matter (grass clippings and kitchen waste—but no animal products) into the container. It's essential to keep the compost moist and aerated, neither too wet nor too dry. The bin at left is a worm composter for kitchen scraps. Separate compartments help screen the compost. The bin below can easily be rotated by hand to "turn" composting material, which speeds decomposition of the contents.

Pairing the formal with the informal, the refined with the rustic, and the ornamental with the utilitarian gives this Northwest garden plenty of visual impact.

July

Pacific Northwest Checklist

PLANTING

☑ ANNUALS. It's a long way to frost, so if you get annuals into the ground or containers quickly, you'll have a long season of summer flowers ahead. Buy plants in sixpacks and 4-inch pots.

☑ HARDWOOD CUTTINGS. Propagate azaleas, fuchsias, hydrangeas, and wisteria by taking tip cuttings and rooting them in a sterile sandy potting mix.

☑ SHRUBS. If you plant a shrub now, be sure to water it well for the next 3 months. Before planting, soak the root ball overnight in a tub of water. Dig a generous hole, fill it with water, and let it soak down 3 times so that the soil around the root ball is saturated. Mix organic matter such as compost or peat moss into the backfill soil, plant, and water again.

☑ VEGETABLES. Zones 4–7: Sow seeds of beets, broccoli, bush beans, carrots, chard, Chinese cabbage, kohlrabi, lettuce, radishes, scallions, spinach, sugar pod or snow peas, and turnips for fall and winter harvest.

MAINTENANCE

☑ PERENNIALS. If the foliage of earlier-blooming perennials such as lady's-mantle or daylilies is tattered, cut it to the ground and water well. Fresh new growth will emerge within a few weeks.

☑ CARE FOR MUMS. For bigger and more abundant flowers, feed chrysanthemums every 3 weeks with a liquid plant food (5-10-10 is a good choice) until buds start to show color. When the first blooms open, feed weekly.

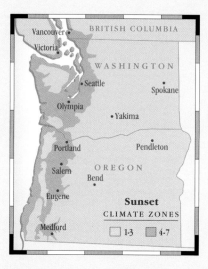

☑ FUCHSIAS. As flowers fade, snip them off to keep blooms coming. Feed plants monthly with a complete liquid plant food or twice a month with a half-strength dilution.

☑ GROUND COVERS. After they've bloomed, shear plants back to keep them compact and neat. Scatter a complete dry fertilizer around beds and water in well.

☑ MULCH. Conserve soil moisture by spreading a 3- to 4-inch layer of organic mulch around the root zones of shrubs.

☑ MANAGE THE COMPOST PILE. Keep adding organic matter and turn the pile. If it's dry, give it a good soaking.

☑ STRAWBERRIES. Remove dead leaves and stems. Fertilize and water plants thoroughly.

☑ WATER. Water perennials in the early morning hours so plants can soak up as much moisture as possible but still have the day ahead to dry out, reducing risk of mildew. Lawns can be watered in the evening.

PEST & WEED CONTROL

☑ BATTLE SLUGS. The heat may chase them into hiding, but they're there. A little bait in the cool spots will go a long way right now. Set out bait under stones, along the edges of walks, and near foundations.

☑ CHECK FOR SPIDER MITES. If you find any, treat the infested plants as necessary.

☑ THISTLES. Get them before they set seed. In small gardens, dig thistles out by the roots. If you have big spaces with lots of thistles, cut them back. As flower heads form, cut thistles to the ground.

Northern California Checklist

PLANTING

☑ MAKE A POND. Use a preformed pond or flexible liner, or fill a large glazed urn that has no drainage hole. Plant water plants such as Japanese water iris *(Iris ensata)*, parrot feather *(Myriophyllum aquaticum)*, water lilies, and water poppy *(Hydrocleyes nymphoides)*. If you like, add mosquito fish, goldfish, or koi.

☑ PLANT FALL VEGETABLES. Zones 1–2: For fall harvest (except in highest altitudes), plant beets, broccoli, bush beans, cabbage, carrots, cauliflower, green onions, peas, spinach, and turnips. Below 5,000 feet, plant winter squash among spinach plants; the spinach will be ready to harvest before the squash takes over.

☑ SET OUT MUMS. To add rich color to the fall garden, plant chrysanthemums now. If plants haven't formed flower buds, pinch growing tips to keep plants compact.

☑ PLANT A PATRIOTIC POT. Nurseries sell many plants in full bloom right now. For a celebratory display, fill a pot with red-, white-, and blue-flowered plants. For red, try annual phlox, celosia, flowering tobacco *(Nicotiana)*, geranium, petunia, and scarlet sage. For white, try alyssum, annual phlox, dahlia, dwarf cosmos, flowering tobacco, heliotrope, petunia, and a white variety of scarlet sage. For blue, choose from gentian sage, lobelia, mealy-cup sage, petunia, and verbena.

MAINTENANCE

☑ ADJUST CONTROLLERS. Depending on where you live, the weather this month can be hot and dry, or cool and foggy. If you water with an automatic controller, make sure the system runs often enough for plants to get adequate water but not so often

that the soil stays overly wet. As a test, check soil moisture just before the system is due to come on by digging down with a trowel or using a soil probe. If the soil seems too dry or too moist, adjust the controller.

☑ CARE FOR FRUIT TREES. To prevent breakage, use wood supports to brace limbs of apple, peach, pear, and plum trees that are sagging with fruit. Since insects and disease thrive in fruit that has fallen to the ground, pick up and discard grounders regularly.

☑ CARE FOR CONTAINER PLANTS. Flowers and shrubs growing in containers dry out quickly in summer, and constant watering drains the soil of nutrients. Water pots often enough to keep the soil moist. Every time you water, fertilize with a half-strength dilution of liquid fertilizer or use the dosage recommended on the label every couple of weeks.

☑ CARE FOR LAWNS. Keep mowing height high during summer's heat; mow when the grass is about a third taller than the recommended height. For bluegrass and fescue, mow when the grass is 3 to 4 inches tall, with your mower set at 2 to 3 inches. Cut Bermuda grass when it's not quite 2 inches tall, with the mower set at 1 inch.

☑ LET ROSES REST. Zone 17: Heat-stressed roses will bloom more spectacularly in fall if you allow them to rest a bit now. Let rose hips form, and stop fertilizing the plants. Water often enough to keep roses healthy, but don't water heavily. In late summer, trim off hips and apply fertilizer to encourage a magnificent fall flush of bloom.

PEST AND WEED CONTROL

☑ CONTROL YELLOW JACKETS. One simple way to control these stinging wasps is to use a yellow-jacket trap that contains a wasp lure. Yellow jacket traps are available at nurseries and home centers.

☑ CONTROL TOMATO HORNWORMS. Look for chewed leaves and black droppings, then hunt through foliage for these fat green worms. Hand-pick the worms and destroy them. If they're still small, spray with BT *(Bacillus thuringiensis)*.

☑ CONTROL CRABGRASS. If your lawn is full of crabgrass and it has set seed, collect the clippings after mowing to keep the weed from spreading.

Southern California Checklist

PLANTING

☑ PLANT SUBTROPICALS. Look for landscaping staples like datura *(Brugmansia)*, hibiscus, and princess flower, or consider one of the many gorgeous vines. Other choices include bougainvillea, coral vine *(Antigonon leptopus)*, mandevilla, passion flower, stephanotis, thunbergia, and trumpet vines (blood-red, vanilla, or royal).

☑ PLANT SUMMER ANNUALS. Fill empty spots in the garden with heat lovers like portulaca, verbena, vinca, and zinnias. Plant bedding begonias, coleus, and impatiens in the shade.

☑ PLANT SUMMER VEGETABLES. For a late-summer harvest, continue to plant vegetables in coastal and inland gardens (Zones 22–24 and 18–21, respectively). Set out cucumber, eggplant, pepper, squash, and tomato plants. Sow snap beans and corn. Don't forget culinary herbs. Plant basil, chervil, chives, parsley, rosemary, sage, savory, and thyme. Start dill and cilantro from seed. In the low desert (Zone 13), plant pumpkins and winter squash.

☑ SOW FLOWERS. Plan ahead for color next spring. Sow seeds of Canterbury bells, foxglove, hollyhocks, verbascum, and other biennials in flats or pots now. In September, transplant to the garden when seedlings are 4 to 5 inches tall. July is a good month to start spring perennials and annuals from seed, too.

MAINTENANCE

☑ CARE FOR FRUIT TREES. Prune fire blight damage from apple, loquat, pear, and quince trees. Make cuts 12 inches below infected tissue on large branches, 4 to 6 inches below on

Bishop

NEVADA

CALIFORNIA

San Luis
Obispo

Bakersfield

• Tehachapi

Santa
Barbara

• Lancaster

Los Angeles

• Palm Springs

Sunset
CLIMATE ZONES

• San Diego

1-3 7-9 11 13 14-24

MEXICO

smaller ones. Wash foliage periodically to remove dust and honeydew secretions and to dislodge aphids, spider mites, whiteflies, and other pests. Clean foliage also encourages beneficial insects such as parasitic wasps.

☑ FERTILIZE PLANTS. Feed actively growing plants such as annual flowers and vegetables, cymbidium orchids, ferns, fuchsias, roses, tropicals, and warm-season lawns. If not done last month, fertilize avocado and citrus trees. Feed camellias and azaleas with an acidic fertilizer. Feed bromeliads (use an acidic fertilizer, diluted to half-strength or less). Don't neglect hard-working foundation plants like rhaphiolepis and pittosporum. If they weren't fertilized this spring, feed them now.

☑ HARVEST CROPS. For further production, harvest beans, cucumbers, squash, and tomatoes frequently.

☑ PRUNE HYDRANGEAS. After flower clusters fade to brown or green, cut back stalks to 2 or 3 buds from the base of the plant. The pruned stems will spring back rapidly, and next

year's flowers will come from this new growth. (Don't prune stems that haven't bloomed yet. They'll bear flower later this year or next.)

☑ CARE FOR LAWNS. Cool-season grasses are slowing down. Leave ryegrass 1½ to 2 inches tall, and fescues 2 to 2½ inches tall so there will be enough foliage left for the lawn to produce food. Warm-season grasses such as Bermuda, St. Augustine, and zoysia, on the other hand, are growing rapidly. Keep them shorter than 1 inch to lessen thatch buildup.

PEST CONTROL

☑ BAKE AWAY FUNGUS AND NEMATODES. Use the sun to destroy fungus, bacteria, and nematodes. Level the soil in the troublesome area with a rake or hoe, thoroughly moisten it, and cover tightly with a thick, transparent plastic tarp, weighted down around the edges. Leave tarp in place 4 to 6 weeks, then replant in fall in a new, healthy bed. Solarization works best in full sun and warm inland locations.

☑ CATERPILLARS. Geranium, nicotiana, and petunias are favorites of geranium budworm (alias tobacco budworm). At first sign of the green larvae, spray with *Bacillus thuringiensis* (Bt). Inspect tomato plants for tomato hornworms. Treat small worms with Bt; pick off larger ones.

☑ WASH AWAY PESTS. Aphids, mites, thrips, whiteflies, and other small pests can be kept to manageable levels with water. Use a sharp stream of water to dislodge the pests from plant foliage. Avoid using pesticides—they kill beneficial insects, too.

Mountain Checklist

PLANTING

✔ **PLANT FALL VEGETABLES.** In all but the highest elevations, plant beets, broccoli, bush beans, cabbage, cauliflower, carrots, green onions, peas, spinach, and turnips. Below 5,000 feet, plant winter squash among spinach plants: It will fill in when you harvest the spinach. Above 7,000 feet, plant warm-season vegetables in large pots. If temperatures are predicted to drop below 60°F, move pots under cover.

✔ **PLANT IRISES.** Dig overcrowded clumps of bearded irises 3 weeks after flowers fade. Discard any dried-out or mushy rhizomes, cut apart healthy ones, trim leaves back to 6 inches, and replant in fast-draining soil in full sun. Plant new rhizomes in the same way.

✔ **PERMANENT PLANTS.** Summer is an especially good time to plant ornamental trees and shrubs, ground covers, and vines. Planted now, they have the rest of the season to settle in. Nurseries are selling many new crabapple trees. If you're in the market for shrub roses, consider plants of the Carefree, Explorer, or Morden series, all of which are outstanding performers in cold country.

✔ **HARVEST VEGETABLES AND FLOWERS.** As vegetables mature, pick them often to keep new ones coming and to keep ripe ones from becoming overmature or downright rotten. Also pick flowers before they go to seed to encourage continued bloom.

Sunset
CLIMATE ZONES

☐ 1-3   ☐ 10-11

MAINTENANCE

✔ **CARE FOR BULBS.** In coldest climates, pluck faded flowers and seed heads from daffodils, tulips, and other spring-flowering bulbs. Let leaves remain until they brown. When bloom is finished, feed plants with high-phosphorus fertilizer.

✔ **STAKE TALL PLANTS.** If you haven't already done so, stake beans, delphiniums, peas, peonies, and tomatoes against high winds. Drive stakes at least 1 foot into the ground and tie plants securely to the stakes.

✔ **COMPOST.** Keep your compost pile as moist as a damp sponge during dry spells. If it is attracting fruit flies, sprinkle lime on it.

✔ **FERTILIZE.** Feed annuals and vegetables with high-nitrogen fertilizer, watering it in well.

✔ **CARE FOR ROSES.** After each bloom cycle, remove faded flowers, cutting them off just above a leaf node with 5 leaflets (nodes closest to the flower have 3 leaflets). Then fertilize and water deeply to encourage the next round of bloom.

✔ **MULCH.** To conserve moisture and reduce weeds, spread organic matter such as compost or straw under and around plants. Use black sheet plastic for heat-loving vegetables such as eggplants, peppers, and tomatoes.

✔ **PRUNE CANE BERRIES.** After harvest, remove old raspberry canes when they begin to die. This helps prevent mildew by encouraging air circulation. In coldest climates, wait until August.

✔ **THIN FRUIT TREES.** On trees with heavy fruit set, thin plums to 2 inches apart, and apples, nectarines, and peaches to at least 4 inches apart.

✔ **WATER.** Continue a regular deep-watering program for ground covers, lawns, shrubs, and trees.

PEST CONTROL

✔ **SPIDER MITES.** Mottled leaves and fine webs indicate spider mites. Spray with insecticidal soap or a stronger miticide. Keep foliage clean by rinsing with water.

Southwest Checklist

PLANTING & HARVEST

☑ HARVEST CROPS, FLOWERS. As vegetables mature, pick them often to keep new ones coming, and to keep ripe ones from overmaturing or rotting. To encourage continued bloom, pick flowers before they go to seed.

☑ PLANT VEGETABLES. Zones 1–2, 10–11: Plant beets, broccoli, cabbage, carrots, cauliflower, green onions, leaf lettuce, peas, spinach, and turnips for fall harvest. Zone 10 (Albuquerque and El Paso): Plant cantaloupe, eggplant, okra, peppers, pumpkins, tomatoes, watermelons, and winter squash. Potatoes can go in at month's end.

MAINTENANCE

☑ CARE FOR ROSES. After each bloom cycle, remove faded flowers, cutting them off just above a leaf node with 5 leaflets (nodes closest to the flower have 3 leaflets). Then fertilize and water deeply to stimulate the next round of bloom.

☑ FERTILIZE. Zones 1–2, 10–11: Feed annuals and vegetables with high-nitrogen fertilizer, and water it in well.

☑ COMPOST. Add leafy garden debris, grass clippings, and annual weeds to the compost pile. Turn and water it regularly to keep it working.

☑ LAWNS. Stop fertilizing lawns during the hottest part of the summer. Aerate the lawn if needed. A core-aerator removes thin, cigar-shaped plugs of turf, power types can be rented.

☑ STAKE TALL PLANTS. Stake beans, delphiniums, peas, peonies, tomatoes, and other plants that could be damaged by high winds.

☑ PINCH HERBS. Your herbs will be bushier if you pinch the growing tips of the plants.

☑ MULCH. Apply a 3-inch layer of organic mulch around permanent plants to retain soil moisture, keep down weeds, and give plants a cool root run.

☑ THIN TREES. Open up top-heavy trees like acacia, Brazilian pepper, mesquite, and olive to protect them from strong winds. Take out suckers; dead, diseased, or injured wood; and branches that run closely parallel to each other.

☑ WATER. Water annual vegetables and flowers only after the top inch of soil has dried out. Basins and furrows help direct water to the roots. Deep-rooted permanent plants can be watered less often, but water them deeply whenever you do irrigate.

PEST & WEED CONTROL

☑ BUDWORMS. These tiny worms eat the flower buds of geraniums, nicotiana, penstemons, and petunias, preventing further bloom. If they attack, spray plants every 7 to 10 days with *Bacillus thuringiensis* (Bt), a biological control.

☑ SPIDER MITES. Mottled leaves and fine webs indicate spider mites; spray affected plants with insecticidal soap or a stronger miticide. Keep foliage clean by rinsing with water.

☑ TOMATO HORNWORMS. If you see chewed tomato leaves spotted with black droppings, look for green worms with white stripes and green horns with black sides. You can control the small ones by spraying Bt; hand-pick the big ones (they can reach the size of a cigar).

☑ SOLARIZE SOIL. To clean soil of weeds, cultivate and water the soil, then cover with a sheet of clear plastic for 2 to 3 weeks. The sun will heat the soil under the plastic and kill the weed seedlings.

Container Gardening

Decorative containers can augment patios, decks, or balconies, contribute to an existing planting bed, or create an entire garden on their own. In any role, it's easy to keep containers at peak attractiveness during all but the dead of winter. But note that the container material, its size, and your plant selections will determine whether the container is high- or low-maintenance.

Look for places in your garden where a container—whether or not it is filled with plants—could add color, height, or provide a focal point. Its shape, hue, and finish should complement the plantings it contains and its surroundings.

Container choices

The container's material affects the way it retains soil moisture—and that, in turn, affects the plants growing in it. Unglazed clay, terracotta, and untreated wood are porous—water and air can easily penetrate them, which means they'll need more frequent watering. If you do choose wood, make it rot-resistant redwood, cedar, or cypress, with galvanized hardware and rustproof metal bands that prevent the wood from splitting or separating.

Glazed ceramic, plastic, fiberglass, concrete, metal, and treated or lined wood containers don't allow free passage of air and water. You'll need to control the amount of water they receive, or plants may suffer from overwatering.

Clay and even plastic can freeze and crack in cold weather—even without plants in them. Stone, concrete, and fiberglass containers can be emptied and left outdoors. If you need to bring in container plants (of citrus, for example) during the cold months, remember that plastic is the most lightweight option. If you have big pots that you can't move indoors, double-pot them: Put the plants in plastic pots set inside larger containers.

Finally, don't restrict yourself to store-bought containers. Old teapots, wheelbarrows, clay pipes—almost anything can become a container as long as you make sure there is adequate drainage.

An architectural cupola trellis provides charming support for a vine.

Lots of pots

Color crazy. Three different colors are plenty for any grouping of plants. Visit a nursery and walk around comparing different plants against each other. Add one "temperer"—gray or silver-foliaged plants, or a foil such as lime green, as a backdrop.

Don't spoil the soil. Buy lightweight, disease-free indoor/outdoor soil mixes at your local nursery. (Bulbs require a mix of equal parts peat moss, organic material, and builder's sand.) To allow for maximum root growth, fill the container with soil to within an inch of the rim.

Size matters. A large container has more visual impact than a group of smaller ones. And large pots provide more root insulation.

Settling in. Set bulbs close together, pointed ends facing up, at the depth recommended by the supplier.

Outer space. Space container plants close together—they won't grow as large as it says in plant descriptions.

Mulch and mulch again. A 2-inch layer of bark, gravel, or cobblestones retains water and suppresses weeds. Stone mulches also discourage animals from digging in the soil in the containers.

Water, water everywhere. Irrigation is critical. Use a watering wand to deliver a gentle stream to the soil without blasting it out of the pots or damaging plant roots. Or install drip irrigation.

Hungry plants. Container-grown plants require frequent feeding. If you renew containers often, dig in some granular, time-release fertilizer. Otherwise, regularly apply water-soluble fertilizer through the growing season—every 4 weeks is sufficient for most plants.

Plants that work

Almost any plant can live in a container for a while. But what characteristics distinguish a really outstanding container plant?

Success depends largely on taking into account the restrictions that container life puts on a plant. A container—even a large one—is a self-contained environment: a kind of closed system that restricts a plant's space as well as the amount of water and nutrients it receives. In addition, plants in pots are often on display in a more focused way than they might be in-ground, making them subject to closer attention.

For these reasons, you'll want to select plants whose growth habits and requirements are suited to a container environment. You'll also want to choose plants that offer maximum eye appeal—color, form, texture, or all three. Such plants will deliver the most enjoyment for the amount of care they require.

This appealing stairstep grouping proves you don't need a big plot of earth to grow an abundant crop of vegetables. Colorful pots hold lettuces, herbs, tomatoes, and peppers.

A breezy collection of spring daffodils in clay pots, set about in clusters, helps to create a smooth transition between the yard and a step-up deck.

A charming garden-in-miniature blooms in Chinese ceramic pots outside a window. Bright Martha Washington geraniums (Pelargonium) on a simple shelf can be enjoyed from both indoors and out.

Look for plants that have these characteristics:

- Naturally compact growth habit
- Long (or repeat) flowering season
- Attractive foliage
- Multiple interest—flowers, attractive foliage, berries, autumn leaf color

Conversely, *avoid* plants that have these characteristics:

- Straggly growth habit
- Vigorous climbing or spreading habit (unless you are willing to prune heavily)
- Short flowering season
- Lackluster foliage
- Greedy, dense root system
- Water-guzzling demands
- Very large size when mature

Annuals are the exception to these "rules"—since they only live for a season, you can choose just about any kind.

Of course, you may choose your container plants for a variety of reasons. Maybe you want to grow tropical plants that can only stay outdoors for a short period in your area, and containers will let you move them come cold weather. Or you may opt for plants with special requirements—like acid-loving camellias or rhododendrons—that won't grow in your garden soil. Perhaps you want to grow edibles but don't have the space. Or maybe you enjoy coddling plants and don't mind if the ones you pick will need extra attention.

Consider the conditions

When you are plant-shopping, keep in mind your general climate as well as the particular conditions on your patio, deck, or balcony. Your local nursery will usually carry only those plants that thrive in your area, but it doesn't hurt to be aware of a plant's special needs, such as protection from frost, special soil or nutrients, and exposure. Remember, the container itself will affect your plants. Highly porous pots allow quick evaporation of moisture; other containers (such as plastic) keep the soil damp longer, so they're better for moisture-loving plants than for plants that like drier soil.

Plant categories

Annuals, perennials, and bulbs… trees, shrubs, and vines. What kinds of plants will you choose? Do you want a display that's more or less permanent, varying little from season to season? Then you'll want to choose shrubs, vines, small trees, or perennial plants that can live in a container for a long time and respond well to pruning, shaping, and dividing.

Or do you want instant color—either to dress up your patio for a party or to provide a summer's worth of bright flowers and fragrance? You'll want to choose annuals—flowering plants that live only for a single growing season.

What you're looking for may well be a combination of these approaches. You might select perennial plants and shrubs for interesting texture, foliage, and flowers over several seasons and put them together with a changing assortment of annuals and bulbs for additional shows of color. Your combination could be in a single pot or in a grouping of pots.

Side by side, a lemon tree and a purple-flowered clematis vine are good container choices from two distinctive plant categories.

A quiet, all-green garden artfully positions evergreens against slatted wood elements in a way that's reminiscent of a serene Japanese garden.

Ways to Water

An irrigation system should fit the lay of your land and the arrangement of your plants. But you should also choose a system that doesn't demand more time than you have to spend in the garden. Choose wisely and watering becomes a leisurely and rewarding process, paid off by healthy, good-looking plants. Choose poorly and watering becomes a dreaded task, an obligation that takes away from the joys of gardening. Worse, a poorly designed irrigation system results in unhealthy plants and a lot of wasted water.

A wealth of equipment—from micro-sprinklers to automatic timers to soil moisture sensors—can help you water your garden efficiently, even when you're busy or out of town.

Hoses

A hose can make the task of watering your garden easy or difficult. If you buy an inexpensive type that is prone to kinking, you'll spend more time cursing than watering. But if you purchase a durable, kink-free type, it will last much longer and work more efficiently.

Unreinforced vinyl hoses are inexpensive and lightweight, but they are also the least durable and most prone to kinking. Reinforced vinyl hoses are less likely to kink and are lightweight—important if you have to move the hose around a lot. Rubber hoses, which have dull surfaces, are the heaviest and toughest types. They kink in hot weather but work well in cold weather. Reinforced rubber-vinyl hoses are flexible, kink resistant, moderately heavy, and durable.

Hoses are sold by length and have various inside diameters (½-inch, ⅝-inch, and ¾-inch hoses are common). Though the difference in hose diameter may seem slight, the water volume each carries varies greatly. If you have low water pressure or if you must run your hose uphill, you'll need all the pressure and flow you can get. Buy the largest diameter, shortest hose that is practical for your situation.

Hose-end sprinklers

These come in a variety of forms, from large impulse sprinklers that can cover hundreds of square feet to small bubblers ideal for watering shrubs or containers. Choose models with a spray pattern that matches the areas you'll be watering. If you have clay soil or sloping ground that is slow to absorb water, select models that apply water slowly to avoid wasteful runoff.

The downside of hose-end sprinklers is that they have to be moved around by hand to cover large areas and they deliver water unevenly; some areas they cover get wetter than others. To get an idea of how much and how evenly your sprinklers apply water, place five identical, straight-sided cups randomly in the area of

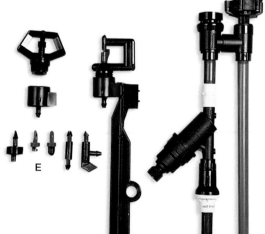

A. **Soaker hose** with factory-drilled holes lets water slowly drizzle out.

B. **Water from emitter line** spreads slowly through soil to irrigate grass roots.

C. **Porous polyvinyl tubing** soaks soil at high pressure; at low pressure, water seeps.

D. **Delivery tubes** for irrigation systems range from (left to right) ½-inch-diameter tube, spaghetti tube, and two soaker tubes.

E. **Other components** of an irrigation system include (left to right) emitters, mini-sprinklers, and piping that leads from the water source.

F. **Hose** is good-quality, reinforced type that bends without kinking.

D

E

coverage. Run the sprinklers for 15 or 30 minutes, then measure the water accumulated in each cup. The cups nearest and farthest from the sprinkler will probably have the least water. In any case, both the amount of water and the unevenness of the distribution will give you an idea of how long to run the sprinklers (use timers so you don't forget the sprinklers are on) and how to move them so that patterns overlap and everything is watered evenly.

Soaker hoses

One of the simplest and least expensive ways to water plants is with soaker hoses. Unlike sprinklers or a complete drip-irrigation system, they attach to hose bibs quickly and with little fuss.

Of the two types of soaker hoses available, one applies a fine spray, the other small droplets. Both are generally sold in 50- and 100-foot lengths.

Perforated plastic emits streams of water from uniform holes drilled along one side. The hose can be used face down, so water goes directly into the soil, or turned up for broader coverage. Output depends on pressure and how far you turn the hose. This type of soaker hose is very useful for irrigating narrow areas of lawn or bedding plants, or around the bases of trees that need slow, deep irrigation.

Ooze tubing is made from recycled tires. The water seeps out of tiny pores. It requires a filter to prevent clogging and applies water slowly—as little as 4 gallons per minute per 100-foot length. If you don't use a pressure regulator, turn on the water until it seeps out of the pores. If you see pinhole sprays, turn down the faucet. To prevent mineral deposits from clogging tubing, bury the tubing 2 to 6 inches deep or cover it with mulch.

This tubing can be used like perforated plastic pipe or it can be run out in rows (spaced about 2 to 3 feet apart) to irrigate large beds.

Drip irrigation

For any size garden and all kinds of plantings except lawns, drip irrigation is the most efficient way to get water down to plant roots. Drip irrigation applies water at slow rates so it can be absorbed without runoff. Because the water is applied directly where it is needed, it results in greater conservation and fewer weeds.

Even though a drip-irrigation system may look intimidating, it is easy to install, even for a beginner. The key is good planning and design. Laying out the water lines requires only cutting with pruning shears and punching holes for emitters.

Start your design with a detailed drawing of your garden, including the positions and spacing of plants. Learn the water needs of your plants. Are they drought tolerant or do they need frequent irrigation? If you are starting a new garden, group the plants according to their water needs.

Rough out your plan on paper, and take it to an irrigation supply store for some expert help with the design and installation of your system.

Rigid-pipe sprinkler systems

Traditionally used for watering lawns, underground pipe systems with risers for sprinkler heads remain the best method for watering medium-size to large lawns and low-growing ground covers. For the greatest water savings, however, use drip irrigation for trees, shrubs, perennials, annuals, and vegetables. A good electronic controller can run both systems automatically, saving time for other garden chores.

Residential water lines seldom have enough water pressure to service the house and water the entire garden at one time. Unless you have only a small area to water, you'll need to divide your sprinkler system into several circuits, each serving only part of the lawn or garden and operated by its own valve. You then operate one circuit at a time to avoid exceeding the maximum flow rate for your water supply. Valves can then be operated by an automatic controller.

Automated irrigation

An automatic sprinkler system is the most efficient way to water. Manufacturers now offer a dazzling array of equipment that can make it work even better.

Controllers. Electronic controllers are far more accurate than mechanical timers—and most have useful features that mechanical timers do not offer.

Controllers capable of daily multiple cycles reduce runoff. When water is applied faster than the soil can absorb it, some will run off the property. If you have this problem, set a repeat cycle to operate the sprinklers for 10 or 15 minutes at, for example, 4, 5, and 6 a.m.

Dual- or multiple-program controllers let you water a lawn on a more frequent schedule than that needed for ground covers, shrubs, and trees.

Sprinklers. New low-precipitation-rate nozzles reduce runoff, improve spray uniformity, and allow a large area to be irrigated at one time. They are particularly useful on sloping ground or on soil that absorbs water slowly.

Moisture sensors. Linked to an electronic controller, a moisture sensor in the open air or in the ground takes the guesswork and day-to-day decisions out of watering. Sprinklers equipped with moisture sensors won't go on if it's raining or if the ground is sufficiently moist.

F

A sample drip system

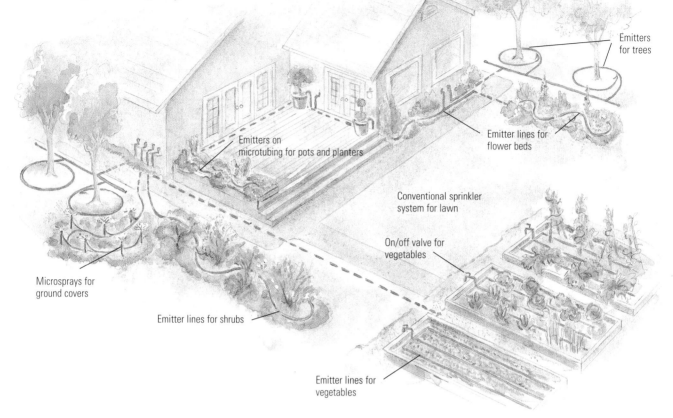

Emitters for trees

Emitters on microtubing for pots and planters

Emitter lines for flower beds

Conventional sprinkler system for lawn

On/off valve for vegetables

Microsprays for ground covers

Emitter lines for shrubs

Emitter lines for vegetables

Coreopsis

Some drought-tolerant plants

The following are some widely grown plants naturally equipped to prosper without regular water during the growing season. You'll probably find numerous others, many better adapted to your particular growing conditions. Check your local nurseries for drought-tolerant plants, especially ones native to your area or to similar climates.

In these listings, ☼ means that the plant grows best in full sun, and ◑ means that it needs partial shade (that is, shade for half of the day or for at least several hours during the hottest part of the day).

TREES
☼◑ *Albizia julibrissin* (Silk tree)
☼◑ *Celtis* (Hackberry)
☼◑ *Elaeagnus angustifolia* (Russian olive)
☼ *Gymnocladus dioica* (Kentucky coffee tree)
☼ *Koelreuteria paniculata* (Goldenrain tree)

Lagerstroemia

☼ *Lagerstroemia* (Crape myrtle)
☼ *Pistacia chinensis* (Chinese pistache)
☼ *Robinia* (Locust)
☼◑ *Sophora japonica* (Japanese pagoda tree)
☼ *Tilia tomentosa* (Silver linden)

SHRUBS
☼◑ *Arbutus unedo* (Strawberry tree)
☼ *Artemisia*
☼◑ *Buddleia davidii* (Butterfly bush)
☼ *Callistemon* (Bottlebrush)
☼ *Caragana arborescens* (Siberian peashrub)

Cerastium tomentosum

Installing drip irrigation

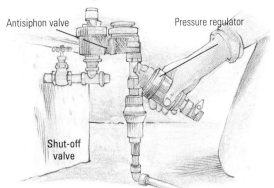

Antisiphon valve Pressure regulator

Shut-off valve

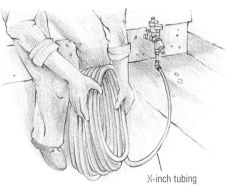

¾-inch tubing

2. Connect ¾-inch flexible polyvinyl tubing *and lay out main lines on the surface of the soil or in shallow trenches. For a more sturdy system, use buried PVC pipe for main lines.*

1. Drip-irrigation system assembly *starts with connecting the control valve, filter, and pressure regulator to the water supply line (for hose-end system, use a hose bib).*

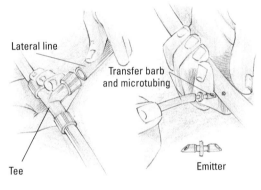

Lateral line

Transfer barb and microtubing

Tee

Emitter

Microtubing

3. Lay out and attach lateral lines *using tee connectors (left). Many kinds hold tubing without cement. Attach end caps, then insert emitters or transfer barbs for microtubing (right).*

4. Flush system *to ensure that all emitters work properly. Cover the lines with a thin layer of mulch, if desired, but leave the emitters and microtubing above ground.*

☼ *Caryopteris* (Bluebeard)
☼ *Cotinus coggygria* (Smoke tree)
☼ *Cotoneaster*
☼ *Lavandula* (Lavender)
☼◑ *Myrtus communis* (Myrtle)
☼ *Phlomis* (Jerusalem sage)
☼ *Pyracantha*
☼ *Rosmarinus officinalis* (Rosemary)
☼ *Santolina*

GROUND COVERS

☼◑ *Aegopodium podagraria* (Bishop's weed)
☼◑ *Cerastium tomentosum* (Snow-in-summer)
☼◑ *Ceratostigma plumbaginoides* (Dwarf plumbago)
☼◑ *Cotoneaster*
☼◑ *Hypericum calycinum* (Creeping St. Johnswort)
☼ *Lantana*

☼ *Oenothera* (Evening primrose)
◑ *Potentilla neumanniana* (Spring cinquefoil)

PERENNIALS

☼ *Achillea* (Yarrow)
☼ *Asclepias tuberosa* (Butterfly weed)
☼ *Baptisia* (False indigo)
☼◑ *Centranthus ruber* (Red valerian)
☼ *Coreopsis*
☼◑ *Dietes* (Fortnight lily)

Cosmos

☼ *Echinacea purpurea* (Purple coneflower)
☼ *Gaura lindheimeri*
☼◑ *Iris* (Bearded iris)
☼◑ *Kniphofia* (Red-hot poker)
☼ *Liatris* (Gayfeather)
☼◑ *Potentilla* (Cinquefoil)
☼◑ *Sedum* (Stonecrop)
☼◑ *Stachys byzantina* (Lamb's ears)

ANNUALS

☼ *Celosia* (Cockscomb)
☼ *Cosmos*
☼ *Eschscholzia californica* (California poppy)
☼ *Gazania*
☼◑ *Gomphrena* (Globe amaranth)
☼ *Limonium sinuatum* (Statice)
☼ *Portulaca* (Rose moss)
☼ *Tithonia rotundifolia* (Mexican sunflower)

Plant Diseases

Fungi, bacteria, and viruses are the pathogens most often responsible for plant diseases. Unlike green plants, these organisms are incapable of manufacturing their own food and must instead take it from a host plant. Fungi can live in the soil, but the bacteria and viruses that cause plant problems cannot survive outside their host.

Fungi multiply by tiny reproductive bodies called spores (their equivalent of seeds), which they produce in great quantity. Spores of some fungi enter plants through the roots; others land on leaves, where they attach and complete their life cycle. A single fungus-infected leaf may release 100 million spores, which drift through the garden and onto new hosts with even the slightest breath of air.

Bacteria need water and warmth to multiply, so the diseases they cause tend to be more prevalent in warm, wet climates. Since they are unable to manufacture their own food (as green plants do), they obtain nutrients from the host plants.

Viral diseases invade plant tissue and reproduce in it. Some viruses damage the host plants by stunting growth or damaging leaves, but others are more benign. Since viruses are carried by insects, try to keep insect populations down.

Powdery mildew fungi appear as white or gray patches on leaves and flowers, never stems. Infected leaves eventually turn yellowish green to brown. New growth may be stunted or distorted.

Oak root fungus can live for many years in old tree roots, so watch for it when planting on newly cleared land. The disease is initially characterized by yellowing and wilting leaves. Later on you'll see white fans of feltlike fungus growing at ground level. If oak root fungus is a problem in your soil, plant resistant species—your local Cooperative Extension agent can give you suggestions.

In the early stages of disease, rust fungi are characterized by powdery pustules on the undersides of lower leaves. As the disease progresses, upper leaf surfaces develop spots, then turn yellow.

The black spot fungus, which targets roses, starts as small black circles that eventually widen to about ½ inch. Look for irregular margins—that's how you can distinguish black spot from other fungi and spotting caused by cold or chemicals.

Since camellia petal blight fungus is more prevalent during blooming season, the best defense is to pick up all dropped petals and blossoms from the ground immediately.

The aster yellows bacteria turns plant foliage yellow, stunts and distorts growth, and prevents flowering. The disease is spread by leafhoppers and affects edibles such as lettuce and ornamentals such as cosmos, marigolds, and petunias.

Preventing diseases

Diseases often thrive where plants don't get enough light or air circulation. Space plants generously to encourage air to move and moisture to evaporate.

Practice good garden hygiene. Discard infected plants promptly. Clean up fallen plant debris and discard it, especially in fall, to prepare for wet weather.

When working with or around infected plants, disinfect the tools you've used in a solution made with 1 part household bleach to 9 parts water.

Disease prevention

You can't always prevent a disease from attacking a prized plant. The bacterial infection fireblight, for example, can enter blossoms readily if there is rain just at the time of bloom; you'd have to control the weather to stop it. A mosaic virus–infected bare-root rose won't exhibit symptoms until it leafs out.

Luckily, good gardening practices will fend off many diseases. To keep plant problems under control, take the following steps.

Buy disease-resistant plants. You'll find tomatoes resistant to verticillium wilt and flowering pear trees less likely to succumb to fireblight, for example. Vegetable seed packets are labeled to indicate the particular plant's disease resistance; plant tags on fruit trees or ornamental trees and shrubs sometimes also include this information.

Transplant carefully to minimize root damage. When broken, roots are susceptible to certain soilborne diseases.

Take care not to injure plants when you work in the garden. An open wound on a plant stem or tree trunk readily admits bacteria and fungi.

Avoid wet-weather garden work. You may unwittingly spread waterborne pathogens.

Install a drip-irrigation system or use soaker hoses to minimize the splashing water that can spread waterborne diseases.

Remove diseased plants. If certain plants are constantly afflicted by disease, eliminate them from the garden and replace them with less trouble-prone choices. This solution is simpler than attempting to control the disease.

Keep the garden clean. Do a thorough fall cleanup each year. Remove weeds, since pathogens may overwinter on them. In mild-winter areas, strip off any diseased leaves remaining on plants; rake up and discard all diseased leaves on the ground. You may also want to rake up other garden debris; though it can serve as a good mulch (if undiseased), it also shelters ground-dwelling pests.

Flowers and foliage form a rich tapestry of colors and textures in this end-of-summer garden, including an eclectic mix of perennials.

August

Pacific Northwest Checklist

PLANTING

☑ ANNUALS. Zones 4–7: With a couple of months of warm weather ahead, you can still plant annuals for a good, long show. Impatiens, marigolds, and pelargoniums are all good candidates. For partially shady places, try New Guinea hybrid impatiens—their robust blooms and colorful foliage light up dark spots.

☑ BULBS. Plant fall-blooming crocus as soon as available in nurseries.

☑ FALL CROPS. Zones 4–7: Early in the month, set out beets, Chinese cabbage, mustard, onions, radishes, spinach, and any of the cole crops.

☑ PERENNIALS, SHRUBS. This is the worst time to put new plants in the ground, especially in full sun. But if you see a plant you can't resist, you have two choices. Keep it in the container out of direct sun and water it religiously until October, when you can plant it in the ground. Or put it in the ground now and water it super-religiously until the weather cools and fall rain begins.

MAINTENANCE

☑ HARVEST HERBS FOR DRYING. Pick herbs in the morning just after dew has dried. Place a clean window screen horizontally atop concrete blocks (one under each corner) in a cool, dry spot out of direct sunlight and where dust won't blow on it. Lay the herbs out on the screen, leaving enough room for air to circulate around the plant parts; when herbs are completely dry, store them in jars.

☑ PROPAGATE SHRUBS. Take cuttings of your favorite shrubs to grow new ones. Evergreen candidates include azaleas, camellias, daphne, euonymus, holly, rhododendrons, and viburnum. Deciduous plants such as hydrangeas and magnolias can also be propagated by cuttings. By next spring, you'll have rooted plants to bed or transplant to 1-gallon cans.

☑ PRUNE CANE BERRIES. On June-bearing plants, remove all canes that produced fruit this season. On ever-bearing plants, cut back by half any canes that have already borne fruit.

☑ WATER. Where permitted by water-use ordinances, irrigate moisture-loving plants like rhododendrons deeply twice a week. Spray the foliage too; it washes dust off leaves and helps stressed plants absorb water quickly.

☑ FERTILIZE ANNUALS. There is enough summer left that annuals will benefit from a feeding with a liquid plant food that is low in nitrogen and high in phosphorus and potassium.

☑ GROUND COVERS. To keep flowering ground covers compact, shear them after they've bloomed.

PEST CONTROL

☑ CARPENTER ANTS. If you use logs or other pieces of dead wood as natural garden sculptures, keep an eye out for carpenter ants. They tend to march along on well-defined trails. If you see them going toward your house, you're likely to have an infestation. Unless you really know what you're doing, call a professional exterminating service.

Northern California Checklist

PLANTING

☑ PLANT FOR EXTENDED BLOOM. Zones 7–9, 14–17: Perennials that bloom now into fall include achillea, asters, begonias, coreopsis, dahlias, daylilies (some), fortnight lilies, geraniums *(Pelargonium)*, lantana, *Limonium perezii*, Mexican bush sage, scabiosa, and verbena. Check hardiness before shopping. A few plants, such as *Limonium perezii* and Mexican bush sage, aren't hardy in all zones.

☑ SOW COOL-SEASON ANNUALS. Zones 7–9, 14–17: Start seeds of fall- and winter-blooming annuals, including calendula, Iceland poppy, pansy, primrose, stock, and viola.

☑ PLANT A SHADE TREE. For optimum cooling effect, plant a tree on the southwest side of the house in a spot where it will shade windows. Use a deciduous tree for shade in summer and sun in winter. In milder climates, try Chinese hackberry, Chinese pistache, Japanese pagoda tree, 'Raywood' ash, or red oak. In cold climates, try American hornbeam, Eastern redbud, honey locust, or little-leaf linden.

☑ SOW COOL-SEASON CROPS. Zones 7–9, 14–17: To start broccoli, cabbage, cauliflower, chard, lettuce, and spinach seeds in containers, choose a well-drained potting mix and fill flats or pots. Moisten the mix thoroughly. Sow seeds according to package directions. Fine seeds are usually planted ½ inch deep. Sow carrots, onions, peas, and radishes directly in the ground: Mix compost into the soil, soak it thoroughly, and plant. Sow peas about 1 inch deep. Zones 1–2: Where frosts aren't expected until late October, sow seeds of beets, carrots, spinach, and radishes.

Sunset CLIMATE ZONES

☐ Mountain (1-2)
☐ Valley (7-9)
☐ Inland (14)
☐ Coastal (15-17)

Eureka • Redding • CALIFORNIA • Mendocino • Santa Rosa • Sacramento • San Francisco • San Jose • Monterey • Fresno • NEVADA

☑ SOW PERENNIALS. Zones 7–9, 14–17: For bloom next spring and summer, sow seeds of carnations, columbine, coreopsis, feverfew, gaillardia, hardy asters, hollyhock, lupine, penstemon, phlox, purple coneflower, Shasta daisy, statice, and yarrow. Plant seeds in flats or small pots filled with a peat-based potting mix.

MAINTENANCE

☑ CARE FOR FLOWERS. To keep warm-season annuals blooming through the end of summer and into fall, water and feed plants regularly with fish emulsion or another fertilizer. Remove spent flowers before they go to seed.

☑ FEED ROSES. Zones 7–9, 14–17: Now's the time to feed roses to get a big fall flush of blooms. A good, homemade recipe consists of 1 cup 12-12-12 fertilizer, ½ cup bonemeal, 2 tablespoons Epsom salts (available at pharmacies), and ½ cup sulfur (iron sulfate, ironite, or soil sulfur). Mix together. Apply this amount to each established (well-watered) rose by mixing it into the soil.

☑ IRRIGATE TREES AND SHRUBS. Large trees and shrubs may need a deep soaking now, even if they're watered by an irrigation system (some systems don't run long enough for water to penetrate the soil deeply). Use a soaker hose or a deep-root irrigator, or build a berm of soil around the plant and slowly soak the area inside with a hose. Let the water run until the soil beneath the drip line of the plant is soaked to a depth of 12 to 18 inches (use the deeper amount for larger shrubs and trees). Check moisture penetration by digging down with a trowel.

☑ HARVEST FRUITS AND VEGETABLES. Search bean, summer squash, and tomato plants thoroughly so you don't miss ripe ones. If you want to preserve tomatoes by canning them, harvest while they're still firm; soft tomatoes may contain harmful bacteria that can spoil the contents. Harvest corn when the tassels have withered and the kernels are well formed and squirt milky juice when punctured.

☑ TREAT NUTRIENT DEFICIENCIES. Inspect foliage for signs of nutrient deficiencies. Pale yellow leaves indicate that plants need nitrogen. Yellow leaves with prominent green veins indicate an iron deficiency; apply chelated iron according to the package directions.

Southern California Checklist

PLANTING

☑ **PLANT FINAL SUMMER CROPS.** Coastal gardeners (Zones 22–24) can set out transplants of eggplant, peppers, squash, and tomatoes. ('Champion', 'Celebrity', and 'Super Sweet 100' cherry tomatoes are good varieties to try for fall harvesting.) Coastal, inland (Zones 18–21), and low-desert (Zone 13) gardeners can sow a final crop of beans or corn.

☑ **START WINTER CROPS.** Coastal, inland, and high-desert (Zone 11) gardeners can start sowing cool-season vegetables in flats mid-month. After 6 to 8 weeks, the seedlings will be ready to transplant to the garden. Good candidates include beets, broccoli, Brussels sprouts, cabbage, carrots, cauliflower, collards, kale, kohlrabi, leeks, lettuces, mustard, peas, radishes, spinach, Swiss chard, and turnips.

☑ **START SWEET PEAS.** For sweet peas by December, plant seeds now. To speed germination, soak seeds overnight before planting. Provide a wall or trellis for vines to climb.

☑ **SPRING BULBS.** Freesias, sparaxis, and other South African bulbs that naturalize easily in Southern California begin to appear in nurseries this month. Plant them immediately after purchase.

☑ **BIENNIALS.** Start seeds of Canterbury bells, foxglove, hollyhocks, lunaria, and other biennials now. When seedlings are about 3 inches tall, transplant them into the garden. Plants will become established during fall and bloom next spring.

MAINTENANCE

☑ **FEED ANNUALS, VEGETABLES.** Continue to fertilize warm-season flowers and crops every 2 to 4 weeks, especially those in containers.

☑ **TRIM SPENT BLOOMS.** To promote late flowering, lightly trim coreopsis, dianthus, felicias, foxglove, marguerites, penstemon, yarrow, and other perennials.

☑ **PRUNE WATER SPROUTS AND SUCKERS.** Tall, thin shoots that grow straight up from citrus and stone fruit tree trunks and branches should be removed as soon as they are noticed. They drain the tree's energy away from fruit production. Cut shoots off flush with the bark. Suckers that develop at the base of the plant should be removed, too. Pull them off rather than cutting them away.

☑ **WATER AS NEEDED.** Give mature trees and established shrubs a slow, deep soak once a month. Water avocado, citrus, and stone fruit trees thoroughly and deeply every 7 to 10 days, depending on location. Water tropicals deeply every 5 to 7 days. Water Bermuda grass lawns once or twice a week, tall fescues two or three times. Plants in containers, especially hanging baskets, may have to be watered daily, especially during Santa Ana winds. A good rule of thumb for everything: If the top few inches are dry, water.

PEST CONTROL

☑ **COMBAT LAWN GRUBS.** Irregular brown patches in summer lawns may be caused by beetle larvae that feed on grass roots. Pull up sections of dead turf to expose them. If grubs are a problem, treat with parasitic nematodes. Following label instructions, spray the nematode-water mixture in late afternoon after watering.

☑ **CONTROL FIREBLIGHT.** This bacterial disease makes affected plants look as if they have been scorched by fire. Cotoneaster, evergreen pear, pyracantha, toyon, and members of the rose family are susceptible. Prune out diseased twigs and branches; cut small branches 4 to 6 inches below the infection, large branches at least 12 inches below the infected part.

☑ **WASH AWAY PESTS.** Aphids, mites, thrips, whiteflies, and other small pests can be kept to manageable numbers with regular syringing. Use a sharp stream of water to dislodge them from plant foliage. Avoid pesticides; they kill beneficial insects, too.

Mountain Checklist

PLANTING & HARVEST

☑ **PLANT FALL CROPS.** Where frosts aren't expected until late October, sow beets, carrots, radishes, and spinach for fall harvest. In mildest climates, set out transplants of broccoli, cabbage, and cauliflower.

☑ **SOW WILDFLOWERS.** Sow seeds of annual and perennial wildflowers now for bloom next spring. Try bachelor's buttons, coreopsis, Mexican hat, perennial blue flax, poppies, prairie asters, Rocky Mountain penstemon, and yellow coneflower. Cultivate the soil lightly, spread seeds, then mulch with ¼ to ½ inch of ground bark or other organic matter.

☑ **HARVEST CROPS.** Even if you can't use them right away, pick apples, beets, broccoli, bush beans, cauliflower, peaches, potatoes, raspberries, strawberries, summer squash, sweet corn, tomatoes, and zucchini. Never let the crop rot on the plant; it cuts production and spreads disease.

☑ **HARVEST FLOWERS FOR DRYING.** Pick blossoms with long stems, strip off the leaves, bundle flowers together, and hang them upside down in a garage or basement until dry.

☑ **HARVEST HERBS.** Pick them after the dew has dried in the morning. Use herbs fresh, or air-dry them on a screen in the shade or hang bundles in a dry, shady place.

Sunset
CLIMATE ZONES
☐ 1-3 ☐ 10-11

MAINTENANCE

☑ **CARE FOR ANNUALS.** Shear or pinch off faded flowers, then water and fertilize to encourage bloom through summer's end.

☑ **CHECK FOR CHLOROSIS.** If leaves are yellowish, but their veins are green, apply chelated iron to correct iron deficiency (chlorosis). If leaves are yellowish overall and you can spot no insect or cultural problems, apply a complete fertilizer.

☑ **DIVIDE PERENNIALS.** After delphiniums, German iris, Oriental poppies, and Shasta daisies bloom, divide large clumps. Dig up and cut the root mass into several sections. Add organic matter to soil and replant. (In shortest-season areas, wait until spring to dig and replant.)

☑ **PROTECT VEGETABLES.** In high-elevation gardens, protect vegetables from early cold temperatures by placing cardboard, glass, or row covers over plants by late afternoon. Remove covers before mid-morning.

☑ **PRUNE WATER SPROUTS.** Water sprouts are vigorous shoots growing from trunks or branches of birch, crabapple, hawthorn, lilac, Russian olive, and willow. Suckers grow from a plant's rootstock. Prune off both.

PEST CONTROL

☑ **POWDERY MILDEW.** Dahlias, peas, roses, squash, and zinnias are particularly susceptible to this powdery white fungus. To keep it from spreading, avoid overhead watering and remove and destroy diseased stems and leaves. In severe cases, control with a sulfur-based spray or a fungicide such as benomyl.

☑ **SLUGS.** Beer traps, hand-picking, and bait containing metaldehyde or mesurol are all effective in slug-prone plantings. Keep the bait away from children and pets—it's poisonous.

Southwest Checklist

PLANTING

☑ PLANT COOL-SEASON CROPS. Zone 10: Sow beans, cabbage family members, collards, corn, cucumbers, potatoes, spinach, squash, and Swiss chard early in the month; put in transplants at month's end. Zone 11: Sow beets, carrots, radishes, and spinach, and put in transplants of broccoli, cabbage, and cauliflower for fall harvest. Zones 12–13: Late in August, sow beans, cabbage family members, carrots, collards, corn, cucumbers, green onions, leeks, lettuce, and squash for a late harvest.

☑ SOW WILDFLOWERS. Cultivate soil lightly, broadcast seed, then cover with ¼ to ½ inch of organic mulch such as ground bark. Some flowers to try include Arizona lupine, blackfoot daisies, blue flax, chia, coreopsis, desert marigolds, firecracker pentemon, firewheel, goldfields, Mexican gold poppies, Parry's penstemon, scented verbena, and sticky asters.

MAINTENANCE

☑ CARE FOR ROSES. To help roses get ready for strong fall bloom, acidify the soil with soluble sulfur (Dispersul), fortify it with a complete fertilizer, and apply iron chelate to correct chlorosis. Water plants thoroughly.

☑ GROOM PLANTS. Keep deadheading annuals, and feed plants every 2 weeks with a liquid fertilizer.

☑ WATER. Container plants, nursery stock, recently planted seedlings, and anything growing under house eaves need extra attention this time of year. Thoroughly drench the roots of permanent landscape plants with a soaker hose, a deep-root irrigator, or a hose running slowly into a watering basin built around the plant.

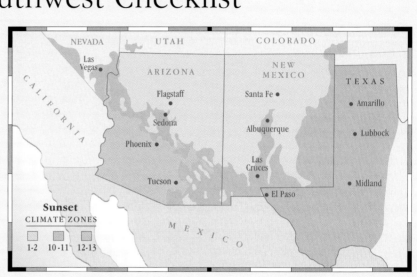

☑ FEED SHRUBS. Give shrubs a half-strength application of a complete fertilizer, watering it in well, to help them recover from heat stress.

☑ MAKE COMPOST. Haul garden waste to the compost pile, mixing weeds, lawn clippings, and nonmeat kitchen waste. Keep the pile evenly moist and turn it regularly.

PEST CONTROL

☑ LAWN PESTS. Just as chinch bugs can cause St. Augustine grass to dry out and die back, microscopic Bermuda grass mites can do the same to Bermuda lawns, giving them a classic shaving-brush look. The treatment for both is the same: an application of chlorpyrifos (Dursban) or diazinon.

☑ SOUTHWESTERN CORN BORERS. If translucent patches skeletonize leaves of corn plants, corn borer larvae are the likely culprits. They can also kill the plants' growing tips. Spray plants with *Bacillus thuringiensis* (Bt), a biological control.

☑ SPIDER MITES. Mottled leaves and fine webs signal the mites' presence. Control infestations by spraying with a miticide.

☑ WHITEFLIES. Yellow sticky traps are the best control measure.

(Front row, from left) 'Konserva' kale and 'Dorat' chard; (center row) bok choy; (back row) 'Red Russian' kale and 'Red Giant' mustard.

Easy-to-Grow Greens

In late fall and winter, when many plants are finished blooming or going dormant, cool-season greens bring a leafy beauty to garden beds. Their leaves, bold and voluptuous as jungle plants, combine handsomely in wide beds. They're also flavor favorites with cooks around the world. In Portugal, kale or collards mix with potatoes and sausage in the soup *caldo verde*. Italians are fond of spinach or chard pie; the French use chard in a seasonal vegetable soup. Asians add bok choy to stir-fries. Creative cooks in the West are catching on by blending, braising, and flavoring a wide array of leafy winter greens—among the most healthful vegetables you can grow.

Leafy greens are fast and easy to grow either from seed or seedlings. (You'll have more varieties to choose from if you start plants from seed.) Start seed indoors about 6 weeks before planting time. Do it this month in the Pacific Northwest, September and October in Northern California, September to November or later in mild areas of Southern California, and October and November in the low desert. Plant in full sun and mix in plenty of compost. Keep the soil moist; greens turn bitter if soil moisture fluctuates between wet and dry.

To harvest greens, you can either pick one leaf at a time or pull out the entire plant when it matures. Then you can simply sauté them in a little oil with garlic, cover, and cook for a few minutes until tender.

Some great greens

Bok choy (pak choi). This Asian green tastes similar to Swiss chard, but its leaves are thicker and less wrinkled. 'Joi Choi' has wide, white stems and tender, succulent leaves that grow to 15 inches long. 'Mei Qing Choi Hybrid' (baby bok choy) grows only 6 to 8 inches long.

Collards. The mild, cabbage-flavored leaves are high in vitamins A and C and calcium. 'Vates' is nonheading, compact (to 24 inches tall), and slow to bolt. 'Georgia' is vigorous, growing to 36 inches tall.

Kale. Gorgeous heads of succulent green or red leaves, some curled. Plants are hardy to 10°F. If you can't find 'Konserva', try 'Winterboro.'

Mustard. Large, green-leafed 'Savannah Hybrid' has a mild flavor; 'Red Giant' and 'Southern Giant Curled' are spicier. Cooking removes some of the spiciness. Most varieties are very fast-growing, maturing in 20 to 45 days.

Spinach. 'Olympia' has smooth leaves and is productive in spring and fall. 'Tyee' has semi-savoyed (crinkled) leaves and is very vigorous. 'Vienna Hybrid' has fully savoyed leaves and matures very early. All three are resistant to downy mildew (which can limit winter production).

Swiss chard. 'Ruby Red' and 'Rhubarb' have dark red leaves and crimson stems that are very ornamental in the garden. 'Dorat' has beautiful light green leaves. 'Bright Lights' is actually a mix of chards whose rainbow-colored stems include crimson, orange, pink, white, and yellow. Its leaves range from green to red.

Hot colors in the desert: Under a palo verde, the reddish spikes of Parry's penstemon and gold Mexican poppies (Eschscholzia mexicana) *put on a spring show.*

Wildflowers

Miner's lettuce, milk maids, sugar-scoops, and shooting stars—these are just a few of the many wildflowers that grow in the West. With their evocative names and brilliant colors, wildflowers offer the gardener a chance to bring pioneer history, Native American lore, and ecological conservation into the garden. For example, you can sow wildflowers in a 4- to 8-foot border to create a cheery transition between lawn and woods; you can sprinkle wildflowers in gaps between ground covers; or you might simply designate a corner or circle of your property as a "wild" patch where children can explore and play. Although wildflowers are often naturalized in the garden, don't be afraid to include such flowers as the delicate western columbine *(Aquilegia formosa)* in formal borders. And feel free to intersperse native species with their modern hybrid offspring (such as Pacific Coast irises, hybrids of *Iris douglasiana*) and other garden flowers.

The wildflower gardens sold in cans at garden centers typically contain wildflowers along with annuals for immediate color and a smattering of perennials. Specialty seed companies offer regional mixes, and there are plenty of showy western natives to make these worthwhile.

After the show

Weeds are the primary cause of failure for wildflower gardens. So whether you are seeding a wildflower border or painstakingly planting an area with small starts of perennial grasses and flowers, you must prepare the planting bed as carefully as you would for any flower border.

With luck, you will get a good display the first year. (Continue to remove weed seedlings as they start to emerge.) But once the plants have finished blooming, your natural meadow may take on a ragged, or even weedy, appearance.

Let all the plants in your wildflower garden set seeds, allowing them to dry out on the plants. The seeds will spill onto the ground and sprout new plants the following year. And they'll attract wild birds. You can gather some seeds by hand, too, and save them for later plantings or to fill out any bare spots.

In early winter or very early spring, mow or cut the dry stems down to 6 to 8 inches. At the same time, pull out any weeds, such as oxalis or dandelion. This once-a-year trim will give perennial wildflowers room and light to spread, before the next crop of annuals has emerged from their seeds. In regions that typically have a lot of rain in winter, irrigate a wildflower patch only when rains are light.

The Desert Botanical Garden in Phoenix has nearly perfected the art of wildflower displays, as shown here. But even if you don't have the space to plant a whole meadow, you can still enjoy wildflowers by planting them in small patches.

Wildflower secrets

Choose a sunny spot, then loosen the soil to a depth of 3 to 4 inches. Soil amendments are generally not necessary for native wildflowers.

Water the area to encourage weed seeds to germinate. Pull or hoe the weeds as soon as they appear. Cultivate no deeper than 1 inch; deeper cultivation exposes more weed seeds that will germinate along with the wildflower seeds. Failure to get rid of the existing weed and native grass seeds that are in the soil and germinate along

with the wildflowers is the most common mistake when planting wildflower seeds. The fast-growing weeds and grasses smother out the slower-growing wildflowers. (You can also spray weeds with an herbicide, such as glyphosate, and then cultivate the soil after the weeds have died, but this is less kind to the environment.)

Scatter a mix of annual and perennial seeds over the area. Use about ¼ ounce of seed for a 25-square-foot garden. Lightly rake the soil to cover the seeds. As a

quicker (but costlier) alternative, set out 1-gallon-size plants of perennial wildflowers.

Water right away and as often as needed to keep the soil moist until wildflower seedlings appear. Then reduce watering to two or three times a week. Pull weeds by hand as soon as you can tell them from the wildflowers.

Protect the garden with a ring of chicken wire if rabbits or other rodents are a problem in your area.

A wildflower sampler

NAME	LIGHT	BLOOMS	DESCRIPTION
YELLOW			
Baileya multiradiata Desert marigold	Sun	Late spring to fall	Bright, daisylike flowers; grows 1 to 1½ ft. tall. Thrives in hot-summer areas.
Coreopsis tinctoria Annual coreopsis	Sun	Spring	Bright, daisylike flowers with purplish brown centers; good for cutting; grows 1½ to 3 ft. tall.
Layia platyglossa Tidytips	Sun	Late spring	Daisylike flowers with white tips; grows to 1 ft. tall.
Mentzelia lindleyi Blazing star	Sun	Spring to early summer	Bright, showy, saucer-shaped flowers; grows 2 to 4 ft. tall.
RED AND ORANGE			
Dimorphotheca sinuata African daisy	Sun	Winter and spring	Masses of daisylike flowers, orange to white; grows to 1 ft. tall.
Eschscholzia californica California poppy	Sun	Winter to summer	Orange, cup-shaped flowers, also available in red, pink, yellow, and white; grows to 1½ ft. tall.
Gaillardia pulchella Indian blanket	Sun	Summer	Masses of daisylike flowers with yellow tips; good for cutting; grows 1 to 2 ft. tall.
Papaver rhoeas Shirley poppy	Sun or partial shade	Spring to summer	Crinkled, saucer-shaped flowers in range of reds; long blooming; grows 2 to 5 ft. tall.
Penstemon eatonii Firecracker penstemon	Sun	Spring to summer	Grows 1½ to 3 ft. tall, with tubular scarlet flowers in spikelike clusters.
Ratibida columnifera Mexican hat	Sun	Summer	Drooping, red-ray flowers touched with yellow surrounding a black central cone. Grows to 3 ft. tall.
BLUE AND VIOLET			
Centaurea cyanus Cornflower	Sun or partial shade	Spring to summer	Bright, button-shaped flowers; good for cutting; grows 1 to 2½ ft. tall.
Clarkia amoena Farewell-to-spring, godetia	Sun	Late spring to summer	Large, cup-shaped flowers; good for cutting; grows 1 to 2 ft. tall.
Iris douglasiana hybrids Pacific Coast iris	Light shade; sun in cool areas	Spring	Sword-shaped evergreen foliage; blue, white, and yellow flowers on 8- to 24-in. stems.
Nemophila menziesii Baby blue eyes	Sun or partial shade	Spring	Small, cup-shaped flowers with a white eye; grows ½ to 1 ft. tall.
Phacelia campanularia California desert bluebells	Sun	Spring	Long-blooming, brilliant, bell-shaped flowers; grows ½ to 1½ ft. tall.
Sisyrinchium bellum Blue-eyed grass	Sun	Spring to summer	Grassy leaves, ½-in. blue flowers on 6- to 24-in. stems.
WHITE			
Oenothera pallida Evening primrose	Sun	Summer	Large, fragrant, saucer-shaped flowers; grows to 1 ft. tall.

Iris douglasiana hybrid

Ratibida columnifera

Sisyrinchium bellum

Penstemon eatonii

Crocus sativus *is lovely to look at—and you can harvest the stigmas for saffron, too.*

Planting for Fall Color

Looking for a quick return on your garden investment? Try autumn-blooming bulbs. If you plant these bulbs in the middle of this month, you can expect to see blooms just weeks later. The refreshing flowers are a welcome lift to gardens languishing in hot, dry weather. Under the right conditions, most come back annually.

For best results, plant autumn-blooming bulbs by mid-September. If you plant later, they likely won't bloom until the following year. The bulbs require well-drained soil. Water deeply when you plant, then sparingly until the fall rains come. After that, they'll need no additional water.

Once fall bloom is over, leaves emerge in winter and spring. The bulbs lie dormant in summer and do fine without water. In fact, too much water during dormancy may cause rot, so it's best to plant bulbs among similarly unthirsty plants. If your garden requires watering in the summer and has heavy clay soil, grow the bulbs in containers.

Four for fall

Colchicum (meadow saffron, autumn crocus). *C. autumnale* has large crocuslike flowers in white or shades of pink and purple. The corms, which are poisonous, can bloom with or without soil or even water, although the flower colors are more intense when planted outdoors. In the ground, clusters of long-tubed flowers bloom shortly after planting, growing as much as 8 inches high and 4 inches wide. Two especially showy varieties are 'The Giant', with its lavender-to-violet flowers, and 'Waterlily', a double-petaled violet. In mild-winter areas, bulbs usually flower for only a couple of seasons.

Crinodonna (Amarcrinum). This hybrid of *Amaryllis belladonna* and a *Crinum* species produces a cluster of pink trumpet-shaped flowers, each 4 to 5 inches wide and equally long; they bloom atop bare 2½-foot stems. The flat, straplike leaves, which make inviting runways for snails, are mostly evergreen.

Crocus (fall-flowering). These species crocus grow as tall as 5 inches and are attractive planted in clusters. The showiest is *C. speciosus*, with deep blue-violet flowers; it multiplies rapidly. The variety called 'Conqueror' has blue 1½- to 2-inch flowers. The long-tubed, scented flowers of *C. goulimyi* are pale to dark purple; the bulb naturalizes especially well in Southern California. *C. kotschyanus* (also sold as *C. zonatus*) has lilac flowers with yellow throats. Flowers of fragrant *C. karduchorum* are lilac with white throats. And *C. sativus* is the saffron crocus; harvest its orange red stigma for seasoning.

Lycoris (spider lily). These are unpredictable bulbs. Even if planted by mid-September, there's only a 50% to 75% chance your *Lycoris* will bloom this year. Also, the plants do well when crowded, so don't disturb the roots for several years. *L. radiata* is the most exotic of the group. It has coral red flowers that bloom in clusters on bare stems growing as tall as 1½ feet.

Bulb sources

You'll find autumn-blooming bulbs available at most garden centers. *Colchicum* arrives this month; most others arrive in early September. With the exception of *Crinodonna* and *Crocus* 'Conqueror', bulbs are all also available by mail order.

Lycoris radiata is exotic and somewhat unpredictable.

Harvesting and Storing Edibles

Picked too soon, vegetables and berries may lack not just size but also flavor. The resulting taste may be tart, bitter, or simply bland. If you wait too long, you may again sacrifice flavor and texture as well. The sugar of peas and corn turns to starch, beans become stringy, beets woody, and berries mushy, for example. Some vegetables will stop producing if their crop is not harvested regularly.

Homegrown vegetables and berries have the kind of flavor you can't buy in a store—especially when you get them to the table immediately after picking. If you have more than you can eat, though, you may want to store the surplus.

The objective of storage is to keep vegetables and berries from aging quickly. In storage, the process of aging uses the crop's stored food; the faster this stored food is used, the faster the crop's flavor and texture decline. As aging continues, the produce eventually rots. The shortest-lived crops must be refrigerated and used promptly; others, stored correctly, can last for many months. To enjoy vegetables and berries all year, preserve them by canning, freezing, or drying, as appropriate to the particular crop.

Cool and damp storage (32° to 40°F). Whether provided in a refrigerator or a root cellar, cool and damp conditions prolong the storage life of vegetables and berries that have a high moisture content and fairly thin skins through which moisture transpires. This type of storage slows the aging process by creating an atmosphere moist enough to prevent dehydration. Relative humidity of about 90% is satisfactory for most vegetables and berries in this category. The major point of difference is length of successful storage time. The extremes range from several days for some berries and tender vegetables to months for root crops.

For vegetables and berries with a short storage life, the vegetable crisper in the refrigerator provides a good environment; for best flavor, use them as soon as possible. Bumper crops that overflow the crisper should be canned, frozen, or dried—or given to a food bank—to keep them from going to waste.

Store the more long-lived vegetables in this category—the root crops, for example—in a root cellar or cold frame. In cold-winter areas, prepare crops for root cellaring before severe frosts hit. For root crops, such as carrots, beets, turnips, rutabagas, and parsnips, dig up the roots and remove the leaves. For heading crops, such as cabbage, Brussels sprouts, and Chinese cabbage, dig up the plants—roots and all—when their foliage is dry; if it's wet when the plants are harvested, they'll rot when piled up.

Knock the soil off the roots and remove the outer leaves, but don't wash the vegetables. Make a 6-inch layer of dry leaves or hay; lay the vegetables on it in a shallow layer. Mound a layer of hay 12 to 24 inches deep over the vegetables, and cover them with a plastic sheet held down with soil, to prevent the vegetables from freezing. Locate your root cellar under an overhang or in an area that's protected from extreme cold and heavy rains.

In a modern house, it's not easy to find a cool, damp room for storing vegetables. You can improvise a root cellar in a basement by insulating a room that stays cool. The insulation protects the area from frost on the outside and from furnace heat on the inside. Use a window for ventilation. The crops can be stored on shelves or in wooden crates or bins.

It's important to prevent the stored crops from withering. To maintain adequate humidity, use natural evaporation from bare earth, gravel, or sand; or sprinkle the floor occasionally with water.

Above: Golden and 'Cylindra' beets need cool, damp storage.
Top left: Garlic bunches are left to cure in a dry, airy place.

If a basement isn't available, you can use a cold frame for fall storage of heading and rooting vegetables; place the vegetables on the ground, and then fill the frame with dry leaves for insulation. Or store vegetables in a trash can sunk into the ground, a method that works particularly well with root crops. Dig a hole deep enough so you can lower the can to within 3 to 4 inches of the rim. Use moist sand at the bottom of the can and between layers of vegetables to prevent them from drying out. For added insulation, place straw or leaf mulch over the can cover, and top the mulch with a sheet of plastic.

Cool and dry storage (35° to 50°F). Cool and dry conditions are needed to store the two most widely grown bulb crops: onions and garlic. If kept in a moist environment, they will continue to grow or quickly decay—or both.

These crops require an initial curing time at room temperature in a shady, dry spot—about 1½ weeks for garlic, up to 3 weeks for onions. Then they should be stored where it's cool, dry, and well ventilated.

In colder parts of the country, a basement or garage may offer ideal conditions. For good air circulation, either spread the bulbs out in shallow boxes or trays with slatted bottoms, or tie them up by the stubs of their dried tops, or put them in mesh bags or in old nylon stockings.

Warm and dry storage (55° to 60°F). Pumpkins, sweet potatoes, and hard-skinned winter squashes store well under warm and dry conditions. Right after harvest, cure these crops at a fairly high temperature (80° to 85°F) for about 10 days. Then place them in an upstairs storage room or a warm garage. Make sure the vegetables are not touching one another.

These green, red, and curly-leaf Savoy cabbages should be stored under cool and damp conditions.

Whatever their size or color, onions keep well given cool, dry storage.

FRESH HERBS

Harvesting herbs such as basil, oregano, rosemary, or thyme this month? If so, bunch them together and pop them into a water-filled pitcher. You can snip from this fragrant kitchen bouquet as needed.

Drying Herbs

Harvest herbs for drying just as the first flower buds begin to open. The oils in the leaves are most concentrated at this time, and the herbs will maintain their flavor when preserved. Cut sprigs or branches in the morning, after dew has evaporated; tie them together at the cut ends and hang them upside down in a warm,

dry, well-ventilated place out of direct sunlight. When the leaves feel crisp, strip them from the stems and store in airtight jars.

You can also dry herbs by removing the leaves from the stems and spreading them on screens placed in a warm, dry, airy place out of direct sunlight. Stir the leaves in the trays

every few days. When they feel crisp and crumble easily, store them in airtight jars.

If you are growing herbs for their seeds, harvest seed heads or pods when they turn brown. Dry them in paper bags until you can shake the seeds loose; then store the seeds in airtight jars.

Making Cuttings

Propagating plants from cuttings allows you to increase your supply of a special perennial, shrub, or tree already in your garden, or to start plants from a friend's garden. Unlike most plants raised from seed, those grown from cuttings are identical to the parent plant. Cuttings taken from the stems of plants are of three types, depending on the maturity of the parent plant: softwood, semihardwood, and hardwood. Some can also be started from leaf or root cuttings.

Softwood and semihardwood stem cuttings. Taken during the active growing season from spring until late summer, *softwood cuttings* are the easiest stem cuttings to take and the fastest to root. They come from relatively soft, flexible new growth. Many perennials, shrubs, and trees can be propagated by softwood cuttings, including coleus, forsythia, crape myrtle (*Lagerstroemia*), geranium (*Pelargonium*), penstemon, mock orange (*Philadelphus*), plum, pomegranate, rose, and weigela. *Semihardwood cuttings* are taken somewhat later in the growing season, usually in summer or early autumn. A semihardwood stem is firm enough to snap if

bent sharply; if it just bends, it's too mature for satisfactory rooting. Among the plants that can be propagated from semihardwood cuttings are boxwood, camellia, citrus, euonymus, holly, olive, and rhododendron.

Hardwood cuttings. You make hardwood cuttings in autumn or early winter, when plants are dormant. Many deciduous shrubs and trees can be propagated by this method, including most of those mentioned under softwood and semihardwood cuttings; others include currant, fig, gooseberry, grape, privet (*Ligustrum*), and mulberry (*Morus*).

Leaf cuttings. Some plants will root successfully from a leaf or a portion of one; examples include rex begonia, African violet (*Saintpaulia*), and mother-in-law's tongue (*Sansevieria*).

Root cuttings. Any plant that produces sprouts from its roots will grow from root cuttings. Some examples are bear's breech (*Acanthus*), Japanese anemone, blackberry, trumpet vine (*Campsis*), and Oriental poppy (*Papaver*). Make root cuttings when the plant is dormant—in late fall or early winter, for most species. Dig up the plant or a section of its roots. With a sharp knife, remove healthy pieces of root 2 to 4 inches long; those growing close to the crown will form new plants most quickly. You don't need

rooting hormone; it may delay rooting.

After planting, water the containers well. Place them in a greenhouse or cold frame protected from direct sun. Once stems and green leaves have formed, move the containers into full light and water as needed. When the shoots are several inches tall and new roots have formed (check by gently digging up a cutting), transplant to individual pots and feed with liquid fertilizer.

THREE TYPES OF LEAF CUTTINGS

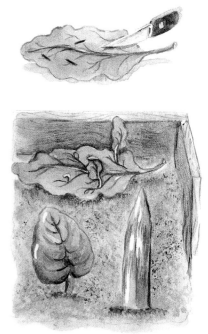

Rex begonias are propagated by making cuts in the large veins on the underside of mature leaves. Lay the leaf flat, cut side down, on the rooting medium; then enclose the container in a plastic bag. In time, new plants will grow at the point where each vein was cut.

To root leaf cuttings of African violets, insert a young leaf with an inch or two of stem into a rooting medium made of 1 part peat moss and 1 part vermiculite, perlite, or coarse builder's sand. Enclose the container in a plastic bag to retain humidity. New plants form at stem base.

To root leaf cuttings of mother-in-law's tongue, cut a leaf into 3- to 4-inch-long sections. Insert these pieces into the rooting medium, covering to three-fourths of their length. A new plant will eventually form at each base.

ROOT CUTTINGS

To start a few root cuttings, insert them upright in a pot, with the top cut ends at soil level. For a larger number, lay the cuttings in a flat filled with potting soil and cover them with ½ inch more mix.

Rooting softwood and semihardwood cuttings

1. Prepare containers first. Use clean pots or flats with drainage holes. Fill them with a half-and-half mixture of perlite and peat moss, or with perlite or vermiculite alone. Dampen the mixture.

2. Gather cuttings early in the day, when plants are fresh and full of moisture. The parent plant should be healthy and growing vigorously. With a sharp knife or bypass pruners, cut off an 8- to 12-inch length of stem.

Prepare the cuttings by removing and discarding any flower buds, flowers, and side shoots. Then slice the stem into 3- to 4-inch pieces, each with at least two nodes (growing points). Make each cut just below a node, since new roots will form at this point. Strip the lower leaves from each cutting.

3. Dip the cut end in rooting hormone powder, if desired. (Many kinds of plants will root without the use of hormones.) Tap off excess powder.

Using the end of a sharp pencil, make holes in the rooting medium an inch or two apart; then insert the cuttings. Firm the medium around the cuttings and water with a fine spray. Label each container with the name of the plant and the date. Set containers in a warm spot that's shaded but not dark.

Enclose each container in a plastic bag, fastening the bag closed to maintain humidity. Open the bag for a few minutes every day to provide ventilation.

4. Once the cuttings have taken hold and are growing roots, they will begin to send out new leaves. To test for rooting, gently pull on a cutting; if you feel resistance, roots are forming. At this point, expose the cuttings to drier air by opening the bags; if the cuttings wilt, close the bags again for a few days.

When the plants seem acclimated to open air, transplant each to its own pot of lightweight potting soil. By the next planting season, the new plants should be ready to go out in the garden.

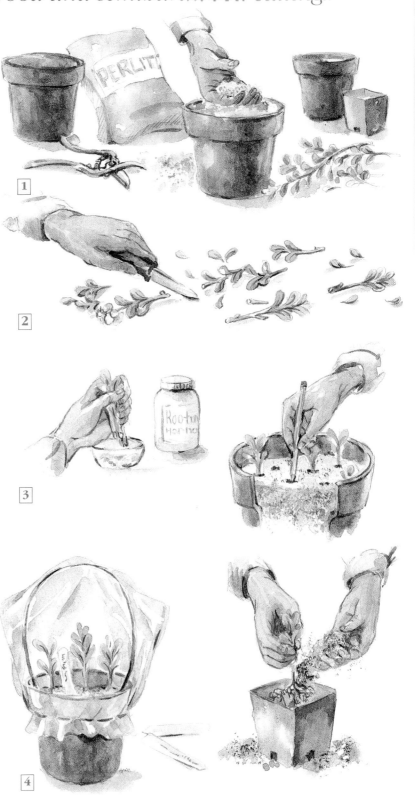

Rooting hardwood cuttings

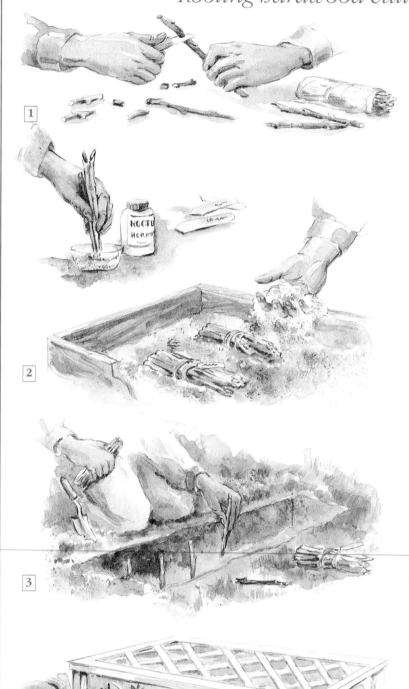

1. Take cuttings from a healthy, vigorous parent plant. Use wood from the previous season's growth, which is often lighter in color than older wood. With a sharp knife, cut pencil-thick stems 1 to 2 feet long.

To prepare the cuttings, slice off and discard the top inch or two of each stem (this is unripened wood and does not contain enough nutrients to survive). Then cut the stems into 6- to 9-inch lengths, each with two or three nodes. Make the cuts about ½ inch above or below a node; to help you remember which end of each cutting is the top, make the top cuts at a slant. Dip the bottom ends in rooting hormone powder and tap off the excess.

2. In climates where the ground freezes, store the cuttings, bundled together and fastened with rubber bands, in a box filled with slightly moist vermiculite, sawdust, or sand (cover the cuttings completely). Place the box in an unheated (but not freezing) garage or shed. In warmer areas, you can bury the bundles in an outdoor trench filled with regular garden soil. During winter, the lower ends of the cuttings will begin to form calluses from which the roots will grow.

3. In early spring, plant the cuttings in a nursery area protected from strong winds. Dig a narrow trench and set in the cuttings, top end up and about 6 inches apart. Fill in the trench with soil mixed with compost or perlite, leaving only the top bud of each cutting exposed. Firm soil around the cuttings.

4. During the growing season, water as needed to keep soil moist; protect cuttings from direct sun with shade cloth or a lattice supported on stakes. By fall or the next spring, the new plants should be ready for the garden.

Ground layering

1. In spring, select a young, healthy, pliable shoot growing low on the plant to be layered. Loosen the soil where the shoot will be buried and work in a shovelful of compost. Dig a shallow hole in the prepared area. With a sharp knife, make a cut where the shoot will touch the soil; cut about halfway through the shoot, starting from the underside. Dust the cut with rooting hormone powder and insert a pebble or wooden matchstick to hold it open.

Lay the shoot (the layer) in the hole and fasten it down with a piece of wire or a forked stick. Some gardeners tie the layer's tip to a stake to help it grow upwards.

2. Fill in the hole, firming the soil around the layer. A rock or brick can be placed on top to help hold the layer in place.

During the growing season, keep the soil around the layer moist. Adding a few inches of mulch will help retain moisture.

When you are sure roots have formed (this may take anywhere from a few months to more than a year; gently dig into the soil to check), cut the new plant free from the parent. Dig it up, keeping plenty of soil around the roots, and move it to its intended location.

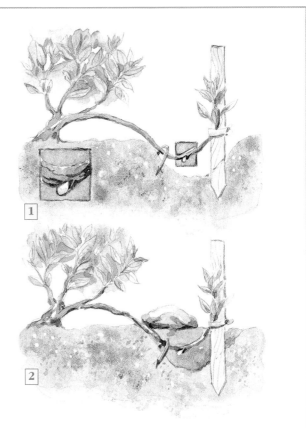

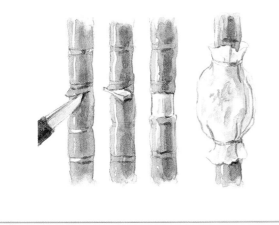

Air layering

Air layering is most successful while a plant is growing actively. To encourage growth in houseplants, fertilize the plant, then place it in a sunny window. When new leaves appear, proceed with layering.

Begin below a node. Make a slanting cut (insert a wooden matchstick to keep it open) or remove a ring of bark. Dust cut with rooting hormone, encase in damp sphagnum moss, and cover with plastic wrap to keep moss moist.

Layering

Layering is a propagation method that encourages new roots to form on branches still attached to the parent plant. The parent supplies the layer—the new plant—with water and nutrients during the rooting process.

Ground layering. Also called simple layering, ground layering is an easy way to produce a few new plants, though it may take as long as a year. Some plants, such as trailing blackberry, reproduce naturally by ground layering. Numerous others are well suited to this method, among them forsythia, gooseberry, grape, hazel-nut, mountain laurel *(Kalmia)*, rhododendron, rose, spiraea, and lilac *(Syringa)*.

To ground layer plants, follow the steps above.

Air layering. Air layering (shown above) involves the same principle as ground layering, but it's used for branches higher on a plant. It is often employed to propagate large house plants (overgrown rubber plants, for example), but it's also generally successful in some outdoor shrubs and trees, including citrus, witch hazel *(Hamamelis)*, magnolia, and rhododendron.

If the air layering in a container is successful, roots will appear in the sphagnum moss after several months; you can then sever the newly rooted stem from the parent plant and pot it in a container or plant it out. At this point, it's usually a good idea to remove about half of the new plant's leaves, to prevent excessive moisture loss through transpiration while the new plant gets established on its own.

If no roots form, the place where you cut will probably form a callus, and new bark will eventually grow over it.

Misty wands of Muhlenbergia capillaris *wave over* Trachelium caeruleum *to create the effect of sea spray without water. Yet the plants stand up to late-summer heat and drought.*

September

Pacific Northwest Checklist

PLANTING

☑ **LANDSCAPE PLANTS. Zones 1–3:** Now through October is the best time to set out trees, shrubs, ground covers, and many perennial plants. Zones 4–7: Do this through November.

☑ **SPRING BULBS.** Daffodils, tulips, and other spring-blooming bulbs show up in nurseries around Labor Day. Shop early to get the best selection, choosing bulbs that are plump and firm. For strong growth and early flowers, plant immediately.

☑ **LAWNS.** Start or overseed lawns this month.

☑ **COOL-SEASON CROPS.** It's your last chance to sow seeds for fall and winter salad crops, including arugula, leaf lettuce, mustard greens, radishes, and spinach.

MAINTENANCE

☑ **CARE FOR LAWNS.** Apply about 1 pound of actual nitrogen per 1,000 square feet of turf. If lawns have bare spots, remove all weeds, rake the ground, scatter and cover seed with a thin layer of soil, then water well. The grass should be up and robust by next spring.

☑ **CARE FOR ANNUALS, PERENNIALS.** Snip spent flowers from annuals and perennials, and water as needed to keep plants looking their best. You can squeeze another few rounds of blooms from summer annuals by feeding the plants with a liquid fertilizer early in the month and again at mid-month.

☑ **GROOM ROSES.** Cut flowers to bring indoors, shaping plants as you cut. Later in the month, allow a few of the flowers to form hips. This encourages plants to head into dormancy. Hips also brighten the garden in fall and winter, and serve as a food source for birds.

☑ **DIG AND DIVIDE PERENNIALS.** Plants that have finished their bloom cycle can be dug and divided. Use a spade or sharp knife to cut clumps into quarters. Replant divisions in weed-free, well-amended soil.

☑ **MAKE COMPOST.** Start a new pile or bin with grass clippings, spent annuals, prunings, and vegetable scraps. Keep both piles as moist as a wrung-out sponge to speed up decomposition during hot weather, and turn weekly.

☑ **MULCH. Zones 1–3:** Before freezing weather hits, weed around plants thoroughly, then spread a 2- to 3-inch layer of organic mulch (compost or pine needles work well) to insulate roots and reduce soil erosion.

☑ **TEND FUCHSIAS.** Continue your feeding program. Keep spent flowers pinched off. Water regularly.

☑ **WATER.** September can be one of the hottest, driest months. Water deeply so plants won't be drought-stressed as they enter fall and winter.

☑ **CLEAN GREENHOUSES.** Before cold weather arrives, clean out the greenhouse. Empty the old soil from flats and seed beds. Hose down the inside. Replace broken glass and cracked weatherstripping. Check the vents and heating and watering systems.

Northern California Checklist

PLANTING

☑ **PLANT COOL-SEASON GREENS.** Zones 7–9, 14–17: Mesclun, a colorful selection of salad greens, is easy to grow at home. Some contain almost a dozen varieties of lettuce as well as arugula, kale, and other greens.

☑ **PLANT NEW LAWNS.** Zones 1–2, 7–9, 14–17: Toward the end of the month, sow seed or lay sod over soil that's been rotary-tilled and amended with plenty of organic matter. Zones 1–2: Plant new lawns early in September (at highest elevations, wait to plant seed until October; it will germinate in spring when snow melts).

☑ **PLANT A NATIVE GARDEN.** Zones 7–9, 14–17: You don't have to have a big garden to grow native plants. Any small bed away from heavily irrigated plants can make an attractive native border. Try *Arctostaphylos*, blue-eyed grass, bush anemone, fremontodendron, lyme grass, mahonia, monkey flowers, Pacific Coast irises, *Penstemon heterophyllus purdyi,* and *Salvia clevelandii.*

☑ **SET OUT FALL-BLOOMING PERENNIALS.** Zones 7–9, 14–17: Some good choices include asters, chrysanthemums, gaillardia, gloriosa daisies, purple coneflower, Japanese anemones, lion's tail, and salvia.

☑ **PLANT VEGETABLES.** Zones 7–9, 14–17: Set out seedlings of broccoli, Brussels sprouts, cabbage, cauliflower, and spinach. Plant seeds of beets, carrots, leeks, onions, peas, radishes, and turnips.

Sunset
CLIMATE ZONES

☐ Mountain (1-2)
☐ Valley (7-9)
☐ Inland (14)
☐ Coastal (15-17)

MAINTENANCE

☑ **DIVIDE PERENNIALS.** From now through October (Zones 1–2, early this month) is the time to divide many perennials—such as agapanthus, candytuft, coreopsis, daylily, and penstemon—that are either overgrown or are not flowering well. Perennials can also be divided to increase the number of plants for your garden.

☑ **FERTILIZE.** Zones 7–9, 14–17: To get annuals, perennials, and fall-planted vegetables off to a strong start, mix compost into the garden bed before planting. Follow up with fish emulsion or a fish-kelp mixture every 2 to 4 weeks, or use a commercial fertilizer.

☑ **PREPARE WILDFLOWER BEDS.** Weeds are the nemesis of wildflower beds. To help control them, soak the soil thoroughly to germinate the seeds, then hoe down, wait for the weeds to pop up, and remove them.

☑ **CARE FOR CITRUS.** Zones 7–9, 14–17: To prevent citrus fruit from drying out as it matures, give trees regular deep soakings during warm fall weather. Irrigate the entire root zone of the tree.

PEST CONTROL

☑ **CHECK FOR SPIDER MITES.** Zones 7–9, 14–17: This tiny pest sucks juices from plant leaves, causing stippling; tiny white eggs on the undersides of leaves and fine webbing may also be noticeable. Control by spraying the tops and bottoms of the leaves thoroughly with a lightweight summer (horticultural) oil.

Southern California Checklist

PLANTING

☑ **ADD COOL-SEASON COLOR.** Coastal and low-desert gardeners (Zones 22–24 and 13, respectively), can set out winter/spring-blooming annuals starting mid-month, including calendulas, English daisies, Iceland poppies, linaria, snapdragons, nemesia, pansies, and stock. Wait until October to plant inland (Zones 18–21). This is also a good month to set out foxgloves, Canterbury bells, and other biennials found in small pots at the nursery or started from seed earlier.

☑ **PLANT SWEET PEAS.** For flowers by December, plant seeds now. To speed germination, soak seeds overnight before planting. Provide a wall, trellis, or 6-foot poles for vines to climb.

☑ **BUY BULBS.** Spring-flowering bulbs arrive in nurseries this month. Shop early to get the best selection. Bulbs that naturalize easily include babiana, daffodil, Dutch iris, freesia, homeria, ixia, leucojum, narcissus, oxalis, sparaxis, *Starnia*, and watsonia. They can be planted immediately. For a long season of cut flowers, plant groupings of anemone and ranunculus bulbs at 2-week intervals starting now.

☑ **CHILL BULBS.** Buy crocus, hyacinth, and tulip bulbs now but chill for 6 to 8 weeks before planting. Store in a paper bag (away from ethylene-producing fruit like apples) in the crisper section of your refrigerator. Plant after Thanksgiving. High-desert gardeners (Zone 11) don't need to prechill these bulbs.

Sunset
CLIMATE ZONES
1-3 7-9 11 13 14-24

☑ **PLANT BULB COVERS.** Planted directly over bulbs, forget-me-nots, Johnny-jump-ups, lobelia, and sweet alyssum provide color until the bulbs flower (bulbs push through them with ease) and hide bulbs' yellowing foliage after they stop blooming.

☑ **START COOL-WEATHER CROPS.** From mid-month on, coastal (Zones 22–24) and inland (Zones 18–21) gardeners can begin planting winter crops. Sow seeds for arugula, beets, carrots, chard, collards, endive, kale, lettuces, bok choy, peas, radishes, spinach, and turnips. Set out broccoli, Brussels sprouts, cabbage, cauliflower, and celery seedlings. Plant sets of garlic, onions, and shallots. In the high desert, plant lettuce, radishes, and spinach.

☑ **TRY A FALL TOMATO CROP.** Gardeners in frost-free areas (except those who live close to the beach) are reporting success with tomato seedlings planted in late summer, especially when planted near a south-facing wall. 'Champion', 'Celebrity', and 'Sweet 100' work well.

MAINTENANCE

☑ **FEED PERMANENT PLANTS.** Feed established trees, shrubs, ground covers, and warm-season grasses, such as Bermuda, now. Repeat in a month. Coastal gardeners can also fertilize tropical plants with a fast-acting product one last time, if needed. Don't feed California natives or drought-tolerant Mediterranean plants.

☑ **PROTECT AGAINST BRUSHFIRES.** Dead vegetation adds fuel to flames. If you live in a fire-prone area, cut and remove all dead leaves and limbs from trees and shrubs, especially those that grow near the house, before the onset of Santa Ana winds. Also clear leaves from gutters and remove woody vegetation growing against structures.

☑ **REPLENISH MULCH.** A thick (3- to 4-inch) layer of organic mulch around permanent plants will help protect them from Santa Ana winds by conserving moisture and insulating roots. Renew mulch around shrubs, trees, rosebushes, and woody perennials. But keep mulch off the crowns, stems, and trunks of plants to discourage pests and disease.

PEST AND WEED CONTROL

☑ **PROTECT CABBAGE CROPS.** Those little white butterflies flitting around your cole crops are laying eggs that will turn into hungry caterpillars. Cover crops with row covers or dust with *Bacillus thuringiensis* to kill the young larvae.

☑ **FORCE WEED SEEDS.** When preparing a new bed for planting, water to start weeds growing. As soon as weeds germinate, pull them out or remove with a hoe.

Mountain Checklist

PLANTING AND HARVESTING

☑ BULBS. Set out bulbs of daffodil, crocus, hyacinth, *Iris reticulata*, scilla, and tulip in loose, well-amended soil. To protect them from soil temperature fluctuations, plant daffodils and tulips 10 to 12 inches deep and small bulbs 5 inches deep. Also, pot up amaryllis and narcissus bulbs by month's end to force blooms for indoor display between Thanksgiving and Christmas.

☑ LAWNS. Early fall is ideal for seeding a lawn or laying sod. Keep the turf well watered until cold weather stops its growth.

☑ PLANT PERENNIALS. Set out campanula, candytuft, catmint, coreopsis, delphinium, dianthus, foxglove, gaillardia, geum, penstemon, phlox, salvia, and yarrow. If you live in a place where the ground freezes hard every winter, mulch plants well to keep them from being heaved out of the ground.

☑ HARVEST CROPS. Cantaloupes are ready to pick when the skin is well netted and the fruit slips easily from the vine. Pick watermelons when tendrils near the fruit start to brown, and winter squash when the rind colors up and hardens. Pick cucumbers and summer squash any time: They're excellent when young and tender. Ripe kernels of corn should be milky inside—if the liquid is watery, the corn is immature; if pasty, the corn is past its prime. Harvest raspberries when the sun is high and berries are warm to the touch. If a light frost threatens, protect eggplants, peppers, and tomatoes under floating row covers.

Sunset
CLIMATE ZONES
☐ 1-3   ☐ 10-11

MAINTENANCE

☑ DIVIDE PERENNIALS. In all but the highest elevations, lift and divide crowded clumps of bleeding heart, daylilies, hostas, peonies, Shasta daisies, and Siberian irises. Use a spade or sharp knife to cut clumps into quarters, and replant immediately.

☑ STORE SUMMER BULBS. When foliage dies down, lift cannas, dahlias, and gladiolus. Let them dry for a few days, then store at 35° to 50°F in a well-ventilated space. Store cannas and dahlias in sand, peat moss, or vermiculite. Leave tuberous begonias in pots that are also in a frost-free place.

☑ FERTILIZE LAWNS. Apply about 10 pounds of 10-10-10 fertilizer per 1,000 square feet of turf.

☑ WATER. Don't forget to water plants growing under eaves and in containers.

☑ MAKE COMPOST. Compost the weeds, vegetable remains, bean vines, grass clippings, and leaves that come out of your garden this month. If you keep the pile turned and well watered, you should have finished compost in time to dig into beds before winter.

PEST CONTROL

☑ PREVENT SNOW MOLD ON LAWNS. To discourage snow mold from forming, rake the dead thatch out of the lawn, then spray with a fungicide, such as benomyl.

Southwest Checklist

PLANTING

☑ ANNUALS. Zone 12 (Tucson): Plant calendula, larkspur, lobelia, pansies, snapdragons, stock, sweet alyssum, and violas.

☑ BULBS. Zones 1–2, 10–11: Plant spring-flowering bulbs, including crocus, daffodils, grape hyacinth, hyacinth *(Muscari)*, irises, and tulips. In Zones 12–13, prechill bulbs (except irises) by placing them in paper bags and storing them in the refrigerator. Plant the chilled bulbs after the soil has cooled down, around Thanksgiving. In all zones, pot up amaryllis and narcissus bulbs by month's end to force blooms for indoor display between Thanksgiving and Christmas.

☑ SOW COOL-SEASON CROPS. Zones 10–13: As soon as temperatures drop below 100°, sow beets, carrots, celery, chard, endive, green onions, kale, kohlrabi, leeks, parsley, parsnips, peas, potatoes, radishes, spinach, and turnips. Sow lettuce and cabbage family members (such as broccoli, cauliflower, and Brussels sprouts) in flats now for transplanting in October.

☑ PLANT WARM-SEASON CROPS. Zones 12–13: If you plant beans and corn in the low and intermediate deserts around Labor Day, you'll be harvesting both crops by Thanksgiving.

☑ PLANT LAWNS. Zones 1–2, 10–11: Seed a lawn or lay sod; continue to water well until grass is established.

☑ PLANT PERENNIALS. Zones 1–2, 10–11: Plant campanula, candytuft, catmint, coreopsis, delphiniums, dianthus, diascia, foxglove, gaillardia, geum, penstemon, phlox, salvia, and yarrow. Zones 10–13: Start seeds of carnations, columbine, coreopsis, feverfew, gaillardia, hardy asters, hollyhock, lupine, penstemon, phlox, Shasta daisies, statice, and yarrow. They'll be ready for transplanting in about 8 weeks.

☑ PLANT FOR PERMANENCE. Zones 10–11: Set out hardy trees, shrubs, and ground covers from nursery containers.

MAINTENANCE

☑ DIVIDE PERENNIALS. Zones 1–2, 10: Lift and divide crowded clumps of daylilies, peonies, and Shasta daisies. Use a spade or sharp knife to cut clumps into quarters. Replant divisions in well-amended soil.

☑ FEED ROSES. Water deeply, apply a complete fertilizer with chelated iron, water again, and apply a 3-inch layer of organic mulch.

☑ WATER CITRUS. Irrigate citrus deeply every 10 to 14 days; it will help reduce fruit split.

☑ CARE FOR LAWNS. If you plan to overseed your Bermuda lawn, stop feeding it. If you don't plan to overseed, apply a pound of actual nitrogen per 1,000 square feet of turf and water it in well.

PEST CONTROL

☑ SPRAY CABBAGE LOOPERS. To kill the little green worms that eat the leaves of cabbage family members, spray with *Bacillus thuringiensis*.

Dividing Perennials

Gardeners divide perennials for at least two reasons: first, to improve the health and flower production of overgrown, crowded plantings; and second, to gain new divisions to increase a planting. Note that division is usually feasible only for perennials that grow in clumps with an expanding root mass. It is not practical to divide those that grow from a taproot; if you attempt to divide the taproot, you'll probably kill the plant. Such plants are usually increased by root cuttings or from seed.

Though there are exceptions, fall is usually the best time to divide plants that bloom in spring or early summer, while those that bloom in late summer to fall should be divided in spring.

Once divided, a large clump may yield several dozen divisions (or even more), but keep in mind that the smaller the division, the longer it will take to mature and bloom well again. For faster results, divide plants into fewer, larger sections.

To divide most perennials, follow these steps:

Wet the soil thoroughly a day or two before dividing to make the clump easier to dig.

Cut into the soil around the clump with a spading fork or shovel, digging 6 to 12 inches beyond the perimeter of the clump. Then dig under the roots to the depth of the fork or shovel, working around the perimeter until the entire area is loosened.

Remove excess soil from the clump (rinse it off with water from a hose, if necessary) so you can find natural dividing points.

Now begin the actual division. The best tool to use depends on the size of the clump and the type of roots it has. Some perennials have such thick, tough roots that a shovel (or even an ax) may be the only practical dividing tool. Others have mats of small fibrous roots that are easily sliced with a knife or pruning saw. Sometimes hand-held pruners or a trowel will do the job easily; if clumps are very loose, you can even separate by hand.

Cut foliage of large plants back to 4 to 6 inches once you've made the divisions. Keep the divisions' foliage and roots damp while you prepare the planting area; place them in a shady spot if the day is sunny and warm.

Amend the soil with organic matter, whether you are replanting in the same area or in another part of the garden. Many gardeners also work in a dry granular fertilizer high in phosphorus and potassium in order to promote healthy root development.

Plant divisions and keep them well watered while they're getting established. You can also plant divisions in containers and hold them for planting later or for sharing with fellow gardeners.

1. *Lift the plant from the ground after loosening soil around and under the clump with a spading fork.*

2. *Slice through the clump with a trowel, dividing it into four sections. Then break each section by hand into 4-by-4-inch pieces.*

3. *Immediately plant divisions in prepared bed.*

4. *Some plant clumps, such as this red hot poker, may need to be split with a sharp shovel or a fork. Take sections that contain both roots and green stems, trim the stems, and replant.*

Creating a Beautiful Border

Mixing and matching colors is like painting with plants. These strategies can help you compose your own work of art.

Use shades of a single color. When you stick with one basic color, everything automatically goes together. Take purple, for instance. You can mix lavender, violet, and mauve flowers and plum-colored foliage with impunity. Or pastel, rose, and cerise pinks. You can add accent colors later if you decide the look is too sedate. Some suggestions:

- A pink-flowered spiraea with 'Apple Blossom' penstemon and pink coral bells.
- Yellow iris and 'Coronation Gold' yarrow with yellow and cream columbine.
- Burnished orange lion's tail (*Leonotis leonurus*) with bronze rudbeckia and a brown sedge like *Carex buchananii.*
- Dark pink azaleas with pink Lenten rose and pink primroses.

Use complementary colors. Colors directly opposite each other on the color wheel—red and green, orange and blue, yellow and violet—are always complementary partners. Muting one or both colors makes these combinations subtler. Apricot and lavender are easier to live with for the long haul than citrus orange and grape-juice purple, for instance. Following are some possibilities:

- Blue catmint with golden yarrow and buttery yellow Jerusalem sage.
- Apricot foxglove and diascia with blue salvia and iris.
- The deep reddish blue leaves of *Loropetalum* 'Plum Delight' with the chartreuse green ones of 'Sunset Gold' diosma.
- Bright gold Japanese forest grass with 'Blue Panda' corydalis and a chartreuse and blue hosta.

Lime blooms of Euphorbia *'Palustris' with purple Siberian irises.*

Above left: Pinkish Sedum telephium *'Autumn Joy' with gray* Artemisia *'Powis Castle'. Right: Creamy yellow* Hypericum inodorum *'Elstead' and violet* Veronica longifolia subsessilis.

Use color echoes. This is the Mother-Nature-makes-no-mistakes approach. Choose a focal plant and then build on its colors.

- Variegated 'Norah Leigh' phlox: Repeat the cream in the foliage with cream-colored foxglove and the pink in the flowers with 'Evelyn' penstemon. Back the whole vignette with cream-colored roses.
- *Aster frikartii:* Back the lavender-blue of the flowers with the mauve haze of purple muhly grass, then pick up the aster's yellow centers with golden coreopsis.

Texture

Foliage is the heart of a good planting. Putting together plants with different leaf shapes and surfaces is the object. Balance big and small leaves, smooth and fuzzy, strappy and feathery. All are instant texturizers.

Artemisia. These perennials are grown for their lacy, silver-gray foliage. They work as foils for spring pastels.

Use: Try billowy 'Powis Castle' with pink roses and blue delphiniums. Or plant common wormwood *(A. absinthium)* between white marguerites and green santolina. Or (along the coast) try dusty miller *(A. stellerana)* between sea lavender and variegated society garlic.

Euphorbia. The dome-shaped bushes of fleshy blue-green leaves and chartreuse flowers *(E. characias, E. amygdaloides,* and *E. martinii)* add instant architectural interest to gardens.

Use: Combine the species listed above with rosemary and santolina; basket-of-gold *(Aurinia saxatilis)* and blue and yellow bearded irises; or sword ferns and green-flowered Corsican hellebore.

Hosta. These plants have gorgeous heart-shaped leaves with prominent veins. (All forms are deciduous in winter.) There are many green, blue, gold, and mixed colors to choose from. Hostas are great for woodland gardens.

Use: Try blue-leafed types with the fall gold of laceleaf Japanese maple *(Acer palmatum* 'Dissectum'*)* and lady's-mantle; gold ones with 'The Rocket' ligularia and ferns; and green varieties with Japanese barberry and astilbe.

New Zealand flax *(Phormium).* Its upright, swordlike leaves always create dramatic tension. Flax adapts to most soils and exposures (Zones 7–24).

Use: Combine apricot-tinged P. 'Maori Queen' with orange African daisy *(Arctotis)* and purple Mexican bush sage; reddish brown P. 'Bronze

Baby' with 'Siskiyou Pink' gaura and Santa Barbara daisy *(Erigeron karvinskianus)*; or *P. hookeri* 'Cream Delight' with a cream- and green-striped agave and brittlebush *(Encelia farinosa).*

Ornamental grasses. They are unparalleled for their ability to add movement to the garden.

Purple fountain grass—which, unlike other pennisetums, won't reseed and make a pest of itself—is a winner in the garden. Try it with lavatera and lavender.

Use: In a large garden, grow tall, urn-shaped *Miscanthus sinensis* with asters and veronica. In a smaller one, pair Mexican feather grass with ornamental oreganos and small salvias like *S. greggii* and 'East Friesland'.

Other good texturizers. *Acanthus mollis,* aloes, barberry, breath of heaven *(Diosma ericoides),* ferns, heavenly bamboo, helichrysum, hellebores, lamb's ears, *Leptospermum,* and rosemary.

Exclamation points

If you plot out the shrubs and perennials you're considering on a piece of paper, or in your head, you'll see that they all occupy oval or circular spaces. Don't let the empty spots between them go to waste. Tuck in some virtually vertical plants—flowers that bloom along tall, leafless stalks.

Biennial foxglove, with its cluster of tubular flowers at eye level, is a perfect example. Tall flowering bulbs and many kinds of irises also fit into this category. These plants may put on only a brief performance, but they make up for it in showmanship. Consider these:

- Lavender foxglove with pink roses and lamb's ears.
- Pale blue delphiniums with dark blue salvia and *Iris pallida.*
- Pale yellow *Verbascum bombyciferum* 'Arctic Summer' with yellow and pink alstroemeria and a pink true geranium like 'Ballerina'.
- Rose-pink watsonia with pink rockrose and artemisia.
- *Verbena bonariensis* with yellow roses and French lavender.

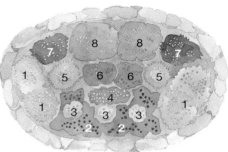

Perennials provide color from spring to fall in this 6-foot-wide oval raised bed. Design: Bud Stuckey.

1. Catmint *(Nepeta faassenii)* **2.** *Verbena canadensis* 'Homestead Purple' **3.** *Diascia vigilis* **4.** Santa Barbara daisy *(Erigeron karvinskianus)* **5.** Spanish lavender *(Lavandula stoechas)* **6.** *Salvia greggii* (pink) **7.** Border penstemon *(P. gloxinioides* 'Midnight') **8.** Mexican bush sage *(Salvia leucantha)*

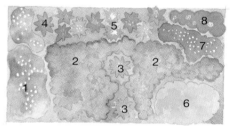

Tulips and lettuce make a surprising combination in this spring border. Design: Robert Clark, Oakland.

1. 'White Flower Carpet' rose **2.** 'Red Oak Leaf' lettuce **3.** 'Mount Tacoma' tulip **4.** 'Twinkle' tulip **5.** 'Maureen' tulip **6.** Lime thyme **7.** Pansy **8.** *Chrysanthemum paludosum*

Nine steps to building a border

1. Make a plan. Determine the size of your bed or border, then sketch out a plan on paper. Mix together annuals, bulbs, perennials, and shrubs, arranging them according to height (low edgers in front, tall plants in the rear). Choose spiky-leafed plants for accents amid horizontal drifts and rounded clumps of annuals and perennials. Avoid a hodgepodge look by planting at least three of each plant.

For a succession of blossoms, choose spring-, summer-, and fall-blooming plants.

2. Design a watering system. Drip irrigation is the most efficient way to water. And since there's no spray to dampen foliage, plants are less prone to disease and taller perennials

aren't knocked over. You can seek professional help to design and install a system or do it yourself.

Install the valve and connect the main water line first, then lay the final drip tubing and install emitters after plants are in the ground.

3. Prepare the soil. For a successful border, first test the soil's drainage: Dig a 12-inch-deep hole and fill it with water. If the water doesn't drain away in 12 to 24 hours, install a tile drain, plant in a raised bed, or choose a new site.

Using a shovel or rotary tiller, turn the soil to a depth of about 12 inches. Mix in 2 to 4 inches of organic matter such as garden compost or well-composted manure.

Two lush borders edge a mossy path in this spring-summer garden. Plant the perennials, roses, and flowering maple in fall, the feverfew and dahlias in spring.
Design: Robert Clark.

1. *Oxalis rubra* 2. *Verbena tapien* 'Pink'
3. Feverfew 4. 'Newport' rose 5. *Liriope muscari* 'Silvery Midget' 6. 'First Light' rose
7. White-flowering maple (*Abutilon hybridum*)
8. New Zealand flax 9. Magic Fountains blue delphinium (*D. elatum*) 10. 'Park Princess' cactus dahlia 11. *Phygelius capensis* 'Moonraker' 12. *Penstemon* 'Midnight'
13. 'Bonica' rose 14. 'Lucky Number' dahlia 15. *Penstemon* 'Elizabeth Cozzens'
16. 'Eden' climbing rose 17. Pink-flowering maple 18. 'Mary Rose' standard rose
19. 'Dream Weaver' climbing rose
20. 'Lavender Beauty' yarrow 21. Scotch moss (*Sagina subulata*) 22. Lobelia
23. *Acorus gramineus* 24. 'Shirley' dahlia

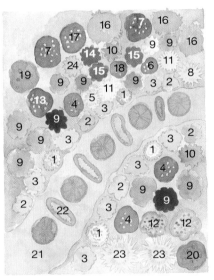

4. Shop for plants. Take your plan to the nursery. Choose small plants (sixpack-size annuals, sixpack or 4-inch perennials, and 1-gallon shrubs); they're more cost effective, and they get established faster than larger plants.

5. Arrange perennials and shrubs. Set the pots of perennials and shrubs out on the prepared soil. Make minor adjustments and rearrange plants if some colors or textures don't work well together.

6. Set plants in the ground. Remove plants from the nursery containers. Loosen their root balls with your fingers or, if the roots are circling, make several scores down the sides of each root ball with a knife. Dig holes and place the plants in the ground, setting the tops of the root balls even with the top of the soil. Fill in the holes; firm the soil.

7. Plant annuals and bulbs. Interplant bulbs among the perennials and shrubs. Overplant with cool-season annuals, so when spring comes, the bulb flowers pop up through them.

8. Mulch the soil. Cover soil with a 2-inch layer of mulch to conserve moisture and help control weeds.

9. Water regularly. To get plants established, water two to four times a week to keep the small root balls moist but not soggy. When winter rains arrive, water only if there are extended dry spells between rains. Once plants are established the following spring, water often enough to keep the soil moist.

Gardening Color Calendar

Summer Phlox

Delphinium

Sedum 'Autumn Joy'

Sunflower

Bloom Colors	Common Name	Botanical Name	Apr.	May	June	July	Aug.	Sept.	Oct.
▢■	Peony—single-flowered	*Paeonia*	█	█					
■	Firetail	*Polygonum amplexicaule*	█	█			█	█	
▨	Fleece flower 'Superbum'	*Polygonum bistorta*		█	█			█	
▨■	Siberian iris	*Iris sibirica*		█					
▢■	Peach-leaf bellflower	*Campanula persicifolia*		█	█				
▢▨■	Peony—mid- and late-season	*Paeonia*		█	█				
▨	Checkerbloom	*Sidalcea*			█	█			
▨■	Yarrow	*Achillea millefolium*		█	█				
▢	Yarrow 'Moonshine'	*Achillea*				█	█	█	█
▢	Lady's-mantle	*Alchemilla mollis*			█				
■	Campanula	*C. glomerata*			█				
▢▨	Monkshood	*Aconitum*			█	█			
▨	Helenium	*H. kanaria*				█			
■	Helenium 'Bronzed Beauty'	*H. magnificum*				█			
▢▨■	Balloon flower	*Platycodon*				█	█		
▢	Gooseneck flower	*Lysimachia clethroides*				█			
▢	Penstemon 'Husker Red'	*P. digitalis*				█	█		
▨	Veronica 'Sweet Sue'	*V. spicata*				█	█	█	
▢■	Summer phlox	*P. paniculata*				█	█	█	█
▢■▨■	Summer phlox—Bartels Stek series	*P. paniculata*				█	█	█	█
■	Crocosmia 'Lucifer'	*C. masonorum*				█			
▨	Butterfly weed	*Asclepias incarnata*				█	█		
▨	Lysimachia	*L. vulgaris*				█	█		
▨	Obedient plant 'Summer Spires'	*Physostegia virginiana*				█	█		
■	Oregano 'Hopley's Purple'	*Origanum*				█	█		
▨	Turtlehead	*Chelone obliqua*				█	█		
▨	Veronica 'Blaureisen'	*V. longifolia*				█	█		
■	Veronica 'Lila Karina'	*V. longifolia*				█			
▢■▨■	Delphinium—Barba series	*D. elatum*				█	█	█	█
■	Delphinium 'Volkenfrieden'	*D. belladonna*				█	█	█	█
▨	Solidaster 'Tara'	*Solidago*				█	█	█	
▨	Solidaster 'Yellow Submarine'	*Solidago*				█	█	█	
▨	Gentian	*Gentiana makinoi*					█		
▨■	Joe Pye weed	*Eupatorium maculatum*					█		
▨■	Sedum 'Autumn Joy'	*S. spectabile*					█		
▨	Sunflower	*Helianthus*					█	█	
▨	Monkshood	*Aconitum arendsii*					█	█	
▢▨■	Aster—Master series	*A. ericoides*					█	█	█
▢	Aster 'Monte Cassino'	*A. ericoides*						█	█

Larkspur produce 4- to 5-foot spikes of color. Give them partial shade inland.

Old-Fashioned Annuals

Most people like old-fashioned annuals. Their lavish blooms and graceful forms bestow even the most urban landscapes with romantic country charm. As a bonus, these old-time favorites are excellent in fresh-flower bouquets, and a few of them dry beautifully.

Although you can buy a few types of old-fashioned annuals as seedlings in nurseries every spring, far more varieties are available by seed. In fact, some of these annuals—love-in-a-mist

Shirley poppies and corn cockle are good full-sun companions.

and corn cockle, for example—are usually available only by seed. Others, including larkspur and Shirley poppies, grow taller and are more vigorous when sown in place than when purchased and transplanted. With seed, you can sow at prime time, resulting in plentiful blooms over an extended period. And finally, seeds are more economical than plants: A packet of seeds costs a fraction of what you would pay for a sixpack of the same plant.

Best bets for old-fashioned charm

Corn cockle *(Agrostemma githago)*. 'Milas' is outstanding, with satiny 3-inch plum-colored flowers veined with deep purple and fading to white in the center; excellent cut. Wispy plants reach 2 to 3 feet tall. Sow in fall in warmest climates only; spring everywhere else. Reseeds. Full sun.

Godetia *(Clarkia amoena, Godetia grandiflora)*. Many varieties, with plants ranging from 4 or 5 inches to 3 feet. In spring, clustered buds open to cup-shaped 2-inch flowers;

they may be single or double, or frilly. Flowers are white, lavender, and crimson—usually with contrasting streaks. Cut tall varieties. Sow in fall if winters are mild; spring in cold climates. Sun.

Larkspur *(Consolida ambigua)*. Upright, branching stems of strains such as Giant Imperial give height (4 to 5 feet) to borders. Spring-bloom spikes are dramatic in white, blue, purple, pink, salmon, and carmine. For best results, plant fresh seed. Thin for biggest flowers. Sow in fall. Sun; partial shade inland.

Love-in-a-mist *(Nigella damascena)*. Attractive both fresh and dried, lacy 'Persian Jewels' has 1½-inch double flowers in blue, white, and rose. Eighteen-inch-tall plants come into bloom quickly, followed by papery seed capsules valued for dried arrangements. *N. hispanica* has 2½-inch deep blue single flowers with bright orange anthers and dark seed capsules. Sow in fall. Sun or part shade.

Shirley poppy (Flanders field poppy, *Papaver rhoeas*). Slender stems (2 to 5 feet tall) with elegant crepe paper-like flowers (2 inches or more across) and divided silver green leaves. Flanders field poppy usually refers to the scarlet ancestor of Shirley poppies, which are commonly white, red, pink, orange, and bicolors. 'Mother of Pearl' are delicate pastels. Sow spring through summer for continuous bloom. Full sun. Reseeds.

Stock *(Matthiola incana)*. Spikes of fragrant single or double 1-inch flowers in cream, pink, lavender, purple, red, or white. Column types are ideal for cutting, with a single but impressive 2- to 3-foot-tall flower spike. Giant Imperial has multiple spikes on branching plants to 2½ feet. Sow in fall. Full sun.

Sweet peas *(Lathyrus odoratus)*. Among the dozens of choices is the exceptionally fragrant climber 'Painted Lady' (carmine pink and white). Other fragrant climbing varieties are 'Antique Fantasy' (mixed), 'Lady Fairbairn' (lavender rose), and 'Royal Wedding' (white). 'Snoopea' (mixed) is a sweet-smelling bushy type to 30 inches. In warm areas, plant in September for winter bloom. In Zones 7–9 and 12–24, plant between October and January. Sun.

Fighting Fire

Wildfires have devastated many parts of the West. By late summer and fall, the highly flammable vegetation that cloaks wilderness areas has been stressed by drought, low humidity, or drying winds. It can ignite and quickly build into a raging inferno.

Ironically, the most wildfire-prone properties have some of the characteristics that define the "good life" in the West. They tend to be on hillsides, surrounded by thick stands of trees and brushy open spaces, or packed close together in canyons. Firefighters have difficulty reaching properties up narrow, curvy, tree-lined (even overgrown) roads or dead-end side streets with little bridges that can't support fire engines.

One of the most important things you can do to prevent your house from going up in smoke is to landscape properly. Fire officials claim that you can halve the odds of your home being destroyed if you clear the brush within 30 to 400 feet of the house—the exact distance is determined by slope, wind, neighborhood density, and house architecture and materials.

For years, the common wisdom was to landscape with fire-retardant plants. Fire specialists, horticultural consultants, and landscape architects now say that this practice is misleading, even dangerous. The Oakland Hills, California, fire of 1991 showed that the use of fire-retardant plantings gave people a false sense of security, especially when those plants were affected by drought or poorly maintained, or adjacent to a house with a wooden roof.

In a high-intensity fire, everything burns. But some gardens are safer than others. Be sure to avoid highly flammable plants (see page 173) that contain high levels of oil or resin, have foliage with low moisture content, or can accumulate large amounts of dead foliage.

Above a scrubby canyon, this Santa Barbara garden has been landscaped for fire safety (below). The lawn is a buffer between the house and fire that might encroach up the canyon. Fire-resistant jade plants and low-fuel-volume perennials grow around its perimeter.

Before: A mass of oaks and scrub blankets the steep slope below a Berkeley Hills home.

After: Clearing out the brush and thinning the oaks have made the slope much more fire safe.

The West's worst fires

Every year, hundreds of wildfires burn in the West. California, with its hot, dry winds and low humidity, is especially vulnerable to wildfires; of the 23 major fires in the West in recent times, almost half ravaged the Golden State. Between 1991 and 1995 alone, almost a million acres of California burned. And all across the West, 1996 was one of the worst fire years. Below are some factors that occur or combine to create a disastrous fire season.

Rainfall. Heavy rains encourage abundant grass growth, which increases the hazard of grass fires later in the summer. Low rainfall increases the amount of dead foliage (known as dead fuel).

Freeze. In open spaces, killing freezes turn live-fuel plants into crackling-dry fuel.

Growth. Some fast-growing communities have ignored fire threats in the rush for development, creating an excess of incendiary flora and structures. More thoughtfully designed, fire-safe subdivisions reduce fire hazards by providing buffers between wild land and houses.

Wind. Foehns, sundowners, monos, Santa Anas—these hot, dry winds start in the interior and blow out to the coast. Heavy onshore winds, though cooler and moister, can fan small fires in coastal sage and chaparral, creating infernos.

Fuel loading. Coastal sage becomes tinder 7 to 10 years after a burn (chaparral 15 to 20 years after a burn). Unless this crackling-dry growth is trimmed or burned, it builds up, creating conditions that favor more damaging fires. At any given time, it is not unusual for certain municipalities to carry a fuel load greater than typical loads in Southern California.

Lightning. Warm air, cooling as it rises into the western mountain ranges, creates thunderstorms. As lightning strikes at higher elevations, it sparks fires.

Cedrus

Highly flammable plants

Abies
Fir
Acacia
Adenostoma fasciculatum
Chamise
Arctostaphylos
Manzanita
Artemisia californica
California sagebrush
Cedrus
Cedar
Cortaderia selloana
Pampas grass
Cupressus
Cypress

Cytisus scoparius
Scotch broom
Eriogonum fasciculatum
California buckwheat
Eucalyptus camaldulensis,
E. globulus, E. rudis,
E. viminalis
Red gum, blue gum, flooded gum, manna gum
Heteromeles arbutifolia
Toyon
Juniperus
Juniper
Palms
Picea
Spruce

Pinus
Pine
Pseudotsuga menziesii
Douglas fir
Rhus laurina
Laurel sumac
Rosmarinus officinalis
Rosemary
Taxus
Yew
Thuja
Arborvitae
Umbellularia californica
California laurel

A fire-retardant house and garden

A. Hydrant. Near the street, you can install a standpipe for fire-fighters' use; check size with fire department. Make sure it's accessible. If possible, use a gravity feed from pool.

B. Siding. Nonflammable material such as stucco is preferred. Avoid shingles or other wooden siding.

C. Eaves and vents. Eliminate eaves or enclose them with stucco or other nonflammable material. Place vents at outer edge of soffit and cover them with ¼-inch wire mesh. If feasible, when fire approaches, block the vents with precut plywood panels.

D. Roof. Use noncombustible materials.

E. Glass. Thermal-pane and safety glass are the most resistant to heat-caused damage. If fire threatens, cover the glass outside with shutters, fire curtains, or plywood panels.

F. Pump. Have a well-maintained pump (gas, diesel, or propane) of at least 100-gpm capacity, with standard 1½-inch threaded standpipe. Keep a plastic or cotton-jacket fire hose (long enough to reach far side of house) and nozzle at hand.

G. Walls, fences, and railings. Use non-flammable masonry, wrought iron, or chain-link—particularly adjoining the house; fences of flammable materials can act like fuses. Make wooden arbors or trellises of 4-by-4 or larger lumber.

H. Deck. Nonflammable brick, tile, or concrete decking is safest. If you use wood, recommended 1-hour fire ratings require overscaled decking—at least 1½-inch-thick tongue-and-groove boards over a solid substructure.

I. Substructure. Decks in wild-land areas should either be enclosed with a nonflammable solid skirt—concrete block, gypsum board, stucco, or other exterior sheathing—or built with oversize timbers (at least 6-by-6 posts and beams).

J. Pool, hot tub. Can serve as a ready reservoir for you and the fire department (a typical hot tub holds about 500 gallons—as much as a tank truck). If possible, make the water source drainable to an accessible hydrant or pumphouse.

K. Two hundred-foot reduced fuel zone. Plant low-growing, deep-rooted, drought-tolerant ground covers. Prune regularly to remove woody undergrowth and encourage new growth.

L. Access. Keep fire lanes (preferably on both sides of the house) clear enough for fire fighters to bring in trucks and other equipment.

Before: A wall of pittosporums surrounds a neighbor's garage; redwood, magnolia, and camellia in the foreground create a fire ladder.

After: To open up the garden, all but one pittosporum has been cut down. Pruning has separated the vegetation and broken up the fire ladder.

Landscaping for fire

Eliminate fire "ladders"—plants of different heights that form a continuous fuel supply from the ground up into the tree canopy.

Create a transition zone, if your lot size allows it, 30 to 50 feet from the house. Remove most major plants, but leave enough shrubs to stabilize a slope. Hydroseed (apply a combination of mulch and seed through a high-pressure hose) with native grasses and wildflowers or plant low-volume herbaceous perennials like gazania, poppy, and common yarrow.

Arrange plants into islands, 50 to 300 feet from the house. The distance between shrubs should be three to five times their height.

Cut out weak or diseased trees in heavily wooded areas; thin healthy ones, if needed.

Get rid of stumps, except when slope stability is a concern. Paint stumps with 1 part glyphosate to 3 parts water.

Regularly clean up leaves and other plant litter and remove brush that grows with winter rains.

Clean off all vegetation and debris from the roof and gutters several times during the year.

Keep plants well irrigated and well maintained, especially those within 30 feet of the house (if water supplies permit). Keep grasses watered and green year-round, or let them dry out and cut them back to 4 inches.

Prune vegetation next to the house to under 1½ feet high. In early spring, prune or mow down low ground covers, such as ceanothus and *Coprosma kirkii*. Fertilize and water afterward.

Periodically cut back chaparral plants hard.

Thin crowns of clustered trees, trim limbs up off the ground to 20 feet or more, and cut back any branches to 15 or 20 feet from the house. Prune out all dead branches; remove all dead plants.

Clear out overhanging tree branches along the driveway, and prune back bushy shrubs (to allow fire trucks easy access).

Ground Covers

In areas with hot, dry summers and mild winters, plant ground covers in fall; the winter rains will help get the plants off to a good start. Where winters are cold, plant in spring; this will give the ground cover an entire season to become established before it must face the rigors of winter.

Though ground covers are tough, they'll grow and spread more quickly if you prepare the planting area carefully. Weed, amend the soil, and broadcast a complete fertilizer over the area. (Shrubby plants from gallon containers are often planted in native soil, without amendments.) Install landscape fabric, if desired, and plant.

After planting, water the plants thoroughly; water again every few days. Mulch between plants to conserve moisture.

Ground cover care

Shrubby ground covers are by nature low growing and spreading, but from time to time they send out upright stems that spoil the evenness of a planting. Whenever you see such a stem, cut it back to its point of origin.

Certain ground covers become so thick that only a close trim will restore their attractiveness. Some of these—ivy *(Hedera),* for example—accumulate thatch, a tangled mass of stems that gradually raises the height of the foliage cover; harbor slugs, snails, and rodents; and may even be flammable. Others, such as winter creeper *(Euonymus fortunei)* and creeping St. Johnswort *(Hypericum calycinum),* become rangy and uneven. If the planting is small, trim it with hedge shears; otherwise, mow the plants with a power mower.

Many ground covers need to be restrained. Either prune the plants or use a shovel or spade to slice the growth back to the desired edge.

A ground cover is not a type of plant, but one that is used in a certain way. Perennial gazania (above) flowers throughout the year. The low-growing herb chamomile (right) can replace a lawn. It won't tolerate much foot traffic but is deliciously fragrant. Many succulent plants, such as trailing ice plant (Lampranthus) *(below), form a dense, drought-tolerant ground cover.*

Liriope spicata, *or creeping lily turf, is slow-growing, but spreads widely to form an interesting lawn replacement that will smother out most weeds. The path laid between these grassy banks is simple cobblestones.*

Diamonds are for ground covers

Fall is prime time to plant evergreen ground covers. And you can't go wrong if you set out plants in the diamond pattern shown here. This design works for any size or shape of bed, giving it a neat, geometrical look. Plants will spread and fill in the gaps in a year or less.

To find the best spacing between specific plants, check the nursery tag. For example, 1 foot is the recommended distance for many ground covers, including English ivy and Japanese spurge (pictured). For even spacing, use a ruler or marked stick to measure 12 inches diagonally between plants.

GROUND COVERS WHERE YOU NEED THEM

For shade. Under trees or high decks, in narrow sideyards, or in other places where sunlight barely penetrates, proven performers include ajuga, sweet woodruff, redwood sorrel, fragrant *Sarcococca,* and baby's tears.

For sun. An expanse of heat-tolerant ground cover can add vibrancy to a sun-washed landscape. Drought-tolerant choices include Carmel creeper, Mexican daisy, sunrose, 'Flower Carpet' rose, lantana, African daisy, stonecrop, and ice plant (*Lampranthus*).

For fire protection. A 200-foot greenbelt or "reduced fuel zone" is recommended around the perimeter of properties in wildfire-prone areas. Plants that are suitable for this area include carpet bugle, snow-in-summer, bearberry cotoneaster, gazania, sedum, and star jasmine.

For traffic. No ground cover will tolerate football games as well as does turf-grass, but some can withstand light pummeling, especially if interspersed with stepping-stones. Consider pussy toes (*Antennaria dioica*), chamomile, thyme, blue star creeper, and baby's tears.

For slopes. Plants with dense, strong roots provide the most efficient, low-cost erosion control for slopes. Try planting Carmel creeper, bearberry cotoneaster, cape honeysuckle, periwinkle, or rosemary.

For fragrance. Some plants emit their fragrance only when stepped on; thyme and chamomile are among them. Other ground covers, such as roses, jasmine, rosemary, and *Sarcococca,* release fragrance continually from their flowers or foliage.

Sourwood fires up this Seattle garden in October. It's suitable for even small gardens in the Pacific Northwest.

October

Pacific Northwest Checklist

PLANTING

☑ Nurseries and garden shops will bulge with BULBS this month. Shop early for the best selection, choosing bulbs that are plump and firm. Get them into the ground as soon as possible so they won't wither or freeze.

☑ PERENNIALS. Throughout the Northwest, now (and into mid-November in Zones 4–7) is prime time to plant perennials. Fall-planted stock has the winter to establish good root systems, then take off vigorously when warm weather arrives in spring. If October is hot and dry, water newly set-out plants frequently.

☑ LANDSCAPE PLANTS. Shop for trees and shrubs in autumn colors now. Plant immediately.

MAINTENANCE

☑ CARE FOR LAWNS. After mowing the lawn, rough up bare spots, then scatter a generous amount of grass seed, cover with a fine layer of soil, water well, and keep the seed bed moist until fall rains begin. You'll have healthy new grass next spring.

☑ GROOM ROSES. Remove faded blooms. As you shape plants, cut flowers to take indoors. Allow a few flowers to form hips. This tells the plant that it's time to head into dormancy.

☑ ANNUALS. Zones 4–7: Continue to deadhead, and fertilize one last time early in the month. Zones 1–3: When frost hits, pull plants, shake soil off their roots, and toss them onto the compost pile.

☑ FUSS WITH FUCHSIAS. Continue to snap off faded blooms and keep up with your feeding program until 2 weeks before the first frost is expected in your area.

☑ WATER. Until rains begin, water established plants deeply. Drought-stressed plants are far more likely to be damaged in a hard freeze.

☑ MAKE COMPOST. As you harvest, mow, rake, and prune, pile everything but the diseased stuff onto the compost pile. Turn the pile and keep it moist. By next spring compost should be ready to use.

PEST CONTROL

☑ BATTLE SLUGS. Whatever method you use to control slugs, consistency pays off. Eventually, you'll see a reduction in numbers and the remaining slugs will be smaller.

☑ SET OUT MOUSETRAPS. As the weather gets colder, mice and rats try to sneak indoors, especially into places where you store produce—potatoes and winter squash are favorites. Set out traps and check them daily from now through the winter.

Northern California Checklist

PLANTING

☑ **NATURALIZE BULBS. Zones 14–17:** To create an informal mass of flowers that looks as if it's spreading across the landscape, toss handfuls of a single kind of bulb over the planting area, varying the density. Repeat with a second or third kind, if desired. Plant bulbs where they fall. Choose bulbs that naturalize easily in your climate, soil, and sun exposure; try species daffodils, grape hyacinths *(Muscari)*, leucojum, scilla, or species tulips.

☑ **OVERPLANT BULB BEDS. Zones 7–9, 14–17:** Cool-season annuals planted over bulbs will give a colorful show during the winter before the bulbs pop up. Choose colors that complement the bulbs, such as blue violas with white or yellow daffodils, salmon *Primula obconica* with purple tulips, or purple and white *P. malacoides* with pink tulips.

☑ **PLANT ANNUALS. Zones 7–9, 14–17:** For bloom from winter through spring, plant cool-season annuals now so they get established and start blooming before the weather turns cold. From containers, choose calendula, Iceland poppies, pansies, primroses, snapdragons, stock, and violas. In Zones 15–17, you can also plant calceolaria, cineraria, nemesia, and *Schizanthus pinnatus*. From seed, try baby blue eyes, forget-me-nots, sweet alyssum, sweet peas, and spring wildflowers.

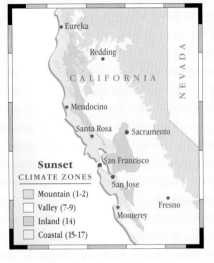

Sunset
CLIMATE ZONES
- Mountain (1-2)
- Valley (7-9)
- Inland (14)
- Coastal (15-17)

☑ **PLANT LANDSCAPE PLANTS. Zones 7–9, 14–17:** This is one of the best months for setting out any kind of plant that's not frost-tender. Ground covers, shrubs, and trees all benefit from fall planting; they get off to a fast start in still-warm soil and then have the long, cool months ahead to develop a healthy root system. Before buying plants, learn their ultimate height and spread. Allow plenty of room to grow, so you won't have to prune to keep them in bounds.

☑ **ORDER GRAPES, FRUIT TREES, BERRIES.** If you plan to purchase special varieties of fruits by mail, get your orders in soon so you're sure to get the type you want, and so they'll arrive in time for dormant-season planting. For a taste treat, try white-flesh 'Arctic Supreme' peach or 'Dapple Dandy' plum.

☑ **PLANT A SALAD POT. Zones 7–9, 14–17:** Start with a large pot (at least 18 inches in diameter and about a foot or so deep) filled with potting mix. Look for seedlings of green- or red-leaf, butter, or romaine lettuce. Plant two or three heads of lettuce along with arugula, curly endive, mache, and mustard. Intersperse with chives and Johnny-jump-ups or other small-flowered violas (which are edible). Or start with seeds of a mesclun salad mix and sow very thinly over the top of the soil. When seedlings need thinning, harvest and use in salad. Harvest additional greens when they're 3 to 5 inches long. Replant when the pot's been completely harvested.

☑ **SET OUT GARLIC. Zones 7–9, 14–17:** Plant in rich, well-drained soil. Break bulbs apart into individual cloves and plant the scar ends down. Cover regular garlic with 1 to 2 inches of soil, elephant garlic (not a true garlic, but a bulbing leek with mild garlic flavor) with 4 to 6 inches of soil. Press the soil down firmly and water. Irrigate if the weather is dry.

MAINTENANCE

☑ **DO A THOROUGH CLEANUP.** To reduce the number of sites that harbor insects and diseases during winter, pull weeds and spent annuals and vegetables. Clean up all fruit and leaves. Compost only pest-free plant debris. Add other material to your city's compost collection, if it has one.

☑ **WATER.** Fall weather is often very dry and warm, so continue to water if winter rains don't come this month or appear infrequently. Check soil moisture before watering by digging down with a trowel.

Southern California Checklist

PLANTING

☑ **PLANT COOL-SEASON ANNUALS.** Coastal, inland, and low-desert gardeners (Zones 22–24, 18–21, and 13, respectively) can set out transplants of calendula, Iceland poppy, lobelia, nemesia, ornamental kale, pansy, primrose, snapdragon, stock, viola, and other annuals.

☑ **CONTINUE PLANTING COOL-SEASON CROPS.** In frost-free areas, you can still put in arugula, beets, broccoli, Brussels sprouts, cabbage, carrots, cauliflower, chard, chives, collards, endive, kale, leaf lettuces, mustard, parsley, peas, radishes, shallots, spinach, turnips, and white potatoes.

☑ **PLANT RANUNCULUS.** Ranunculus have a longer bloom period than most spring bulbs and make great cut flowers, but are susceptible to rot. Water them well after planting, then withhold water until they poke through the ground. (Plant tubers, prong side down, about 6 inches apart.)

☑ **PLANT PERENNIALS.** Fall is the best time to plant perennials. Visible growth will be slow, but the roots will take hold and the plants will zoom into action come spring.

☑ **SOW ANNUALS.** Some cool-season annuals grow faster and perform better when directly seeded rather than transplanted. Starting from seed also gives you more choices. Try corn cockle, flax, forget-me-not, godetia, larkspur, lavatera, linaria, linum, nemesia, Shirley poppy, and sweet pea. Sow in raked-smooth, weed-free soil.

CALIFORNIA
NEVADA
Bishop
San Luis Obispo
Bakersfield
Tehachapi
Santa Barbara
Lancaster
Los Angeles
Palm Springs
Sunset
CLIMATE ZONES
San Diego
1-3　7-9　11　13　14-24
MEXICO

☑ **OVERSEED BERMUDA.** For an emerald-green lawn by December, overseed Bermuda grass with annual winter ryegrass now.

☑ **SHOP FOR NATIVES.** California natives such as ceanothus and Mediterranean plants such as rosemary are excellent for drought-tolerant, low-maintenance, or wildlife-habitat gardens, and fall is the best time to plant them. (They need winter rain and cool temperatures to put down deep roots before summer.)

MAINTENANCE

☑ **PREPARE FOR SANTA ANA WINDS.** Thin top-heavy trees like jacaranda to prevent branch breakage. Give trees, shrubs, and ground covers a deep soaking ahead of time when winds are predicted. Once winds come, mist frequently—especially vulnerable container plants and hanging baskets.

☑ **PROTECT AGAINST BRUSHFIRES.** Dead vegetation adds fuel to flames. In fire-prone areas, before the onset of Santa Ana winds, cut and remove all dead branches and leaves from trees and shrubs, especially those that grow near the house. Clear leaves from gutters and remove woody vegetation growing against structures.

☑ **CARE FOR LAWNS.** Rake up thatch that has built up in your lawn. Fertilize cool-season lawns, such as tall fescue, with a high-nitrogen fertilizer.

☑ **DIVIDE PERENNIALS.** To restrain fast-growing perennials, such as Shasta daisies, or to rejuvenate stagnating ones, such as daylilies, circle plants with a shovel or spade and pop them out of the ground. Wash or shake off excess soil and divide plants with a knife or spade. Partially cut back foliage on divisions; replant immediately.

PEST CONTROL

☑ **MANAGE INSECT PESTS.** Aphids and whiteflies multiply when the temperature drops. Dislodge them from plants with blasts of water from a hose or use insecticidal soap.

☑ **PROTECT CABBAGE CROPS.** Those little white butterflies flitting near your broccoli and cabbage lay eggs that turn into leaf-chomping caterpillars. Protect your crops with row covers to keep butterflies away. Or dust with *Bacillus thuringiensis* to kill young larvae.

Mountain Checklist

PLANTING AND HARVEST

☑ **HARVEST TOMATOES. When** frost threatens, protect tomato plants with row covers, or harvest all fruits and bring them indoors to ripen. Compost dark green fruits, but save those with traces of yellow or red; at room temperature they'll eventually ripen.

☑ **PLANT BULBS.** Set out bulbs of daffodils, crocus, hyacinths, *Iris reticulata,* scilla, and tulips. To protect them from soil temperature fluctuation, plant daffodils and tulips 10 to 12 inches deep, smaller bulbs 5 inches deep.

☑ **PLANT PERMANENT PLANTS.** Set out ground covers, trees, shrubs, and perennials. Make sure to water them well after planting.

☑ **SOW WILDFLOWERS.** Early in the month, broadcast seeds over rock gardens, hillsides, and fields. Lightly rake, and cover seeds with ¼-inch layer of organic matter. If you live in an area that normally gets a light snow cover, wait until spring to sow seeds.

☑ **STORE PRODUCE.** Beets, carrots, turnips, and potatoes keep best at 35° to 45°F in barely damp sand. Onions and shallots need cool, dry storage in slotted crates or mesh bags. Leave a 2-inch stem on winter squash and pumpkins; store at 50° to 60°F. Store apples and pears indoors in separate containers at around 40°F. Carrots, horseradish, kale, parsnips, and turnips can tolerate heavy frost; mulched, they can stay in the ground all winter.

Sunset
CLIMATE ZONES
☐ 1-3   ☐ 10-11

MAINTENANCE

☑ **CUT BACK PERENNIALS.** After the first hard freeze, cut back aster, campanula, daylily, phlox, and veronica to about 2 inches above the ground.

☑ **MULCH FOR WINTER.** Spread 2 to 3 inches of compost, straw, or other organic matter over bulbs, perennial flowers and vegetables, permanent plants, and strawberry beds.

☑ **PREPARE PLANTING BEDS.** Spade planting beds now, working in generous amounts of organic matter. Leave soil rough so it absorbs winter moisture; the freezing-thawing cycle will break apart clods.

☑ **PROTECT YOUNG TREES. Bright** winter sunlight can burn the south-facing side of tender young trunks and cause them to split. Protect them with a coat of white latex paint, tree wrap, or burlap.

☑ **WATER.** After leaves have fallen, water deciduous trees deeply when the temperature is above freezing.

PEST CONTROL

☑ **BARK BEETLES.** Before spring, burn all firewood cut from pines killed by bark beetles. Otherwise, newly hatched beetles may fly into your live pine trees when weather warms.

Southwest Checklist

PLANTING

☑ **OVERSEED LAWNS.** Zones 11–13: Mow Bermuda grass closely (at about ½ inch), overseed with perennial ryegrass, and water deeply.

☑ **PLANT COOL-SEASON ANNUALS.** Zones 10–11: Plant seedlings of common aubrieta, candytuft, English daisy, forget-me-not, primrose, snapdragon, and stock. Zones 12–13: Try seedlings of calendula, dianthus, English daisy, Iceland poppy, lobelia, nemesia, ornamental cabbage and kale, pansy, primrose, schizanthus, snapdragon, stock, and viola.

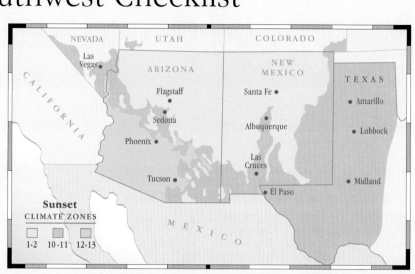

☑ **PLANT COOL-SEASON CROPS.** Zones 12–13: Now is the time to plant beets, cabbage and its close relations (bok choy, broccoli, Brussels sprouts, cauliflower, kale, kohlrabi), carrots, chard, endive, garlic, lettuce, onions, parsley, peas, radishes, and turnips. Many of these are sold as nursery seedlings; sow the root crops yourself.

☑ **PLANT NATIVES.** This is the best month of the year to start all kinds of native plants. Before planting container-grown trees and shrubs, loosen the soil to at least the depth of the root ball and five times as wide.

☑ **PLANT SHRUBS, TREES.** Set out all except frost-tender kinds this month. In windy areas, support young trees with stakes.

☑ **GROUND COVERS.** Zones 10–11: There's still time to plant low-growing junipers. Zones 12–13: Plant *Acacia redolens,* Baja and Mexican evening primroses (plant Mexican evening primrose in a confined area or it will invade the garden), *Dalea greggii,* dwarf rosemary, gazania, lippia, low-growing junipers, snow-in-summer, and verbena.

☑ **PLANT PERENNIALS.** Plant perennials right away for spring bloom. Water them well until they become established.

☑ **PLANT STRAWBERRIES.** Plant any time after mid-month for a crop next spring. 'Sequoia' and 'Tioga' are two varieties that do well in Zones 12–13. In Zones 10–11, try 'Fort Laramie' and 'Ogallala'.

☑ **BULBS.** Zones 1–2, 10–11: Plant all the spring-blooming kinds outside now, and tender bulbs (such as paper whites) indoors for forced winter bloom. Zones 12–13: Plant amaryllis, anemone, calla, crocus, daffodil, grape hyacinth, harlequin flower, hyacinth, iris, oxalis, ranunculus, tulip, and watsonia. (Refrigerate crocus, hyacinths, and tulips for at least 6 weeks before planting.)

MAINTENANCE

☑ **DIVIDE PERENNIALS.** Zones 10–13: Dig and divide perennials such as daylily and Shasta daisy to reinvigorate plants and increase the size and number of blooms.

☑ **FEED ESTABLISHED LAWNS.** Zones 12–13: Apply 1 pound actual nitrogen per 1,000 square feet of lawn.

☑ **TEND ROSES.** Feed and water roses deeply to encourage another round of bloom.

☑ **PLANTING BEDS.** Test your soil now if you suspect it is deficient in nutrients or that the pH may require adjustment.

Bulb Basics

Bulb sizes of 'King Alfred'-type daffodils are graded DN #3 (one flower per bulb), DN #2 (one or two flowers), DN #1 (two or three flowers), and Jumbo (three or four flowers).

Like eggs, bulbs are graded by size. Generally, the bigger the circumference of the bulb, the more flowers you get. The most common sizes of narcissus (daffodils) range from DN #1 down to DN #3. The largest 'King Alfred' types are called jumbos. Narcissus smaller than DN #1 may be labeled in centimeters (typically 14 centimeters and smaller).

Dutch irises and lilies are graded in centimeters. Dutch irises range from 6 to 12 centimeters or larger; 8 to 9 centimeters is typical. Lilies run from 12 to 20 centimeters.

Sizes vary according to variety, too. For instance, large-cupped and trumpet daffodils produce larger bulbs than species and miniatures; blue Dutch iris bulbs are larger than the purple and yellow kinds.

When you're planting a large quantity for the long haul, choosing midsize bulbs makes economic sense. But beware of mail promotions that offer a large quantity of bulbs for just a few dollars: You may end up with undersize bulbs that produce few flowers.

Look for a note in catalogs that indicates the size and quality of bulbs; it may simply say top-size bulbs. When shopping locally, buy early in the season and choose firm bulbs that aren't sprouting. Generally, they should still have their outer skins intact (although sometimes pieces fall off in the box—common with freesias).

Soil preparation

Good soil drainage is the key to long bulb life. If you can't dig in it, you can't expect a bulb to live in it. Where soil is poorly drained, plant on a slope or in raised beds.

Before planting, add organic amendments if your soil is clayey, sandy, rocky, or low in nutrients. Your best bets are leaf mold, redwood soil conditioner, compost, or similar products; unless it's well aged, manure can burn bulbs. If the soil is low in organic matter, spread about 3 inches over the planting area and dig it in; use only an inch or so if the soil is already fairly loose and loamy. In acid soil in the Pacific Northwest, you may need to add lime to make the soil neutral.

At planting time, mix into the soil a bulb food or a balanced fertilizer, such as 10-10-10; these are generally better sources of nutrients than bonemeal. Fertilize again at bloom time or just when flowers fade. The following seasons, broadcast fertilizer over the soil and rake it in when flowers first emerge. When using a dry fertilizer, water it in well unless rain is expected.

Planting

By laying out bulbs on top of the soil before you dig the first one in, you can fine-tune your planting scheme and distribute bulbs evenly. Or for a natural, random effect in a field or large planting area, just toss the bulbs onto the ground and plant them where they land.

In well-prepared or sandy soil, dig holes with a trowel. A bulb planter works best in moist soil that's clayey enough to hold the soil together when the planter is removed. Push the planter into the soil and twist it slightly as you remove it. Some bulb planters have a release mechanism that opens the sides so the soil drops out easily. Otherwise, you have to knock the soil out.

To dig planting holes, grip trowel as shown, stab it into loose soil, and pull toward you; drop in the bulb and cover with soil.

For planting depth, the standard guideline is to set bulbs so they're covered with soil three times as deep as the bulb's diameter. But there are exceptions. In hot climates or sandy soil, plant slightly deeper than recommended; in heavy soil, plant slightly shallower. Some types of bulbs should be planted just below the soil surface.

Watering

Water bulbs well at planting time. Keep the soil moist through winter and spring while roots are growing and flowers blooming. A layer of mulch over the soil helps maintain moisture.

Right after petals have faded or fallen off, remove flower stalks so bulb energy isn't diverted into seed formation. Let the foliage remain and continue photosynthesizing, so bulbs will store up nutrients for next season's show. Don't bundle the foliage. Wait for it to turn limp and yellow, then cut it back to 4 to 6 inches above the soil; pulling it off too soon can damage the bulb. Or wait until foliage dries up and then pull it off.

Bulb division

Many bulbs can be left undivided for years. If bulbs aren't blooming well because of overcrowding, then it's time to divide. Daffodils may need dividing every three to five years, bearded irises every three or four years.

Lift most true bulbs in summer after the foliage dies down. Using a spading fork, carefully dig up and separate clumps into individual bulbs; each new bulb should include a piece of basal plate—the area from which new roots arise.

Divide bearded irises between July and the end of October (the earlier date in cold climates). Use a sharp knife to divide rhizomes, discarding the woody center. Plant only healthy sections with good fans of leaves; allow cuts to heal for several hours or up to a day before replanting.

Divide lilies in spring or fall. You can also propagate them from bulb scales pulled off the main clump, or bulblets. Scales and bulblets can take three years to flower.

Corms (such as freesias) wither each year and grow new ones to replace the parent. They also produce cormels, or small corms, at the base; you can pick these off and replant them, but they generally won't bloom for the first two years.

Troubleshooting

If bulbs decline prematurely, the problem is probably over-watering, not disease. In cool, moist weather, botrytis blight may damage lilies, causing leaf spots and stem rot, but it usually doesn't affect the bulbs. A similar disease may rot narcissus. To prevent infection, give bulbs plenty of air circulation, keep beds free of debris, and keep soil dry when bulbs are dormant. Remove and destroy infected plant parts and rotting bulbs.

In mild climates, aphids can be a problem in spring. You can gently wash them off with water (hard blasts can damage flowers) or spray with insecticidal soap or other insecticide.

Gophers go after most bulbs except daffodils. So do mice, which follow mole tunnels to reach bulbs. To ward off these critters, use hardware cloth to surround bulbs or to line an entire bed. You can fashion a protective basket by bending two rectangles of hardware cloth into U shapes and nesting one inside the other so you have wire on all four sides; bury the basket so the edges are at soil level.

When thickly massed, a display of tulips requires hundreds of bulbs. Here, annual blue forget-me-nots, their seeds sown just after the tulip bulbs were planted, furnish a lacy filler and extend the color as the tulips fade. When the show is over, both plants can be dug out and the bed refilled with summer annuals.

A sea of flowering bulbs proclaims that spring has come. Yellow narcissus and peach pink hyacinths (Hyacinthus) provide a splashy foreground for an imposing clump of orange-red crown imperial (Fritillaria imperialis).

Best Bets for Naturalizing

More important than how you plant is what you plant. The following are good naturalizers in all or most of the West, and they're readily available in October in nurseries and through catalogs. Bloom times are approximate: Expect earlier bloom in Southern California and the low desert, later in northern and high-elevation areas.

Scilla or bluebells *(Endymion)*

There are two groups called bluebells or scilla. Spanish bluebells *(E. hispanicus)* come mostly in blue (though there are white, pink, and rose forms available), grow well almost everywhere, and look like loose woodland hyacinths. Their 20-inch flower stalks rise above grassy foliage in spring.

The true scillas include Peruvian scilla *(Scilla peruviana)*, which naturalizes along the California coast and in most of Southern California, and Siberian squill *(S. siberica)*, which naturalizes only in the Northwest and the high desert. Peruvian scilla has a full dome of blue flowers that rises to the top of 10-inch, strappy leaves in late spring. Siberian squill is low—less than 6 inches high—and has a looser stalk of spring flowers in shades of blue, white, and purplish pink. Both kinds do well in light shade. Plant bulbs 3 to 4 inches deep and 6 inches apart.

Calla *(Zantedeschia)*

From Seattle to San Diego, callas are widely known and sold both as dormant rhizomes and as nursery plants. Plants do best in mild coastal climates, where they're evergreen; in colder areas, foliage dies down in winter. The rhizomes develop clumps you can divide every few years. Plant 4 to 6 inches deep and 1 to 2 feet apart to allow room for the large arrow-shaped leaves.

In spring and early summer, the common calla *(Z. aethiopica)* bears 3-foot stems, each topped by a large white flower (spathe) with a yellow, fingerlike spadix in the center. Dwarf and colored (pink, yellow, and purple) callas are less vigorous but just as beautiful.

Crocus

Dutch crocus *(C. vernus)* naturalize in areas with pronounced winters; that excludes much of California. In late winter through early spring, the lawn-high, urn-shaped flowers—white, yellow, lavender, purple, or striped—appear just above grasslike foliage. Plant bulbs 2 to 4 inches deep and 4 inches apart, arranging them in masses or in highly visible clusters along walkways and borders. Go light on water in summer (often not possible if you plant crocus in lawns).

Daffodil *(Narcissus)*

Drive through western farmland and you'll see daffodils growing along the edges of fields and pastures, as they have for decades. Don't be misled into thinking all daffodils naturalize: Some may give a great show the first year but then decline. You'll do best with mixes sold for naturalizing or by buying any of the following varieties.

Large trumpets or cups for bloom from early to midspring: 'Carlton', large-cupped yellow; 'Ice Follies', early flat-cupped bicolor that fades to cream; and 'King Alfred', the best-known type of yellow trumpet (the name is so popular it's used to identify similar daffodils, including 'Dutch Master' and 'Unsurpassable'). Plant large-flowered types 4 to 6 inches deep, 6 to 8 inches apart.

Cyclamineus hybrids (single, medium-size flowers with swept-back petals), early spring: 'February Gold' and (somewhat later) 'Peeping Tom', both yellow.

Multiflowered daffodils (the most fragrant): 'Thalia', an early-spring, white triandrus hybrid; 'Suzy' (midspring) or 'Trevithian' (late spring), both yellow jonquilla hybrids; and 'Cheerfulness' (white) or 'Yellow Cheerfulness', late-spring doubles. In mild parts of California, single or double paperwhites and the related gold-cupped, yellow 'Soleil d'Or' flower all winter. In the Northwest, the best tazetta is the somewhat hardier 'Geranium', whose red-orange corona and white petals appear in early spring. Set small-flowered types 3 to 4 inches deep, 4 to 6 inches apart.

Most daffodils grow 1 to 2 feet high. If your garden gets a lot of rain or wind in spring, avoid tall and double-flowered kinds, which get knocked down more easily than singles and short varieties.

Freesia

Only mild-winter parts of Arizona and California have a climate benign enough to convince freesias to naturalize. While they reproduce reliably there, their fragrant flowers are smaller the second year. Comeback is iffier in the San Francisco Bay Area and comparable climates, and freesias are one-season plants in the Northwest.

Spindly stems, 12 to 18 inches tall, tend to flop over from the weight of their multiple blossoms, which bloom in succession from late winter to early spring. To prop up the flower stalks, interplant freesias with strong-foliaged annuals or perennials they can lean on.

Hybrid freesias come in all colors. If you don't deadhead spent flowers, they may self-sow—and the offsprings' flowers usually revert to cream marked with purple and yellow. For best fragrance, try 'Safari' (yellow), 'Snow-don' (double white), Tecolote red, and Tecolote yellow. Plant corms 2 inches deep, 2 to 3 inches apart.

Grape hyacinth (Muscari)

The pea-size blue flowers of *Muscari armeniacum* bunch together like clusters of grapes atop 6-inch stems with grassy leaves. The white form is *M. botryoides* 'Album', which also naturalizes well.

For a bold swath of spring color, start with at least three or four dozen bulbs, and set them 2 to 3 inches deep, 3 inches apart. Use them to create a cool riverine corridor that plays up the hot colors of surrounding tulips and daffodils.

Bearded iris

Tall bearded irises come in almost every color and perform well in all climate zones. The tendency among breeders now is to develop strong-stemmed, shorter varieties—in the 3-foot range instead of 4 feet and taller—so they stand up to bad weather and fit easily into the perennial border. There are plenty of varieties with ruffles, great colors, and abundant blooms to choose from. All bloom in April or May.

Breeders charge premium prices for rhizomes of new varieties, but older varieties are far less expensive. By dividing rhizomes every three years, you can really stretch your investment. Breeders have also been working on reblooming varieties, which flower in both spring and fall; they have a way to go in terms of reliability and flower color range, but you might want to experiment with them.

Mail-order sources generally stop shipping bearded irises by the end of September, but you should still find stock in nurseries in October. Place rhizomes 1 to 2 feet apart, with the top just below the soil surface and the roots spread out.

Dutch iris

They come in a wide range of colors and grow in all zones. In the mildest parts of Southern California, naturalizing results are mixed—you may lose some or even all of your bulbs after the first year or two. The farther north you are, the better the return, as long as the ground doesn't freeze down to bulb level.

You can choose from about 12 varieties of Dutch iris in shades of yellow, white, blue, and purple, with some stunning bicolors; all behave about the same. Try setting out pure drifts of 8 to 12 bulbs of each variety you can get your hands on; they flower over about a month, late spring into early summer. Plant bulbs 4 inches deep, 3 to 4 inches apart.

Leucojum

Sometimes called summer snow-flake, leucojum is often confused with snowdrop (*Galanthus nivalis*). Leucojum grows everywhere and has lots of little bell-shaped white flowers on 18-inch stalks; snowdrop, which grows only where winters are chilly, has slightly larger white flowers on plants that are less than a foot tall.

Leucojum takes well to life under deciduous trees and in mixed shrub or perennial borders. Plant bulbs 3 to 4 inches deep, 3 to 4 inches apart. Don't disturb them for the first few years, then divide them. Flowers appear in winter in mild climates, in early spring in colder areas.

Lily

Lilies come in an enormous array of sizes, colors, and bloom seasons (the ones listed here flower in early summer). All are temperate-zone plants, and most are readily available in fall.

A rule of thumb: If you want to naturalize lots of lilies, buy the cheaper ones on any grower's list. They're cheap because they multiply so quickly for the grower.

Asiatic lilies naturalize well in most of the West. Some good Asiatics to try are yellow 'Mary Bernard' or 'Connecticut King', orange 'Enchantment' or 'Pretender', deep peach 'Tiger Babies', red 'Tristar', and white 'Brushstroke', 'Nepal', or 'White Sails'.

Among Oriental lilies, good perennializers include 'Casablanca' (white), Imperial Gold, Imperial Silver, 'Rubrum' (pink to reddish), and 'Stargazer' (red and white), a favorite of almost every grower we talked with. In warm areas, plant these bulbs in light shade and mulch well.

Other good choices are regal lily (*Lilium regale*, fragrant, white), *L. pumilum* (fragrant, coral), and trumpet-flowered lilies. These don't need much winter chill to keep coming back.

Avoid tiger lily *(L. lancifolium)*, which is the Typhoid Mary of the group: Without showing symptoms, it carries diseases that can affect other bulbs in your garden. Give lilies even moisture and cool soil; a thick layer of organic mulch helps. Space bulbs about 1 foot apart, setting small bulbs 2 to 3 inches deep, medium ones 3 to 4 inches, and large ones 4 to 6 inches. Keep beds well weeded; lilies can't compete with grass runners. And bear in mind that lilies are a feast for gophers, squirrels, and deer.

Watsonia

You can grow this South African native in all mild parts of the West, but it's most successful in coastal California. Almost all plants labeled watsonia are *W. pyramidata*, which bears 4- to 6-foot spikes of red, white, lavender, or pink flowers that bloom in late spring and early summer. The deciduous leaves, which grow in fall and winter, reach about 2½ feet tall.

The rare species *W. beatricis* is evergreen, with flower colors that range from peach and apricot to scarlet. Bloom time is mid- to late summer.

Both kinds produce fine, long-lasting cut flowers and survive with little extra summer water. Given their height, watsonias lend themselves to the back of a garden bed. Plant them 4 inches deep, 6 inches apart.

The bulb family

We group them together as bulbs, but only some are true bulbs, with fleshy scales usually surrounded by a papery tunic. (Because they lack this tunic, lily bulbs are more susceptible to drying out.) Corms have solid center tissue instead of scales. Rhizomes are thickened stems that usually grow horizontally near the surface of the soil. Tubers and tuberous roots are also commonly grouped with bulbs.

These pictures represent typical shapes for the leading naturalizers. They're shown oriented the way you should plant them, but if you're not sure which end goes up, setting bulbs on their sides is a good way to hedge.

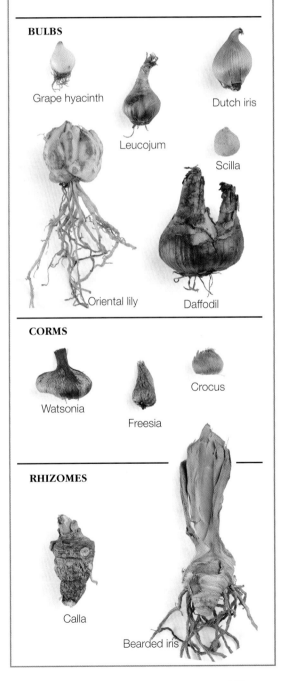

BULBS

Grape hyacinth

Dutch iris

Leucojum

Scilla

Oriental lily

Daffodil

CORMS

Watsonia

Crocus

Freesia

RHIZOMES

Calla

Bearded iris

Left: Scores of 'Carlton' daffodils splash this pasture with yellow as they've done for 30 years running.

Below: Summer show-offs in a 9-by-16-foot perennial bed. Lilies include regal (white), 'Tristar' (red), and 'Connecticut King' (yellow).

Landscaping with Bulbs

Bulbs look best when their flowers are massed in plain sight. They look worst when their dying foliage is massed in plain sight. But if you cut back the foliage before it fades, you cut back the life of the bulb. Here are four landscaping solutions that show off bulbs to best advantage and encourage naturalizing.

Overseed bulbs with annuals. Use tall, lacy-leafed summer annuals such as cosmos and baby's breath. They'll conceal declining foliage without blocking the light it needs. Avoid types that need abundant summer irrigation, which is bad for dormant flower bulbs. Whenever you dig bulbs to divide, you'll need to tear out the annuals too.

Overplant with ground covers. While daffodils will push up through English ivy year after year, in the long run, aggressive ground covers will win the survival contest. Innumerable western pastures are studded with daffodils, and many Northwest lawns sport colorful spots of crocus. To keep bulbs healthy, plant swaths you can mow around until foliage dies down. Bear in mind that ground covers make bulb division a bleak prospect.

Plant clusters in flower beds. Even small groups of bulbs provide impressive spot color. Try planting bulbs in a kidney-shaped pattern. You can stretch out or wrap the bed around other flowers, perennials, or small shrubs, and you can do it with almost any number of bulbs. The only caveat is to dig bulbs every three years or so, as much to clear away invading roots as to divide the bulbs.

Naturalize in mulched earth. Covering bulbs with mulch improves soil, keeps down weeds, retains moisture, and lends a natural effect well suited to a relaxed landscape; the warmer the climate, the thicker the mulch should be.

Among the earliest signs of spring, Dutch crocus carpet a Northwest lawn.

NORMAN A. PLATE

Dividing bulbs

If an established bulb planting has begun to bloom sparsely, the cause is probably overcrowding—and that means it's time to dig and divide. You'll also need to divide bulbs if you want to make more plantings of a favorite kind. Because each of the five bulb types increases in a different way, techniques for division differ as well.

To divide **true bulbs,** carefully break apart the parent and the increase (smaller bulb) at its base. To divide lily *(Lilium)* bulbs, remove outer scales from the basal plate, dip the ends in rooting hormone, and plant.

Corms renew themselves each growing season by producing a new corm and (sometimes) small cormels on top of the old corm. To divide, separate healthy new corms and any cormels from the old corms.

Tubers increase in size and in their number of growing points as they age, but most of them don't form separate increases. To divide, cut a large tuber into two or more sections, making sure each has a growing point.

Rhizomes produce new plants from growth points along their sides. To divide, break the sections apart at the natural divisions between them; be sure each division has at least one growing point.

Tuberous roots form multiple growing points. Some, such as daylily *(Hemerocallis),* form separate plants that can be pulled apart; this is usually done in summer or fall, when the plant is growing. Others, such as dahlia (above), do not separate as easily. To divide the latter, cut clumps apart so that each root has a growth bud; do the job before planting in early spring.

Northwestern favorites, azaleas and rhododendrons transform a simple staircase into a hidden entryway.

Selecting and Planting Shrubs

If you try to visualize your property without shrubs, you'll quickly grasp the importance of these plants in landscape design. Without these shrubs, there would be no hedges to keep children and pets safely in bounds, no lilacs or roses to gather for bouquets. House lines would be stark and angular without the softening effect of feathery evergreens or bushy hydrangeas.

Just as a large sofa or bulky upholstered chair can help fill a room, shrubs can add weight and substance to a landscape. They become permanent fixtures, altering traffic flow and framing views. Planted near a wall,

they create attractive backdrops; set close together, they form a living fence. For example, clipped boxwood, just a few feet high, helps to define a formal garden, while a staggered row of loose, flowery oleander *(Nerium oleander)* works well as a privacy screen. And a hedge of thorny, dense shrubs, such as barberry and natal plum *(Carissa macrocarpa),* makes an effective barrier against unwelcome intruders.

Judiciously placed, a single flowering shrub can punctuate the landscape as a focal point; short or dwarf shrubs, when grouped together, can add heft and structure to a flower bor-

der or create a smooth transition from tree canopy to ground level.

Like trees, shrubs are either deciduous or evergreen. They grow in a variety of rounded, tapered, or fountainlike shapes. With their showy flowers, fruits, or autumn foliage, shrubs offer seasonal appeal. Some, however, have decorative foliage throughout the growing season. Others, such as daphnes, lilacs, and viburnums, are primarily valued for their fragrance.

With hundreds of shrubs available, one key to successful landscaping is to select bushes that suit your garden's site—its soil conditions, available sunlight, and water resources. Certain favorites such as azaleas and rhododendrons, for example, thrive in the semishade of overhead trees and acid soil that is both moisture-retentive and fast draining. Rosebushes, on the other hand, prefer bright light and a slightly alkaline soil.

To ensure low maintenance, choose shrubs with similar cultural requirements, and remember that for shrubs to look their best they must be given adequate space to grow into their natural shapes. A small smoke tree *(Cotinus coggygria)* purchased in a gallon container will ultimately fill an area 6 to 8 feet wide, but it will lose much of its billowy charm if restricted to less space. Plant annual or perennial flowers to add color around newly planted shrubs until they fill out.

Pruning needs

In general, shrubs require regular pruning to keep their shape, to reduce diseases and pest problems, and to produce plentiful blooms. Consider the amount of seasonal work you are willing to do before making your final selections. Most flowering shrubs are pruned after their blossoms fade; for example, a May-flowering lilac should be pruned in June. Other deciduous shrubs bring forth long stems each year from the base and benefit from an early-spring removal of some older stems. Most evergreens, however, can be pruned at any time of year; exceptions are bloomers such as camellias.

As for young or recently installed shrubs, correct pruning at the proper time of year will lead to bushier plants with more flowers—which may or may not be the look you desire.

Shrubs as trees

Some of the best flowering shrubs are medium- to large-size plants trained to a treelike form with a single, upright trunk known as standards. Others are multitrunked shrubs, such as the oleander above, that have been pruned to form a treelike canopy.

Certain shrub standards, such as azalea, flower in spring; others, such as hibiscus and the Paraguay nightshade, bloom for most of the growing season. For an accent near a front door, color on a deck, or a focal point at the bend of a path, consider a rosebush, gardenia, or lantana. Good choices for small standards in containers (2 to 4 feet) are euryops, lantana, rosemary, roses, and Southern Indica azalea. Larger specimens (4 to 6 feet) include camellia, hibiscus, lilac, Princess flower *(Tibouchina urvilleana)*, staghorn sumac, and witch hazel. In mild-winter areas, bottlebrush and tea tree *(Leptospermum)* make perfect patio or street standards.

To prevent the tree from reverting to shrub form, continue pruning and trimming to control growth. Be sure to remove any suckers along the trunk.

Shrubs offer more than green leaves; those with tinted foliage such as this smoke tree can blend into color schemes.

Shrubs in borders

Borders filled with several plant types show shrubs to their greatest advantage. All shrubs, but especially evergreens, lend permanence to flowering borders that change with the seasons; in cold climates, shrubs may be the only source of winter interest. They can be focal points and accents or, conversely, serve as backgrounds for showier plants. Shrubs that reflect the color or texture of nearby trees link the planting scheme to the surrounding landscape. The weight and substance of many shrubs contrast with more delicate herbaceous plants. Flowering shrubs furnish color and fragrance, as well as attract birds and butterflies.

A. This shady corner is brightened with shrubs such as golden-leafed box honeysuckle *(Lonicera nitida* 'Baggesen's Gold'). Its color is complemented by the rosy lavender of flowering onion *(Allium)* and echoed by the chartreuse flowers of euphorbia in the foreground. Various hostas add bold foliage contrasts.

B. Along the path perennials grow. Shrub roses dominate borders on both sides of the walkway. The bluish green leaves of sea kale *(Crambe maritima)* and *Sedum spectabile,* each displaying masses of flowers in season, combine well with the silvery grasses *(Festuca* and *Miscanthus)* and the teal garden shelter.

C. Shrubby lavenders star in this dry California garden, with both French and Spanish species promising a long season of color. Their gray foliage is repeated in the silvery leaves of lavender cotton *(Santolina chamaecyparissus)*; floral color appears again in the broad-leafed sea lavender *(Limonium perezii).* Rosemary and scented pelargoniums offer additional fragrance.

Azaleas and 'White Emperor' tulips add a splash of color.

Planting balled-and-burlapped shrubs and trees

Some kinds of woody plants have root systems that won't survive bare-root transplanting; some are evergreen and cannot be bare-rooted. Instead, such plants are dug from the growing field with a ball of soil around their roots, wrapped in burlap or a synthetic material, and tied with twine or wire. These are called balled-and-burlapped plants (B-and-B for short). Some large specimens of deciduous trees and shrubs, evergreen shrubs such as rhododendrons and azaleas, and various conifers are sold this way in fall and early spring.

When buying B-and-B plants, look for healthy foliage and even branching. The covering should conceal the roots, and the root ball should feel firm and moist. If you have any doubts about the condition of the root ball, untie the covering and check for healthy roots and a solid, uncracked root ball.

B-and-B plants can be damaged if handled roughly. Support the bottom of the root ball when moving the plant; don't pick the plant up by the trunk or drop it, which might shatter the root ball. Because a B-and-B plant is usually heavy, have the nursery deliver it to you or have a friend help you move it in a sling of stout canvas. Once home, you can move the plant by sliding it onto a piece of plywood and pulling it to the planting spot.

1. Dig a planting hole with tapering sides. Make the hole at least twice as wide as the roots. Roughen the sides with a spading fork to help roots penetrate the soil.

2. Measure the root ball from top to bottom. The hole should be a bit shallower than this distance, so that the top of the root ball is about 2 inches above the surrounding soil. Adjust the hole to the proper depth then set in the plant.

3. Untie the covering. Spread out burlap to uncover about half the root ball. Remove a synthetic covering entirely. If planting in a windy site, drive a stake alongside the root ball. Fill the hole to within 4 inches of the top and water gently.

4. Continue to fill the hole, firming the soil as you go. Make a berm of soil to form a watering basin then water the plant. If you staked the plant, loosely tie it to the stake. As the plant becomes established, keep the soil moist but not soggy.

SELECTING SHRUBS

In times past, homeowners sought out bulky shrubs for "foundation plantings," to provide transition from house to garden by hiding the unattractive foundation. But with the disappearance of high foundations in many modern homes, shrubs play new roles. Because they encompass such a diversity of sizes, shapes, and appearances, shrubs can perform many landscape functions well.

In choosing shrubs for your garden, don't be guided solely by flashy color or sentimental attachment. Keep in mind the following points:

- **Adaptability.** No shrub will satisfy you unless it is suited to your climate, your soil, and your garden environment.
- **Plant size.** If you have a space for a 4-by-4-foot shrub but plant one that will reach 12 feet in all directions, you're bound to be unhappy. Remember that the most attractive shrubs (except those intended for sheared hedges) are those that are allowed to reach their natural size.
- **Growth rate.** Hand in hand with knowledge of a plant's ultimate size should go the realization of how fast it will get there. Slow growth is the price you will have to pay for some of the most desirable shrubs, so place those plants where their slowness will not be detrimental to your plans.
- **Texture.** The texture of individual leaves, as well as the texture of many leaves in mass, varies almost as much as do shrubs themselves. Shiny, dull, hairy or fuzzy, smooth, quilted—these qualities, combined with the size and shape of the leaf, give a plant its character. You can do much to highlight a shrub's inherent beauty if you consider how its foliage texture will complement that of neighboring plants and structures. If you capitalize on differences in texture, the individual plants will have a chance to show off.
- **Color.** Though many shrubs are planted for their floral display, foliage colors are just as important in the landscape.

Much of the advice about plant texture also applies to choosing and combining foliage colors. Visualize the combinations and juxtapositions, remembering that too much of a good thing—color, in this case—produces not an artistic statement but a jumble.

Perfect Peonies

Some plants possess the power to stimulate our remembrance of good times past. Peonies, with their soft pastel blossoms and light, clean fragrance, may remind you of long-ago springs when your grandmother cut generous bouquets from the garden to fill her favorite cut-crystal vase.

But peonies have a highly practical side, too. These herbaceous perennials require minimal care, and they can thrive undivided for decades. And peonies have great three-season value in the landscape. In early spring, their large, strong leaf buds poke up. Then bright flower buds form, bursting into spectacular blossoms. And from spring through autumn, peonies form luxurious clumps of greenery.

Some nurseries sell blooming plants in 1-gallon containers in spring. But there's no need to wait: Now is the time to plant peonies from tubers (shown below). Planted this fall, peonies will produce a few flowers next spring, then a full round of bloom the second year.

Peonies thrive in the Pacific Northwest, where gardeners plant them in massed beds or use them in mixed plantings with other perennials and shrubs.

In mild-winter areas of Northern California, where temperatures rarely dip below freezing for long, peonies have a reputation for being difficult to grow since many kinds do need a certain amount of winter chill to set buds and flourish. But a dedicated bunch of peony fanciers in California has discovered a number of plants that bloom well even when they don't get much winter chill.

The peonies listed on the opposite page have proved themselves in gardens from the San Francisco Bay Area to Vancouver, B.C. Most are early-blooming (midspring) varieties. These plants will also flourish in cold-winter areas where hard freezes are common. However, some can't tolerate hot summer climates.

CHOOSY ABOUT THEIR CLIMATES

Herbaceous peonies bloom well only when they experience a period of pronounced winter chill. Winter cold and summer heat are not problems, but flowers do not last well where spring days are hot and dry; in such areas, choose early-blooming varieties and give plants some afternoon shade and ample water. In Zones 1–7, where they grow best, they thrive in full sun.

'Mrs. Franklin D. Roosevelt' makes a showy container plant.

'Red Charm' bears double flowers with pompon-like centers.

Plant peony tubers with reddish "eyes" pointing up.

Pick your peonies
These 11 varieties are proven performers.

Note that peonies grown in mild-winter climates tend to be shorter than the maximum heights given here.

'Charlie's White' has creamy white double flowers as wide as 6 inches on stems that reach 4 feet long. Plants, with deep green leaves, grow as tall as 48 inches.

'Claire de Lune' bears ivory-yellow, 4-inch-wide single flowers with 11 to 13 petals on 32-inch-long stems. Plants mound as tall as 32 inches.

'Coral Charm' bears glowing coral to peach semidouble flowers as large as 8 inches across on 4-foot stems. Plants reach 36 inches tall.

'Coral Supreme' has lush pink, almost iridescent semidouble blossoms as wide as 7 inches on stems that can stretch 4 feet or longer. Plants grow 45 inches tall.

'Eventide' bears coral to pink cup-shaped single flowers 6 inches across on 3- to 3½-foot stems. Plants grow 3 feet tall.

'Festiva Maxima' produces white double flowers with vivid crimson flecks. The 6-inch-wide blooms are borne on 3½-foot stems. Plants, with dark green leaves, reach 36 inches tall. A mid- to late-season bloomer, this one works in coastal climates but has a hard time with inland heat.

'Late Windflower' has masses of white, 3½-inch-wide single flowers, each with a tuft of golden stamens in the center. Stems often grow longer than 4 feet. Plants, with finely cut leaves, reach 3 to 3½ feet tall.

'Miss America' bears white semidouble flowers 4 to 6 inches across on 3-foot stems. Plants form a bush 3 feet tall and as wide as 4 feet.

'Mrs. Franklin D. Roosevelt' has soft, pale pink double flowers 4 to 5 inches across on 38- to 40-inch stems. Plants stand 28 inches tall. A good choice for coastal California, this midseason variety won't be happy inland.

'Red Charm' produces dark red, 5- to 6-inch-wide double flowers on 2½-foot stems. Plants grow 3 feet tall.

'Roselette' bears clear pink single flowers, 5 to 6 inches wide, with crinkly petals. Stems can reach 42 inches long. Plants form a dense bush 22 inches tall.

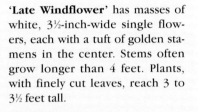

'Festiva maxima' bears 6-inch-wide double flowers with crimson flecks on some petals.

A garden for all seasons, this fall landscape shows off the fiery-hued foliage of maples and liquidambar trees.

November

Pacific Northwest Checklist

PLANTING

☑ SOW ANNUALS. Sown in autumn, the seeds of hardy annuals will germinate as soon as nature wakes them up in the spring. Sow candytuft, clarkia, larkspur, linaria, and wildflower mixes in well-tilled, weed-free soil.

☑ PLANT BULBS. Throughout the Northwest, there's still time to get spring-flowering bulbs into the ground. Nursery bins are full of crocus, daffodil, and tulip bulbs as well as less common bulbs such as allium, anemone, and scilla.

☑ CAMELLIAS. Zones 4–7: Sasanqua camellias are one of the joys of a coastal Northwest winter. Shop nurseries for plants in bloom. Before you put one in the ground, slip it into a decorative pot for display on a porch or patio. These camellias are especially effective espaliered against a wall under a roof overhang where pelting winter rains won't knock the blossoms apart.

☑ EVERGREENS. As leaves drop from deciduous trees and shrubs, you'll see where conifers can make a contribution to your landscape. Shop now for conifers and other evergreen trees and shrubs. When selecting a conifer, consider the ultimate size of the tree in your garden: A young Douglas fir looks adorable in a 5-gallon can, but in 10 years it may look as out of place as an eagle in a canary cage.

☑ PLANT GARLIC. Set out single cloves for harvest next summer. The variety 'Inchelium Red' does especially well in the Northwest.

☑ GROUND COVERS. If slopes planted with turf are eroding during heavy rains, replace lawn grass with ground covers that have dense root systems, such as rosemary, bearberry, or low-growing junipers.

MAINTENANCE

☑ DIVIDE PERENNIALS. Zones 4-7: This is an excellent time to dig and divide perennials. Circle clumps with a shovel or spade, then pop the plants out of the ground. A plant the size of a dinner plate will divide neatly into three or four sections. Replant divisions immediately in soil amended with organic matter.

☑ CUT BACK MUMS. Once blooms fade, cut the plants back to within 6 inches of the ground. Next spring, they'll send up vigorous new shoots.

☑ GROOM BORDERS. Late in the month, cut back frost-downed perennials and rake up leaves and debris. Then spread a 4-inch layer of mulch around plants.

☑ GROOM LAWNS. Mow and edge the lawn one last time. Rake leaves before they mat up and smother the grass underneath. Zones 4–7: There's still time to overseed bare spots; rough up the soil, sow seed, and cover with a thin layer of soil. Water until fall rains take over.

☑ MAKE COMPOST. As you rake, prune, mow, and pull out spent annuals and vegetables, throw the waste on the compost pile. Turn the pile one last time for the season.

☑ PRUNE TREES AND SHRUBS. Remove dead, diseased, and injured wood and any branches that cross. Then prune for shape.

Northern California Checklist

PLANTING

☑ **CHOOSE TREES FOR FALL COLOR.** Trees such as Chinese pistache and maples vary in how well their leaves color up, so this is the time to shop at nurseries while leaves are still on the trees (plant health in the nursery can also affect tree color). Other trees to consider are Chinese tallow tree, crape myrtle, ginkgo, liquidambar, persimmon, Raywood ash, redbud, and sour gum.

☑ **FIGHT EROSION.** If your garden is on a slope, make sure you have enough plants to keep the hillside from eroding if rains are heavy during winter. If the slope is bare or covered with young plants whose roots haven't yet knit the soil together, sow seeds of wildflowers and a perennial grass, such as blue wild rye *(Elymus glaucus)*.

☑ **GARLIC.** Artichoke (common white) types are easiest to grow. Rocambole has a wonderful, intense flavor. Choose a site in full sun with well-drained soil. If your soil is heavy and poorly drained, plant in raised beds. Mix in plenty of compost. Plant cloves so tips are about 1 to 2 inches deep. (Elephant garlic isn't a true garlic and is milder in flavor; plant cloves 4 to 6 inches deep.)

☑ **INSPECT BULBS, CORMS, AND TUBERS.** Zones 7–9, 14–17: As the bulb-buying season comes to a close and bulbs have sat in nursery bins and cartons for a while, make sure to carefully inspect bulbs, corms, and tubers before purchasing them. Bulbs should be firm and not sprouting. Avoid ones with soft spots or any that look dried out.

Sunset
CLIMATE ZONES

☐ Mountain (1-2)
☐ Valley (7-9)
☐ Inland (14)
☐ Coastal (15-17)

☑ **SOW WILDFLOWERS.** Zones 7–9, 14–17: For colorful spring bloom, choose a mix that's suited to your climate or buy individual kinds and create your own color combinations. You can also buy mixes for specific purposes, such as wildflowers that attract butterflies or beneficial insects.

☑ **PLANT PERENNIALS.** Nurseries have a wide assortment in sixpacks and in 4-inch and 1-gallon containers. Some good choices include alstroemeria, artemisia, campanula, catmint, columbine, coral bells, dead nettle *(Lamium)*, delphinium, dianthus, diascia, Oriental poppy, penstemon, perennial foxglove *(Digitalis mertonensis)*, phlox, salvia, scaevola, and species geraniums.

MAINTENANCE

☑ **CLEAN UP DEBRIS.** If you haven't rid your garden of fallen fruit, leaves, and faded summer annuals and vegetables, do so now. A clean garden, free of overwintering sites for insects and diseases, will be a healthy garden come spring.

☑ **CUT BACK CHRYSANTHEMUMS.** Zones 7–9, 14–17: As soon as flowers die, cut back plants to within 6 inches of the ground.

☑ **DIVIDE PERENNIALS.** Zones 7–9, 14–17: Dig out and separate overgrown clumps. For delicate roots, use your hands; for tougher roots, use shears, a pruning knife, or a shovel. To divide acanthus, agapanthus, and fortnight lily, you may need to force them apart with a spading fork. Add organic matter to the soil and replant.

☑ **FERTILIZE COOL-SEASON CROPS.** Zones 7–9, 14–17: If you didn't mix in a controlled-release fertilizer at planting time, your annuals and vegetables probably need feeding. You can use an organic fertilizer, such as fish emulsion, or another liquid or granular fertilizer.

PEST CONTROL

☑ **CONTROL SNAILS AND SLUGS.** Zones 7–9, 14–17: Protect newly planted annuals and emerging bulbs from snails and slugs this month. Hand-pick the pests at night or place copper rings around plants or raised beds. Insecticidal diatomaceous earth (not the type used in pool filters) is also effective if the weather is dry.

☑ **SPRAY FRUIT TREES.** Zones 7–9, 14–17: After the leaves have fallen, spray peach and nectarine trees with lime sulfur to control peach leaf curl. For brown rot on apricots, use a fixed copper spray. Apply it on dry days when no rain is predicted for at least 36 hours. Cover the stems and trunk of each tree thoroughly.

Southern California Checklist

PLANTING

☑ **PLANT FOR FALL COLOR.** Shop carefully for trees whose leaves will change color in mild-winter areas, even in frost-free coastal Zones 22–24. Look for gold-leafed ginkgo, orange-red Chinese pistache, and various shades of liquidambar in nurseries now. Consider adding some late-blooming perennials—such as asters, rudbeckia, or salvias—to the garden as well. These underutilized perennials perform beautifully in the Southern California climate.

☑ **PLANT WINTER VEGETABLES.** In coastal, inland, and low-desert gardens (Zones 22–24, 18–21, and 13, respectively), continue to plant winter vegetables. Sow seeds for beets, carrots, chard, kale, lettuces, mustard greens, onions, peas, radishes, spinach, and turnips. Set out transplants of broccoli, Brussels sprouts, cabbage, and cauliflower.

☑ **OVERSEED BERMUDA.** Sow annual winter rye to cover up dormant Bermuda grass. Mow the Bermuda as low as possible first, then sow ryegrass at a rate of 1 pound per 100 square feet of lawn. Cover with light mulch and keep moist until seeds germinate.

☑ **PLANT COOL-SEASON ANNUALS.** Except in the mountains (Zones 1–3), there's still time to set out early-blooming annuals such as African daisies, calendula, dianthus, Iceland poppies, ornamental cabbage and kale, pansies, snapdragons, stock, and viola. For shady areas, try cineraria, cyclamen, and English and fairy primroses. Some annuals perform best when seeded directly into the garden. Good annuals for direct sowing include flax, forget-me-nots, godetia, larkspur, linaria, linum, Shirley poppies, and sweet peas.

Bishop · NEVADA
CALIFORNIA
San Luis Obispo ·
Bakersfield ·
Santa Barbara
· Tehachapi
· Lancaster
Los Angeles ·
· Palm Springs
Sunset
CLIMATE ZONES
· San Diego
1-3 7-9 11 13 14-24
MEXICO

☑ **FIGHT EROSION.** Make sure you have plant material in place on slopes to prevent erosion during heavy winter rains. On bare or sparsely planted slopes, now is the time to sow a cool-season grass such as a mixture of fine fescues. You can add native wildflower seed for color.

MAINTENANCE

☑ **TEND CHRYSANTHEMUMS.** Support still-blooming plants with stakes and ties. After bloom, cut back plants, leaving 6-inch stems. Lift and divide old clumps; cut roots apart and discard woody centers, then replant.

☑ **PRUNE CANE BERRY PLANTS.** Cut back old canes of blackberry, boysenberry, and loganberry to the ground. Leave the smooth-barked canes that grew this year to bear fruit next year. Wait until December or January to cut back the canes of low-chill raspberries.

☑ **MULCH.** Put a 3- to 4-inch layer of organic mulch around half-hardy plants, trees, and shrubs, and on bulb beds that might heave during winter frosts at high elevations (Zones 1–3) and in the high desert (Zone 11).

PEST & WEED CONTROL

☑ **SPRAY FRUIT TREES.** After leaves have fallen, spray peaches and nectarine trees with lime sulfur to control peach leaf curl, an airborne fungal disease. Rake up debris under trees before applying. Spray entire tree—trunk, branches, twigs—and ground under tree. Mark calendar to spray again at height of dormancy (around New Year's Day) and just before bud break (around Valentine's Day).

☑ **CONTROL SNAILS AND SLUGS.** Put collars or sleeves around vulnerable plants, and copper bands or screens around raised beds. Handpick pests evenings and early mornings. Or let tiny, conical-shelled decollate snails do the job. They feed on the eggs of brown snails, eat dead and decaying vegetation, and won't harm plants. You can buy decollate snails from some nurseries, or through mail-order garden suppliers.

☑ **PROTECT CABBAGE CROPS.** Cover broccoli, cabbage, and other cole crops with row covers to keep cabbage white butterflies from laying eggs that hatch into leaf-chomping caterpillars. Or spray the uncovered plants with *Bacillus thuringiensis*. Focus the Bt carefully to avoid spraying other plants, so you don't destroy the larvae of swallowtails and other butterflies you want in your garden.

☑ **STAY AHEAD OF WEEDS.** Pull out annual bluegrass, chickweed, spurge, and other weeds as they emerge. If they're prevented from setting seed, next year's weeding will be easier.

Mountain Checklist

PLANTING

☑ **SPRING-FLOWERING BULBS.** Nurseries and garden centers are well stocked with spring-flowering bulbs now. Buy before they're picked over, and plant immediately.

☑ **WILDFLOWERS.** Sow them in weed-free beds. Also sow a small amount of the same seed in a flat of sterile soil so you'll have a reference plot. Otherwise you won't know weeds from wildflower seedlings when they emerge next spring.

☑ **HERBS.** Many herbs grow well indoors if they get 5 hours or more of bright light daily. In a sunny window, try oregano, rosemary, sage, sweet marjoram, and thyme. In a window with less light, try bay, chives, peppermint, and spearmint. Nurseries and some supermarkets sell herb plants in 2- or 4-inch pots; transplant these immediately into 6-inch or larger pots filled with well-drained potting soil. Allow the soil to dry slightly between waterings.

MAINTENANCE

☑ **DIG AND STORE DAHLIAS.** Stop watering a few days before digging dahlias, then carefully unearth them with a spading fork. Discard tops, brush dirt off tubers, and let them cure for a few days in a dry, frost-free place. Place tubers in boxes of peat, vermiculite, or sand and store at 45°F.

☑ **GROOM LAWNS.** Mow and edge lawns one last time. Rake the leaves off before they mat up and smother the grass.

Sunset
CLIMATE ZONES

☐ 1-3 ☐ 10-11

☑ **GROOM PERENNIAL BORDERS.** Be judicious as you cut back perennials, leaving ones with seed heads or dried flowers to provide winter interest—and food for birds.

☑ **MULCH.** Spread a 3-inch layer of organic mulch around half-hardy plants, under trees and shrubs, and over beds of bulbs that might otherwise be heaved out of the ground by hard freezes.

☑ **PLAN NEXT YEAR'S GARDEN.** While the memories of this year's successes and failures are still fresh, draw up plans for next year's plantings. When planning your vegetable patch, be sure to rotate crops so that you don't end up growing related plants in the same beds more than once every 3 years. For example, don't replant cabbage or its close relatives—including broccoli, cauliflower, and kale—in the same bed.

☑ **PROTECT ROSES FROM FREEZING.** Cut back 50% to 60% of the top growth, then mound fallen leaves over the plants (use screening to keep the leaves from blowing away).

☑ **PRUNE TREES AND SHRUBS.** After leaves fall from deciduous trees, start pruning ornamental varieties, but wait until spring to do stone fruits. Work on a mild day, removing dead, injured, and crossing or closely parallel branches. Then prune for shape.

☑ **MAKE COMPOST.** As the weather cools off, you can speed decomposition by grinding plants before you throw them into the compost pile.

Southwest Checklist

PLANTING

☑ **ANNUAL COLOR. Zones 12–13:** In sunny places, set out ageratum, aster, bells-of-Ireland, calendula, candytuft, clarkia, cornflower, foxglove, larkspur, lobelia, painted daisy, petunia, phlox, snapdragon, stock, sweet alyssum, and sweet pea. In shade, set out dianthus, English daisy, pansy, primrose, and viola.

☑ **BULBS. Zones 1–2, 10–11:** Plant spring-blooming kinds immediately. **Zones 12–13:** Buy Dutch irises, hyacinths, and long-stemmed varieties of daffodils and tulips; they do better in the heat than short-stemmed kinds. Chill bulbs in your refrigerator for 6 weeks before planting.

☑ **OVERSEED WARM-SEASON LAWNS. Zones 12–13:** Mow warm-season Bermuda grass at about ½ inch, then overseed it with 10 to 20 pounds of ryegrass per 1,000 square feet. You can use annual or perennial rye (coarser-leafed annual rye costs less but needs more frequent mowing than its perennial cousin). A month after sowing, fertilize the young ryegrass to encourage it to fill in quickly.

☑ **TREES AND SHRUBS. Zones 10–13:** Plant hardy trees, shrubs, and ground covers, including acacia, *Baccharis,* cassia, *Cordia boissieri,* desert spoon, fairy duster, mesquite, oleander, palo verde, *Salvia greggii,* and Texas ranger.

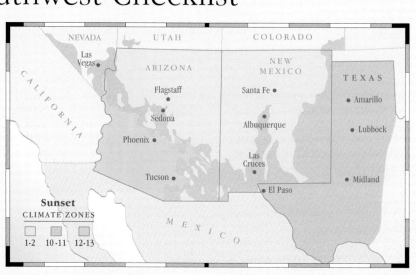

☑ **COOL-SEASON CROPS. Zones 12–13:** Sow or plant asparagus, beets, broccoli, Brussels sprouts, cabbages, carrots, cauliflower, celery, endive, garlic, kale, kohlrabi, leeks, lettuces, mustard, parsley, peas, radishes, spinach, Swiss chard, and turnips.

☑ **WILDFLOWERS. Zones 10–13:** Try blackfoot daisy, desert bluebells, desert globe mallow, firewheel, Mexican hat, Mexican tulip poppy, and owl's clover. Keep seed plots moist until plants are at least 2 inches tall if rain is infrequent.

☑ **SHOP.** Containers, landscape fabric, garden tools, irrigation systems, and other garden staples are available at reduced prices at garden centers.

MAINTENANCE

☑ **PRUNE AND FEED ROSES. Zones 12–13:** Remove faded flowers, pruning lightly as you go. Take out dead, diseased, crossing, and injured canes, and prune for shape. Then apply a complete fertilizer and water it in well to encourage winter bloom.

PEST CONTROL

☑ **APHIDS. Zones 12–13:** Blast them off new growth with a jet of water from a hose, then spray with insecticidal soap.

☑ **SNAILS AND SLUGS. Zones 12–13:** Hand-pick them at night or in the morning after you've watered. Or set out poison bait where children and pets can't get it.

Garden Edging

Neat, crisp edgings define garden spaces and add contrast to paths, low beds, and areas of lawn. To various extents, edgings can also keep plants in and grass and weeds out. Because of the unmortared joints between them, bricks and pavers, while pretty, are less reliable weed-stoppers than continuous materials such as wooden boards or commercial rubber or metal edgings.

Where the edging will abut the lawn, think about how you're going to trim the grass where it meets the edging. If the edging is higher than your mower deck can clear, you're setting yourself up for a tedious running appointment with a string trimmer. Sometimes the best edging of all in this case is nothing more than a beveled edge between the lawn and the garden. It's free, easy to maintain, and simple to create. Just slice 4-inch-deep cuts along the bed with a flat-edged shovel, then force the soil back into the bed to create an angle of about 45°F.

Clockwise from top left: An edging may be as simple as a beveled edge between lawn and bed. Supple branches, such as bamboo or willow, can be fashioned into an edging that defines the transition from pathway to plantings. Flexible plastic edging material prevents turf grass from spreading into adjoining plantings. A loosely laid collection of stones matches the informal style of a gravel path.

Recessed brick edging highlights the curve of a garden bed, draws the eye to the patio in the distance, and serves as a mowing strip.

At Season's End

Perennials and bulbs both need a bit of attention at the end of their bloom periods to keep them going for successive years.

Perennials

When their last flowers fade in summer or autumn, shrubby or branching perennials (such as chrysanthemums and yarrow) need to be cut back to encourage the best bloom the following season. Use pruning shears to remove about one-third to one-half the length of each stem. Don't cut back clump-forming perennials (such as primroses and gerbera).

Bulbs

Not all bulbs require annual digging and storage, and some need to be stored in some climates but not in others. Usually, though, storage is indicated when a bulb left in the ground cannot survive winter cold or summer.

In the first case, dig up the bulbs, then store them over winter under cool but not freezing conditions (35° to 55°F). Container-grown bulbs can often remain in their pots in a dark, dry place.

In the second case, dig spring-flowering bulbs when leaves die back, store them dry over summer, and replant in autumn. Withhold all moisture from container bulbs during the dormant phase.

The two storage methods presented below cover the needs of all popular bulbs. One cautionary note: If mice find your bulb storeroom, they'll have a banquet. Securely cover or enclose stored bulbs with screening or wire mesh to avoid mice.

Ventilated storage. Bulbs that have a protective tunic—such as narcissus and gladiolus—can be stored in mesh bags or piled loosely in boxes or baskets. Exposure to air keeps them dry and discourages rot, while the protective skin helps prevent dehydration.

To prepare bulbs for ventilated storage, dig them up or knock them from containers when foliage has yellowed. Remove leaves and soil, then spread the bulbs on newspapers in a shaded location and let them dry for several days. Don't separate bulbs before storage, since broken surfaces admit disease and encourage dehydration. Store the dried bulbs in a cool, dry, dark place (35° to 55°F) until the proper planting time for your area.

Covered storage. A number of bulbs (caladium and begonia, for example) lack a protective covering; if

Cut back ornamental grasses, salvias, lavender (above), and deciduous perennials to 4 to 6 inches above the ground to make room for new growth. Do this job in winter, when dead plant parts can easily be pulled from the ground.

exposed to the air for long after digging, they'll begin to shrivel. If dehydration continues during storage, the bulb may die or become severely debilitated before replanting time.

Dig and dry these bulbs as directed above, then place them in a single layer in a box or clay pot, making sure they don't touch. Cover with ½ inch of dry sand, vermiculite, sawdust, or peat moss. Replant bulbs at the proper time for your area, dividing them then if needed. If any appear dry or shriveled, plump them up in moist sand before replanting.

Some bulbs may successfully remain in the ground in regions a bit colder than their preferred zones if you cover the soil with a layer of insulating material. During bursts of springlike temperatures, protected ground remains colder than unprotected ground, and the bulbs under cover remain inactive; they aren't tricked into producing growth that would then be killed by a return to subfreezing weather.

Apply a 4- to 6-inch layer of winter protection after the first hard frost in autumn. Use conifer boughs; marsh, prairie, and salt hay; or ground corn cobs—just make sure the material won't pack into an airtight mass. Leave the protection in place until just before the start of the normal spring growing period, then rake it aside.

Store bulbs with hard skins in hanging mesh bags so air can circulate around them (left). Bulbs that lack protective skin need covered storage (right). Keep both kinds of bulbs in a cool, dry place until planting time.

Dormant-season cleanup

Remove all diseased plant material, along with spent annuals and vegetables, to prevent diseases from recurring season after season. In most areas of the West, this cleanup is done in late fall.

Until just a few years ago, it was generally recommended that the garden be stripped bare. While that ensures the most protection from recurring disease, it may make your garden uninhabitable for creatures you want to protect during the dormant season. Some unkempt areas may be just what's needed for birds, small mammals, and other attractive or beneficial creatures to find shelter in the cooler months. Of course, you should remove anything that's badly diseased or has completed its life cycle. But otherwise, moderation is a good rule of thumb. Chemicals sold for "total soil cleanup," for instance, are highly toxic and their use should be avoided.

One task you should plan on completing during the dormant season is dormant-oil spraying. Spraying trees and shrubs with an oil-and-water solution will kill many pests in their dormant stages; it will also prevent some diseases from occurring the following spring. Dormant-oil spraying is one way of keeping next season's aphid, scale, and mite populations under control. (You might want to limit this spraying to those plants that had the greatest infestations in the prior year. Widespread spraying may have the unwanted side effect of killing beneficial creatures.)

Some commercially available oils contain disease-preventing components—sometimes the only control that will prevent certain diseases, such as peach leaf curl, from occurring later during the growing season. Consult your Cooperative Extension agent to learn details about winter spraying of ornamental and fruit trees.

Oil sprays are sold in two formulas. Those applied during winter are heavier and better able to coat tree and shrub branches, suffocating insects in their dormant states. Summer oil is lighter weight. If you apply dormant-oil spray during warmer seasons, it puts too heavy a coating on leaves, making it difficult for them to breathe and making them more vulnerable to burning from sunlight reflected by the oil. As with any material you purchase to spray on your garden, be sure to follow the directions on the label exactly.

If you're growing roses in a mild-winter area, you'll find their leaves don't drop naturally. While the task can seem daunting, you must strip off all old leaves—sometimes you can knock off the majority with a broom—and dispose of them. By winter the leaves have lost their vigor, and most are harboring some evidence of black spot or rust. If you don't remove them, the disease spores will rapidly infect the new leaves next spring. Once you've removed the leaves, do your regular winter pruning and then spray the entire bush with dormant-oil spray.

In colder-winter areas, most rose leaves will drop naturally. However, remember to spray your rosebushes with dormant-oil spray after their annual pruning.

In both types of climates, dispose of rose leaves with the trash, not in the compost. Disease spores will survive in compost, even in a pile that generates high temperatures.

BE CAREFUL WITH DORMANT-SEASON AND SUMMER-OIL SPRAYS

Many gardeners are aware of the dangers to fish from soaps and pesticides. But they often don't realize that oil sprays, such as those used on trees during the winter dormant season or in summer to prevent mildews, will also kill fish.

Far left: Potted bulbs such as tuberous begonias and caladium need to be dug up and stored out of the soil, then repotted in fresh soil in later winter/ early spring for another season.
Left: By contrast, potted bulbs such as lily-of-the-valley can stay in the same container and soil for several seasons. Move them to a sheltered place before the first frost. Amaryllis, cannas, cyclamen, and ranunculus can also be treated this way.

Shade Trees

The path along which the sun travels across the sky from morning to afternoon—and also from winter to summer—determines the best locations for shade trees.

In midsummer, the sun shines on the east side of your house in the morning, passes over the roof near midday, then beats down on the west side in the afternoon. It's in the afternoon, when temperatures are highest, that solar radiation heats the house most and air conditioners work the hardest. Consequently, the west side of your house is the most important side to shade. The east

An Eastern redbud makes a brilliant spring show before flowers ever open.

side, where sun can warm the house early in the day, is the second most important to shade.

As fall and winter approach, the sun is lower in the sky and shines more directly on the south side of your house. With cooler weather, however, the sun becomes a benefit rather than a liability. The warmth it provides reduces heating costs, so in most cases you don't want to shade the south side of the house. Even leafless deciduous trees can reduce sunlight falling on the south side of your house by as much as 40 percent. Leaving the southern exposure open also allows you to use solar collectors for heating water or your home.

There are a few exceptions to these rules. In hot, sunny climates (such as in Phoenix or Palm Springs), the weather can be quite warm in spring and fall. Shading the south side of a house can have some benefits as long as the trees don't block solar collectors. But if you live in a cool-summer or foggy climate (such as in San Francisco or Seattle), any sunshine is a blessing, and planting trees for shade may be a mistake.

In cold climates, a row of conifers that doesn't shade a house can break cold prevailing winds and help save money on heating. But to make the most of solar gain through south-facing windows, avoid planting any trees that would block sunlight falling on the south side of your house.

Where to plant shade trees

Shade windows first. Sun shining directly through a window heats a home quickly. Plant trees on the east or west side near any windows. If possible, position them just to the side of the window so you don't block the view but still provide shade.

■ **Don't plant too close to the house.** The closer you plant to your house, the more you'll shade it. But planting trees too close could cause the roots to damage the foundation. Small trees should be at least 5 feet from the foundation, larger trees at least 10 feet away.

■ **Shade paved areas.** The right shade tree can turn a patio into a special garden retreat. Shade trees also reduce the heat that's stored or reflected by paved surfaces, including patios and driveways. Reflected heat can increase the temperature of your home during the day, and stored heat can slow the cooling of your house after the sun has gone down.

■ **Shade air conditioners.** Keeping your air conditioner cool can reduce its workload and cut energy consumption.

■ **Don't plant near utilities.** Avoid planting trees where limbs will grow into power lines or where roots may damage underground utilities. If you have questions, contact your local utility company.

The West's best shade trees

These trees are recommended by tree experts as being most suitable to the conditions of most *Sunset* climate zones. All the trees illustrated here do a good job of providing shade and helping cut energy costs, but the best choice depends on your particular situation: Fruiting trees, for instance, may be too messy for a patio.

The color bars below indicate leaf color in each season.

CALLERY PEAR	CHINESE PISTACHE	CHINESE TALLOW TREE	EASTERN REDBUD
Pyrus calleryana 'Chanticleer'	*Pistacia chinensis*	*Sapium sebiferum*	*Cercis canadensis*

Zones 2-9, 14-21 Moderate, 25'-50' White flowers, fall color, resists fire blight	Zones 4-16, 18-23 Moderate, to 60' Fiery fall color, shapely with age	Zones 8-9, 12-16, 18-21 Moderate, to 35' Brilliant fall color, may reseed heavily	Zones 1-3, 7-20 Fast, 25'-35' Striking flowers, few problems

East

In the morning, three trees planted on the eastern side of the home help keep the interior cool.

North

In the late afternoon, two trees planted on the western side help keep the interior cool. A third tree partially shades the patio.

HOW MUCH CAN YOU SAVE?

How much energy and money can you save by planting trees around your house? Thanks to a computer program at the University of California at Davis, researchers for the U.S. Forest Service's Western Center for Urban Forest Research and Education can now predict both. Using a model of a 2,500-square-foot unshaded house in Sacramento, the computer predicted that shading the house's east and west sides (including windows) could reduce energy use for air-conditioning by as much as 40 percent annually.

As a bonus, plant tall, narrow trees such as giant redwoods in a row to help block prevailing winds.

Prevailing Winds

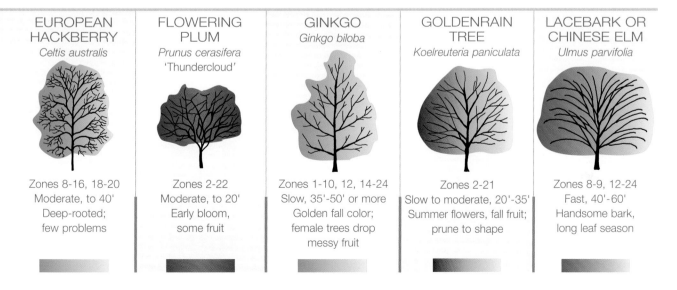

EUROPEAN HACKBERRY	FLOWERING PLUM	GINKGO	GOLDENRAIN TREE	LACEBARK OR CHINESE ELM
Celtis australis	*Prunus cerasifera* 'Thundercloud'	*Ginkgo biloba*	*Koelreuteria paniculata*	*Ulmus parvifolia*
Zones 8-16, 18-20	Zones 2-22	Zones 1-10, 12, 14-24	Zones 2-21	Zones 8-9, 12-24
Moderate, to 40'	Moderate, to 20'	Slow, 35'-50' or more	Slow to moderate, 20'-35'	Fast, 40'-60'
Deep-rooted; few problems	Early bloom, some fruit	Golden fall color; female trees drop messy fruit	Summer flowers, fall fruit; prune to shape	Handsome bark, long leaf season

Same tree, different colors: Autumn turns the Chinese pistache on the left orange, the one on the right golden yellow. Expect some color variability in most species.

What tree to plant?

In most areas, the ideal shade tree is deciduous: The sun can shine through its leafless branches in winter. The tree should have a fairly dense, round to spreading canopy, and ultimately reach 25 to 50 feet—anything much larger may be a liability on an average-size lot. Ideally, the tree will spread its limbs wide enough to partially shade the roof.

Small trees are appropriate where space is at a premium or when you want to shade only a single window. For narrow side yards, a row of several columnar or upright trees works better than a single broad-canopied tree.

If you live in warm-winter climates, evergreen trees may be an appropriate choice to provide year-round shade. But if you live in a cold climate, evergreen shade trees—especially when planted on the south side of the house—can add as much as 20% to winter heating costs.

How many trees should you plant in your yard? Often more than one is needed. Because the sun rises and sets in different places at different times of year, you can get better shading if you plant a pair of trees outside each window that needs shade. (In San Francisco, for example, the sun sets 40°F farther north in June than it does in October, so a tree that shades the house well in summer may not help as much in fall.)

Seasonal shade patterns

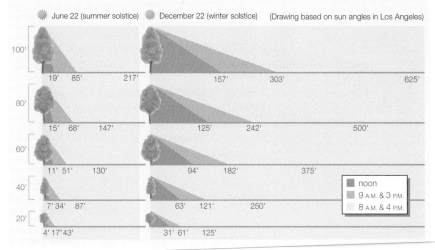

☀ June 22 (summer solstice)   ☀ December 22 (winter solstice)   (Drawing based on sun angles in Los Angeles)

100'	19' 85' 217'	157' 303'	625'
80'	15' 68' 147'	125' 242'	500'
60'	11' 51' 130'	94' 182'	375'
40'	7' 34' 87'	63' 121' 250'	
20'	4' 17' 43'	31' 61' 125'	

■ noon
▨ 9 A.M. & 3 P.M.
░ 8 A.M. & 4 P.M.

Evergreen trees cast shade farther in winter than in summer, when it's most needed.

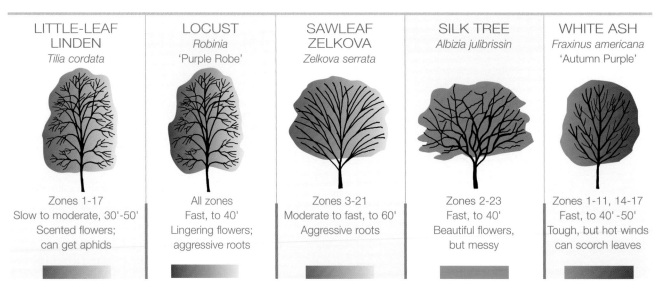

LITTLE-LEAF LINDEN *Tilia cordata*	LOCUST *Robinia* 'Purple Robe'	SAWLEAF ZELKOVA *Zelkova serrata*	SILK TREE *Albizia julibrissin*	WHITE ASH *Fraxinus americana* 'Autumn Purple'
Zones 1-17 Slow to moderate, 30'-50' Scented flowers; can get aphids	All zones Fast, to 40' Lingering flowers; aggressive roots	Zones 3-21 Moderate to fast, to 60' Aggressive roots	Zones 2-23 Fast, to 40' Beautiful flowers, but messy	Zones 1-11, 14-17 Fast, to 40'-50' Tough, but hot winds can scorch leaves

Goldenrain trees (Koelreuteria paniculata) *splash this house and lawn with shade. Summer flowers are followed by buff-colored fruit.*

You can buy most kinds of trees three ways from nurseries:

- Bare-root (available in winter only)—least expensive.
- In standard-size containers (usually 5-gallon size)—more expensive.
- As roof-high "specimen" trees in 2-foot-diameter containers—most expensive. You'll probably also have to pay a delivery charge and perhaps even a planting charge if the tree is too heavy for you to handle by yourself.

According to some landscape contractors, larger, more mature trees are slower to become established than their younger counterparts, so in the long run, a smaller tree may be a better deal and actually surpass a specimen tree in a few years. Because specimen trees are costly, it pays to get a tree with a replacement guarantee if you can. Many nurseries warrant the tree's survival for a year after planting. Good care, of course, is assumed.

Big trees for a big house: Grand old sycamores keep this Sacramento house cool.

Getting a fast start

The sooner a tree starts reducing your energy bills and increasing your comfort, the better. Since trees grow fastest when they're young, most trees will really start to pay off within five years. (If you don't want to wait, start with a tree that's already roof-high when you buy it.) Here's how to pick the best tree and get it off to a good start.

Look before you buy. If the top of the tree is healthy and well formed, check the roots. They should penetrate the root ball's edges, but not densely circle the inside of the container or be growing through the drain holes (a common problem with a tree that's been in the same pot or box for too long). Check roots by sliding the plastic container off the root ball, or if the tree is in an extra-large container,

Palo verde's tracery of branches provides shade even when tiny leaves drop.

Crape myrtle's flowers bloom in the summer hea[t]

dig down a side of it and feel for a matted sheet of roots against the container wall. Avoid trees that have thick surface roots encircling the trunk.

Dig the planting hole. Make it the same depth as the root ball and two to three times as wide. Unless you have extremely sandy soil, you don't need to add amendments; it's enough just to break it up. Plant the tree so that its crown—where the trunk goes into the ground—is slightly above ground level.

Water thoroughly. Build a berm of soil around the tree just outside the root ball. The berm should be at least 6 inches high and 18 to 24 inches wide. Soak the newly planted tree and rock it gently by the trunk to settle it in. Then spread a 4-inch layer of organic mulch over the root zone (but don't let it rest against the trunk). Soak the tree twice a week for the first month and weekly after that until winter rains take over. Next year water the tree weekly during the growing season. In sandy soils or hot desert climates, trees may need deep watering more often.

More great trees

FOR THE NORTHWEST:
Mountain areas (Zones 1–3)
• Hawthorn *(Crataegus* species*)*
• Hedge maple *(Acer campestre)*
• Maples *(Acer freemanii* 'Autumn Blaze', A. *grandidentatum)*

Mild areas (Zones 4–7)
• *Acer freemanii* 'Autumn Blaze'
• Crabapple *(Malus* species*)*
• Hawthorn *(Crataegus* species*)*
• Hedge maple *(Acer campestre)*
• *Magnolia* 'Galaxy'
• Tupelo *(Nyssa sylvatica)*

FOR CALIFORNIA:
Mountain areas (Zones 1–3)
• Hawthorn *(Crataegus* species*)*
• Hedge maple *(Acer campestre)*
• Maples *(Acer freemanii* 'Autumn Blaze', A. *grandidentatum)*

Central Valley (Zones 7–9)
• Chitalpa *(C. tashkentensis)*
• Crape myrtle *(Lagerstroemia indica)*
• Oriental persimmon *(Diospyros kaki)*

Central and Northern California Coast (Zones 14–17)
• Oriental persimmon *(Diospyros kaki;* best in Zones 14–16)

Southern California (Zones 18–24)
• African sumac *(Rhus lancea)**
• Australian willow *(Geijera parviflora)**
• Chitalpa *(C. tashkentensis)*
• Crape myrtle *(Lagerstroemia indica;* best in Zones 18–21)
• Jacaranda *(J. mimosifolia)*
• Strawberry tree *(Arbutus unedo)**
• Victorian box *(Pittosporum undulatum;* best in Zones 21–24)**

FOR MOUNTAIN GARDENS:
• Hawthorn *(Crataegus* species*)*
• Hedge maple *(Acer campestre)*
• Maples *(Acer freemanii* 'Autumn Blaze', A. *grandidentatum)*

FOR DESERT GARDENS:
• *Acacia salicina* (best in Zones 12–13)*
• *A. saligna* (best in Zone 13)*
• *A. smallii* (best in Zones 12–13)
• Arizona ash *(Fraxinus velutina)*
• Blue palo verde *(Cercidium floridum)*
• Chinese photinia *(P. serrulata)**
• Crape myrtle *(Lagerstroemia indica;* best in Zones 10, 12–13)
• Desert willow *(Chilopsis linearis)*
• Hawthorn *(Crataegus* species; best in Zones 10–12)
• *Magnolia grandiflora* (best in Zones 10–12)*
• Mesquite *(Prosopis)*
• Pines *(Pinus eldarica, P. halepensis)**

*Evergreen

Frost and Snow

Mild winters are one of the main reasons that people choose to live at low elevations in the West. But frosts can occur almost anywhere, at any time, even in the mildest climates. Arctic air that flows south can cause low temperatures that last for days, killing even hardy plants. At high elevations, cold winters with heavy snows consistently threaten plant survival. If you live in a zone that regularly experiences frost, choose hardy plants. But no matter where you live in the West, protect your plants during cold weather, especially tender plants like citrus and early blooming fruit trees like Japanese plum.

Preparing for frost

Local weather reports tell you when to expect cold weather. But a common type of freeze can occur in isolated spots on clear, still, dry nights. Known as "radiation" freezes, these happen when warmth that was stored in the ground during the day rises quickly and is replaced by cold air.

Frost pockets are most likely to develop just before dawn and in low-lying areas.

To protect plants from radiation freezes, cover them with plastic or burlap, which slows the loss of heat and insulates against the cold. Prop up the material so it doesn't touch plant leaves. You can add sources of heat, such as outdoor lights, under the covers.

On cold nights, run sprinklers under vulnerable plants like citrus. As the water cools or freezes, it releases heat that warms the air around the plant. (Do this only if there are no restrictions on your water supply and if the tree can support a coating of ice.)

The following precautions will go a long way toward reducing winter damage to your garden.

Precondition plants. As winter approaches, slow down growth and harden plants by withholding nitrogen fertilizer, gradually watering less, and avoiding heavy pruning. Let plants form seeds or fruit to force slower growth.

Keep soil moist and weeded. Dry winter winds and cold temperatures hasten evaporation from the soil and from leaf surfaces, causing them to wilt. Plants weakened by wilting are more susceptible to damage from freezing temperatures. Bare soil absorbs more heat than weedy soil, so remove weeds often.

Mulch. Mulching prevents soil from alternately freezing and thawing, which can damage roots. However, mulching also reduces the amount of heat stored in the soil and can increase the chance of frost damage to foliage. Apply a 4- to 6-inch layer of loose organic material such as leaves, straw, or compost around the base of plants. But if you are expecting frost, remove the mulch so the sun can warm the soil beforehand.

Protect from sun. If plants are frozen overnight, protect them from damage by quick-thawing in morning sun with shade cloth, sheets, or burlap. Paint tree trunks with white latex paint or wrap them.

Frost-damaged banana plant has crackling dry foliage.

Tender citrus are easily injured by frost. This one has shriveled leaves and fruit.

Ice plant in exposed area is damaged; a nearby tree protected the other bed.

After a freeze

In mild-climate areas, rare freezes can leave gardens with wilted foliage and split bark. When this occurs, what can you do? The best advice is to be patient and wait until new growth starts before you pick up the pruning shears. The longer you wait, the more obvious the actual damage will be.

Look for live buds (they will be greenish rather than withered and brown). If you can't find buds, look for healthy plant tissue: Carefully scratch through the bark with your thumbnail, starting near the branch tips and working inward. Greenish or whitish wet tissue is still alive.

For ground covers, look under dead or discolored leaves. Green pieces with roots attached may have survived. If there's enough green growth below, the plants may recover.

Wait to prune conifers and broad-leafed evergreens until they are actively growing. The pruning cuts will heal better than if the plants are dormant, and old wood and foliage help protect live tissue until the chance of frost damage is past.

Twigs and small branches that are blackened, misshapen, soft, or shriveled, however, are almost certainly dead. Remove them; otherwise, they could invite botrytis or other fungi that attack dead or weakened plant tissue (and can later spread to live tissue) when air is still and moist. Grayish or brown fuzz on damaged leaves or other plant parts is a symptom of fungal infection.

If bark is split, there is little you can do except leave the cracks alone and see how they close. If pruning or dropping leaves reveal bark on sun-sensitive trees such as citrus and avocado, paint the exposed areas with white latex paint.

Irrigate frost-damaged plants immediately and continue with a regular watering pattern. But don't water severely damaged soft-stemmed plants like banana until the new growth starts; wet soil could cause them to rot. In all cases, wait until new growth starts to mature before fertilizing. Scale back the amount of fertilizer in proportion to the amount of foliage lost.

Severely damaged plants

Some plants killed to the ground by frost may have undamaged root systems that will resprout, so before removing the plant, wait a year to see if it revives. It may take two or three years to determine the full extent of damage on old, established trees.

If a budded or grafted plant shows signs of life, make sure the new growth is from the grafted portion, not the rootstock.

Frost and freeze protection

Wherever you garden, the best defense against cold damage is to choose trees and shrubs that are hardy in your climate zone. Plants that are more tender to frost should be restricted to summertime display in borders or grown in containers that can be moved to shelter when the weather turns cold.

It's also important to know your garden's microclimates—that is, to learn which areas are warmer, which are cooler. The riskiest spots for marginally hardy plants are stretches of open ground exposed to air from all sides (particularly from the north). Other dangerous locations include hollows and low, enclosed areas that catch cold air as it sinks, then hold it motionless. The warmest part of the garden is usually next to a south-facing wall with an overhang; such a spot offers maximum frost protection and supplies the warmth needed to stimulate buds, blossoms, and fruit on vines, shrubs, and espaliered trees that might not thrive elsewhere in the garden.

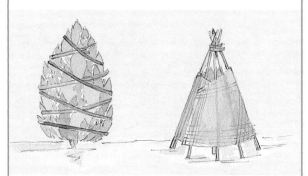

Snow. To prevent heavy, wet snow from breaking upright branches, wrap conifers with a spiral of twine (left). A tent of bamboo stakes covered with burlap (right) shelters plants from snow and wind.

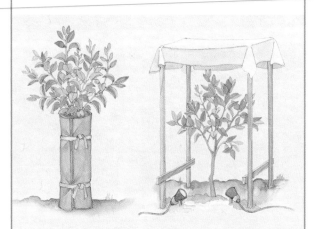

Frost. Insulate the trunks of frost-sensitive plants with corrugated cardboard, newspapers, or batting (left). Or cover the plant and raise the temperature around it with trouble lights (right) or strings of Christmas tree lights.

All-winter protection for broad-leafed evergreens

In very cold climates, some plants require protection all winter long to survive; examples include broad-leafed evergreens such as boxwood *(Buxus)*, euonymus, holly *(Ilex)*, pieris, and rhododendron. Evergreens suffer in winter because the leaves continue to transpire and thus lose moisture (especially on relatively warm, windy days)—but when the soil is frozen, the roots cannot take up water to replace what has been lost, and the plant becomes desiccated.

1 Water thoroughly before the ground freezes, then apply a thick mulch of oak leaves, pine needles, wood chips, or ground bark around the plants. The mulch limits the penetration of frost into the ground, allowing the deepest roots to continue absorbing moisture; it also protects surface roots from alternate freezing and thawing.

2 Apply an antitranspirant around the time the first hard frost is due. Available from garden centers, this product forms a thin film on the leaves, sealing in moisture. You may need to make further applications later in winter; check the label.

3 Construct a windbreak in especially exposed locations, if needed. Drive three or four stakes into the ground around the plant and staple or nail burlap to them. Don't use plastic film for the windbreak; it cuts off needed air circulation.

WINTER PROTECTION FOR ROSES

Where winter lows tend to fall regularly to 10°F or below, some protection is needed for most modern roses. After a couple of hard freezes have occurred, cut canes back to a manageable height and tie them together, then mound soil at least 1 foot high over the base of the bush. After the soil mound freezes, cover it with an insulating mound of straw, hay, cut conifer boughs, or other noncompacting organic material. For greater security, surround the insulated bush with a wire mesh cylinder: This will hold the soil mound and its covering in place while allowing water to drain away easily.

Stately saguaro cactus shimmer like lighted sculptures against the night sky.

December

Pacific Northwest Checklist

PLANTING

☑ **BUY CAMELLIAS.** Zones 4–7: Winter-flowering camellias will be available in full bloom. Slip them into decorative pots, planters, or big baskets to display on a deck or patio for the holidays (you can even string them with lights). When flowers fade, plant them out in the garden.

☑ **GROUND LAYER EVERGREENS.** You can propagate evergreen plants such as daphne, hebe, mahonia, and rhododendrons by using a technique called ground layering. Find a branch near the ground and scrape a bit of bark (about the size of a fingernail) from the underside. Dust the wound with rooting hormone and press the branch down into a shallow hollow in the ground. Cover the branch with a bit of soil and weigh it down with a rock or brick. Keep the area well watered. By next fall, the branch will have rooted; cut the new plant away from the parent and plant it in another site.

☑ **TREES AND SHRUBS.** Zones 4–7: All but marginally hardy trees and shrubs can go into the ground this month. Water them thoroughly after planting.

☑ **DECORATE.** Lightly prune evergreens such as juniper, glossy abelia, and Oregon grape and use the trimmings for holiday decorations.

☑ **AMARYLLIS.** Garden shops and nurseries will have amaryllis bulbs of all kinds, from classic big, red-flowered varieties to new dwarfs with cream-and-pink blooms. Buy several bulbs and pot them up at 2-week intervals; you'll have plants in bloom from mid-December to Valentine's day and beyond.

☑ **HARVEST EDIBLE FLOWERS.** If calendulas or nasturtiums are still blooming in your garden, harvest some flowers to sprinkle on your winter salads—these flowers are edible.

MAINTENANCE

☑ **INSPECT STORED BULBS.** Frost-tender bulbs, corms, and tubers in storage for the winter should be examined for rot. Discard damaged ones. Dahlia tubers are the exception: Cut out the rotten spots and dust with sulfur; store them apart from other tubers.

☑ **COMPOST HOLIDAY GREENS.** Add withered greens from swags and wreaths to the compost pile. Cut boughs into 6-inch lengths to speed decomposition.

☑ **WATER.** Make sure plants in containers and under house eaves get enough water. When temperatures plunge, well-watered plants stand a better chance of surviving than dehydrated ones.

☑ **TEND GIFT PLANTS.** Christmas cactus, cyclamen, and kalanchoe will bloom longer if they are not allowed to dry out. They do, however, need perfect drainage. Remove foil wrapping or cut it from the bottom of the pot. Snip off faded leaves and flowers.

☑ **CARE FOR HOUSE PLANTS.** Snip off faded blooms and yellowing leaves. If leaves are dusty, give plants a shower in lukewarm water. Feed winter-flowering plants, but don't fertilize the others until early April.

☑ **REMOVE MOSS.** Moss on pathways, decks, and stairs can be dangerously slippery; eliminate it with a product that kills moss.

Northern California Checklist

PLANTING

☑ **CHOOSE CAMELLIAS.** Zones 7–9, 14–17: Select *C. sasanqua* and early-flowering *C. japonica* in bloom. Sasanquas are good choices for espaliers, ground covers, informal hedges, and containers. Some are upright, others spreading or vinelike; they tolerate a fair amount of sun. Choices include 'Egao', 'Rainbow', 'Shibori Egao', and 'Yuletide'. Japonicas are handsome as specimen plants and espaliers. Try 'Alba Plena', 'Daikagura', 'Debutante', 'Elegans' ('Chandleri Elegans'), 'Magnoliae-flora', 'Nuccio's Carousel', 'Nuccio's Gem', and 'Wildfire'.

☑ **SHOP FOR BARE-ROOT ROSES.** Zones 7–9, 14–17: Bare-root roses start appearing in nurseries this month. Shop while selections are good.

☑ **PLANT FRUITS AND VEGETABLES.** Zones 7–9, 14–17: Late this month, nurseries begin selling bare-root artichokes, asparagus, cane fruits, grapes, rhubarb, and strawberries. Buy and plant early in the month while roots are still fresh. If the soil is too wet to plant, temporarily cover the roots with moistened mulch to keep them from drying out, or plant in containers.

☑ **PLANT BULBS.** Zones 7–9, 14–17: It's not too late to plant any bulbs you still have stored in the refrigerator or the garage. But if you shop for left-over bulbs at nurseries, choose them carefully. Avoid soft or molding bulbs. Plant healthy ones right away (tulips not chilled in the refrigerator will bloom on slightly shorter stems).

Sunset
CLIMATE ZONES
- Mountain (1-2)
- Valley (7-9)
- Inland (14)
- Coastal (15-17)

☑ **SET OUT CYCLAMEN.** Zones 8–9, 14–17: To protect the flowers from rain spots, set plants in containers, then put the pots under an overhang or on a covered porch. Give cyclamen partial shade or morning or late-afternoon sun. Set crowns (base of plants) slightly higher than the surrounding soil.

☑ **MAKE A LIVING ARRANGEMENT.** Zones 7–9, 14–17: Most nurseries have a good supply of 4-inch pots of color to cluster in large containers. Choose azaleas, calendula, Christmas cactus, cineraria, cyclamen, English primroses, fairy primroses, kalanchoe, pansies, *Primula obconica*, and snapdragons. Protect Christmas cactus and kalanchoe from frost.

MAINTENANCE

☑ **FEED ANNUALS.** Zones 7–9, 14–17: Even though the weather is cooler and foliage growth has slowed, annuals need nutrients for root development. Feed every 2 weeks with fish emulsion or once a month with a commercial fertilizer that's higher in nitrogen than the emulsion.

☑ **KEEP CUT CHRISTMAS TREES FRESH.** Look for trees that are stored in water at the Christmas tree lot. To prolong the tree's freshness after you bring it home, saw an inch off the bottom of the trunk, then temporarily store the tree in a bucket of water in a shady area outdoors. Before setting the tree in a stand, saw another inch off the trunk's bottom. Use a stand that holds water, and keep the reservoir full.

☑ **WATCH FOR COLD WEATHER.** Zones 7–9, 14–17: You never know when the first freeze of the season will hit. Keep an eye on the weather report. If cold weather is predicted, move tender container plants under eaves and suspend covers over plants in the ground using 4 tall stakes (don't allow the cover to touch the leaves). Remove in the morning.

☑ **PRUNE FOR HOLIDAY GREENS.** Long-lasting choices include juniper, pine, and redwood.

☑ **SPRAY.** Zones 7–9, 14–17: After leaves have fallen, apply dormant oil to deciduous flowering and fruiting trees and roses. The oil will smother overwintering insects. Use fixed copper (in wettable powder form) or lime sulfur to control peach leaf curl. Spray on a dry day and follow label directions carefully. Spray again in January or early February.

Southern California Checklist

PLANTING

☑ **BUY BARE-ROOT PLANTS. Roses** seem to turn up at nurseries earlier every year. Deciduous fruit trees, cane berries, grapes, and perennial vegetables such as asparagus and artichokes will start appearing later this month and early next. For the best selection, shop soon; plant all as soon as possible after purchase. If the soil is too wet for immediate planting, plant temporarily in containers.

☑ **PLANT FLOWERING SHRUBS.** Sasanqua and early-flowering japonica camellias are available in nurseries now. Other reliable winter bloomers to look for include breath-of-heaven (*Coleonema*) and New Zealand tea tree (*Leptospermum scoparium*).

☑ **PLANT WINTER VEGETABLES.** Plant replacements for the winter crops you harvest. Beets, carrots, chard, kale, head and leaf lettuces, mustard, peas, radishes, and spinach can go in from seed. Broccoli, Brussels sprouts, cabbage, and cauliflower do best started as seedlings.

☑ **FINISH PLANTING BULBS.** Coastal, inland, and low-desert gardeners can continue to plant spring-blooming bulbs, including crocus, hyacinths, and tulips that have been prechilled at least 6 weeks.

Map labels: Bishop, NEVADA, CALIFORNIA, San Luis Obispo, Bakersfield, Tehachapi, Santa Barbara, Lancaster, Los Angeles, Palm Springs, San Diego, MEXICO

Sunset
CLIMATE ZONES
1-3 7-9 11 13 14-24

MAINTENANCE

☑ **PROTECT FROST-SENSITIVE PLANTS.** Follow weather reports. When a temperature drop is predicted, move tender container plants under the eaves or indoors. Cover citrus and other sensitive plants in the ground with plastic or burlap supported by a frame that will keep the cover from touching the foliage.

☑ **FERTILIZE CYMBIDIUMS.** Feed cymbidiums with a bloom-promoting fertilizer such as 15-30-15, until buds open up.

☑ **CARE FOR CHRISTMAS TREES.** To prolong the freshness of a cut tree, saw an inch off the bottom of the trunk, then store the tree in a bucket of water in a shady area outdoors. When ready to bring it indoors, saw off another inch of the trunk before setting the tree in a stand filled with water. Keep the reservoir full (check it daily during the first week). It's best to keep living trees outdoors until shortly before the holidays. Don't leave them indoors for more than 10 days to 2 weeks.

PEST CONTROL

☑ **APPLY DORMANT SPRAY.** As soon as their leaves fall, spray deciduous flowering and fruit trees with dormant oil to smother overwintering aphids, mites, and scale. If you haven't already treated trees for peach leaf curl, do so now. Add lime sulfur or fixed copper to the dormant oil. Spray branches, crotches, and trunks, as well as the ground beneath the trees' drip lines. If it rains within 48 hours of spraying, repeat the treatment. Spray again at the height of dormancy and at the first bud swell. Gardeners at upper elevations (Zones 1–3) or in the high desert (Zone 11) can treat roses with dormant spray now, too.

☑ **PREVENT BEETLE DAMAGE.** Prune eucalyptus, pine, and other trees susceptible to bark beetles now, while beetles are inactive. Chip the prunings or cover the firewood tightly with a tarp to prevent beetles from laying eggs. (Beetles lay eggs on dead as well as live wood.)

Mountain Checklist

PLANTING

☑ **BUY AND CARE FOR LIVING CHRISTMAS TREES.** Some good choices for mountain areas include alpine fir *(Abies lasiocarpa)*, Douglas fir *(Pseudotsuga menziesii)*, Colorado spruce *(Picea pungens* 'Fat Albert'), Colorado blue spruce *(P. pungens* 'Glauca'), and Engelmann spruce *(P. engelmannii)*. Keep living trees away from fireplaces and heater vents. Water thoroughly.

☑ **HOUSE PLANTS.** Buy new plants (try a bonsai garden), or start new plants from old. To start new plants of Chinese evergreen, dracaena, hoya, philodendron, and pothos, snip off leggy stems and immerse the cut ends in water. When roots form, transplant into fresh potting soil.

MAINTENANCE

☑ **DON'T OVERGROOM.** Leave seed heads on sedums, echinops, ornamental grasses, and any other plants you find attractive; many also provide food for birds.

☑ **PRUNE EVERGREENS.** Lightly prune evergreens such as juniper, Japanese holly, and atlas cedar; bring the branches inside for decorating.

☑ **CHECK STORED BULBS AND PRODUCE.** Examine stored summer bulbs, squash, and apples, throwing out any that show signs of rot. Dahlia tubers are an exception: Cut out the bad spots, dust the wound with sulfur, and store apart from the others.

Sunset
CLIMATE ZONES
☐ 1-3 ☐ 10-11

☑ **MULCH.** It's not too late to put a 3- or 4-inch layer of mulch over perennial, bulb, and shrub beds that might be damaged by alternate cycles of freezing and thawing. Apply mulch on damp, unfrozen ground.

☑ **PROTECT YOUNG TREES.** When the low winter sun shines on the trunks of young trees (any less than 4 inches in diameter), it can burn and split the tender bark. You can prevent this by wrapping the trunks with burlap or commercial tree wrap or by painting the bark with white latex (water base). Or make a protective collar by splitting white PVC pipe lengthwise and fitting it around the trunk. Use pipe that's slightly larger than the trunk so water will drain through the collar.

☑ **SAND ICY WALKWAYS.** Sand is a better choice than salt for use around plants, since it's nontoxic and can be swept into the garden. But don't use sand on decks—it scars wood.

☑ **WATER.** When the temperature is above freezing, water dry spots in the garden and plants under house eaves.

☑ **TEND GIFT PLANTS.** To prolong bloom on Christmas cactus, cyclamen, kalanchoe, and poinsettias, water plants well but make sure they have adequate drainage (remove decorative foil from pots). Snip off faded leaves and flowers.

PEST CONTROL

☑ **FIGHT RODENTS.** Hidden beneath snow and mulch, field mice and voles gnaw on the bark at ground level. To keep them from girdling landscape plants, put rodenticide around the base of garden trees and shrubs.

☑ **KILL OVERWINTERING INSECTS AND DISEASES.** On a clear day when the temperature is above freezing, spray deciduous fruit trees and roses with dormant oil mixed with lime sulfur or fixed copper.

Southwest Checklist

PLANTING

✔ANNUALS AND PERENNIALS. Zones 12–13: Set out seedlings of calendula, candytuft, cyclamen, dianthus, Iceland poppy, larkspur, pansy, petunia, primrose, snapdragon, stock, sweet alyssum, and viola. In Zone 13 (Phoenix), you can also set out bedding begonias and cineraria.

✔BARE-ROOT PLANTS. Berries and roses are among the first bare-root plants in nurseries, followed by fruit trees and perennial vegetables, including asparagus. To keep plants from drying out and dying between nursery and garden, wrap them in damp burlap or place them in a sawdust-filled plastic bag. Plant immediately.

✔BULBS. In early December, plant daffodil, gladiolus, ranunculus, and prechilled tulip bulbs (they need at least 6 weeks of chill in the refrigerator to perform well in the low desert).

✔NATIVE PLANTS. Zones 10–13: Set out nursery stock, water in well, and mulch. If you don't get much winter rain, water regularly for the first year.

✔START PEPPERS, TOMATOES. Zones 10–13: Sow seeds of peppers and tomatoes in a warm, bright spot indoors. They should be ready for transplanting around the end of February.

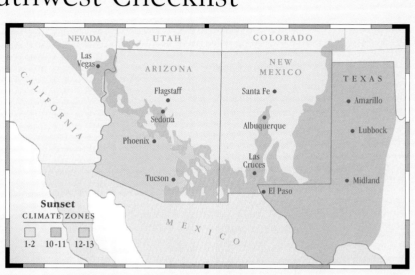

MAINTENANCE

✔FERTILIZE DECIDUOUS FRUIT TREES. Zones 10–13: For trees at least 4 years old, apply 9 pounds of 10-10-10 fertilizer now, then 3 more pounds right after harvest.

✔MULCH. Zones 1–2, 10–11: It's not too late to spread mulch over bulb and perennial beds and over the root zones of permanent shrubs, especially those most vulnerable to cold.

✔WATER. When the temperature is above freezing, water dry spots in the garden as well as plants in containers and under house eaves. Well-watered plants stand a better chance of surviving a deep freeze than dehydrated ones.

✔PROTECT TREES. Zones 1–3: Protect the trunks of young trees from sunscald, which splits the bark and can harm the tree, by painting the trunk with white latex paint.

PEST CONTROL

✔INSECTS ON HOUSE PLANTS. If aphids, mites, or scale insects infest indoor plants, slip a plastic garment cover (the kind you get from a dry cleaner) over the plant, then spray the foliage with insecticidal soap; the plastic "tent" confines the spray.

✔OVERWINTERING INSECTS AND DISEASES. On a clear day when the temperature is above freezing, spray deciduous fruit tees and roses with dormant oil mixed with lime sulfur or fixed copper.

Four jade plants, pruned to reveal branch and trunk pattern, form an instant grove in a bonsai dish. This can go indoors or out (as long as it's protected from frost).

Jade Forest in a Bonsai Dish

December is a perfect time to do some indoor gardening, such as making a miniature forest in a dish. Jade plants *(Crassula argentea)* make good "trees," because they are easy to find, inexpensive, grow well indoors, and don't mind having their roots crowded. The approach shown isn't true bonsai, but many of the techniques and materials are the same.

When you shop for jade plants, you'll find that some have bigger leaves than others. Choose plants with smaller leaves, since they'll be more in scale with the grovelike arrangement.

The materials you need are shown below. The 9-by-13-by-2¼-inch ceramic bonsai dish is in scale with the four small jade plants chosen for the project.

The most time-consuming step is preparing the dish for planting. Jade plants have to be wired in place initially because they tend to be top-heavy and have very small, fibrous root systems for support.

Once you've finished preparing the dish as shown in the steps below, decide how you're going to line up the plants and which direction each will face. Staggering the plants and varying the spaces between them will create a more natural look. You may need to do some preliminary pruning to make the jade plants fit together.

Take the tallest plant out of its pot first, spread its roots, and butterfly them over a mound of soil. Lay a 1- to 2-inch-wide strip of plastic mesh over the roots and tie it snugly in place with two ends of copper wire sticking up through the soil.

Repeat this process for each jade plant until all are securely in place. Then cover with more soil and another thin layer of gravel; water the plants thoroughly.

Jade plants need bright light and occasional feeding; start by mixing some controlled-release fertilizer into the potting soil; repeat feeding every few months.

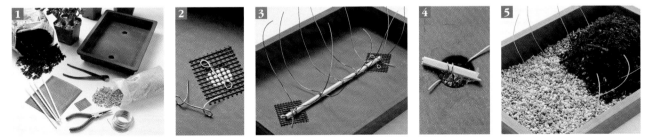

Step-by-step forest: 1. *You'll need potting soil (a cactus mix is good), four jade plants, a bonsai dish, gravel, 24-gauge copper wire, wire cutters, wooden chopsticks, plastic mesh, and pruners.* **2.** *Put plastic mesh over each drainage hole and secure with double-looped wire (bent on underside).* **3.** *Tie five 20-inch lengths of wire around the long chopstick in a spine-and-ribs pattern, as shown.* **4.** *Secure a long chopstick to a short piece of chopstick on the outside of the holes.* **5.** *Cover the bottom of the dish with gravel, then add the potting soil.*

Growing Camellias

In the eastern Asian homeland of the camellia, there are at least 80 different species. But only four are generally available in North American nurseries: *C. japonica, C. reticulata, C. sasanqua,* and *C. hiemalis.* Japonicas, reticulatas, and sasanquas are the camellia gardener's "big three" (hiemalis varieties are usually cataloged with the sasanquas).

In addition, various other species can offer the big three additional desirable characteristics through hybridization. Plant enthusiasts tend to be incorrigible dreamers, and among camellia enthusiasts, three dreams of long standing have been flower fragrance, greater hardiness to cold, and yellow color. Fragrance is already present in several species, and some hybrids now combine fragrance with improved flowers. Persistent hybridizing should, in time, add distinct fragrance to the striking blossoms of japonicas and even reticulatas. Hardiness to cold is also improving. Extra-hardy camellias are good choices if you live in a region considered too cold for standard camellias. Finally, yellow-flowered camellias are becoming available in the United States, on a limited basis.

Camellia care

Camellias thrive and bloom best when sheltered from strong, hot sun and drying winds. Tall plants in old gardens prove that camellias can thrive in full sun when their roots are shaded by a heavy canopy of leaves. Young plants do well when grown in shade cast by tall trees, or on the north side of a building.

Established plants (over 3 years old) can survive on natural rainfall. If your water is high in salts and you irrigate your camellias, deep-soak them twice in summer to dissolve harmful salts and carry them deep below the root zone.

Fertilize with a commercial acid plant food in the weeks and months following bloom. It's best to cut fertilizer in half and feed twice as frequently as the label recommends.

Scorched or yellowed areas on leaf centers are usually due to sunburn. Burned leaf edges, excessive leaf drop, or corky spots may indicate overfertilizing. Yellow leaves with green veins are signs of chlorosis; treat with iron or iron chelates.

For camellia petal blight, sanitation is the best defense. Pick up all fallen flowers and snip infected flowers off plants, dispose in a covered trash bin. Replace old mulch periodically with fresh mulch; 4 to 5 inches will help keep fungal spores down.

Bud drop may be natural; many camellias set more buds than they can open. It can also be caused by overwatering and underwatering (more likely).

Some camellias bear too many flowers. To get the nicest display in midsummer remove all but one or two round flower buds (leaf buds are slender) from branch-end clusters; along stems, leave a single flower bud for each 2 to 4 inches of branch.

Camellia japonica *can be maintained in a 16-inch pot almost indefinitely.*

Prune right after flowering or during summer or fall. Remove dead or weak wood and thin when growth is so dense that flowers have no room to open properly. Prune at will to get the form you want. Shorten lower branches to encourage upright growth. Cut back top growth to flatten lanky shrubs. Make the cut just above a scar that terminates the previous year's growth (often a slightly thickened, somewhat rough area where bark texture and color change slightly). A cut just above this point will usually force three or four dormant buds into growth.

Camellia flower forms

Single   Semidouble   Formal double   Peony form   Anemone form   Rose form

Camellias in the Landscape

Even if camellias never flowered, most would rank high on any list of recommended landscape shrubs. But as they are capable of sending forth beautiful blossoms during the months when garden color is at low ebb, camellias rise above the category of "recommended"—even approaching that of "essential" for some aficionados. Camellias grow best in Zones 4–9, 12, and 14–24. Only climate limits their use, and even then, camellias can be grown in containers or protected from the effects of cold climates. Here is a summary of the many landscaping possibilities camellias offer.

Woodland garden. The gardener lucky enough to have dappled shade from tall trees can use camellias as nature distributed them in the forests of eastern Asia. Casually grouped around meandering paths under high shade according to color, size, type, and bloom season, camellias can help you achieve a fusion of natural beauty and artistic control.

Basic shrubbery. The idea may seem dull, but think of the need in every garden for basic shrubbery, and then reflect on the virtues of using camellias for such plantings. Whether along a fence or walkway, against house walls, or as a backdrop to lower shrubs, perennials, or annuals, camellias can give a landscape dignity and polish throughout the year, punctuated by colorful blossoms in their season.

Accent specimen. Visualize just one camellia plant in full flower, then imagine it placed in a partly shaded garden area that you'd like highlighted during the year's least colorful period. A camellia could greet you beside your front door or welcome you at the garden entrance. A tubbed specimen might become the focal point of an intimate patio, while a large japonica or tall reticulata under high shade trees could be a garden beacon in a picture-window view.

Trained as espaliers, camellias can lend both foliage and floral

Camellias are easily trained as espaliers, which let you show off their beauty against a wall or fence.

beauty to walls and fences where shade or space restrictions rule out other—and less attractive—choices. Among the sasanquas are some of such pliable growth that you can consider them almost as vines.

Container plants. Camellias take so well to container culture that many gardeners actually prefer growing specimens that way. When growing them in containers, you have greater control over water and nutrients, and you always have the option of moving plants to a more favorable or more conspicuous location.

Hedges. Many sasanquas, many hybrids, and some japonicas are both vigorous and dense enough to be massed in a line as hedge and barrier plantings. They'll look their best when only lightly clipped—just enough to remove straggling growth—rather than formally sheared. When camellias are clipped this way, they'll also produce more blooms.

Ground covers. The more willowy or vinelike sasanquas can easily be coaxed into service as ground cover plantings. All year they'll offer handsome, polished foliage, and in autumn they'll nearly smother themselves with blossoms.

A forest of camellias in a wooded garden.

Forcing Bulbs

Because newly purchased bulbs already contain the embryonic bloom for the following season, you can—with a bit of extra effort—manipulate conditions to induce flowering before the normal outdoor bloom season. This process, popularly known as "forcing," takes advantage of the fact that bulbs have certain minimum requirements for each stage prior to bloom. Because outdoor climate slows development, bulbs in the ground usually spend more than the minimally necessary time in these prebloom stages. Under a forcing regime, however, you can control conditions so each stage is completed as quickly as possible.

Not all bulbs respond well to forcing, though many of the most popular spring bloomers do (see list at right). When perusing catalogs, look for species and varieties described as "good for forcing." For the most satisfying results, buy the largest top-quality bulbs you can find: They have the most stored energy and thus are most likely to succeed in a process that draws heavily on their food reserves.

To make sure the bulbs bloom when you want them to do so, you'll need to calculate planting time carefully. Natives of mild-winter areas bloom the soonest after planting, since they don't need a prolonged period of cold. The more tender Tazetta narcissus varieties (often sold as "Paper Whites," though 'Paper White' is more properly the name of one variety) will bloom 5 to 7 weeks after planting. Hardy bulbs (those native to cold-winter regions) typically bloom after 13 to 15 weeks of cold treatment for root and early shoot development, followed by 3 to 4 weeks of warmth and light to induce flowering. Some of the hardy types that bloom earliest in nature—glory-of-the-snow *(Chionodoxa)*, winter aconite *(Eranthis hyemalis)*, and snowdrop *(Galanthus)*—may get by with only 12 weeks of cold before being brought into the light. Hardy bulbs are usually planted in October, November, and December for bloom in January through April.

Some bulbs needing cold treatment, such as hyacinth *(Hyacinthus)* and lily-of-the-valley *(Convallaria majalis)*, can be purchased pre-chilled; you may see the terms "precooled" or "pretreated." In fact, the bulbs are only partially chilled, saving you 3 or 4 weeks of cold treatment. The supplier should indicate how much longer the bulbs must be chilled after you receive them.

Various plants can fill a single pot.

Smaller-growing kinds of narcissus are excellent container subjects.

GIVE COLD TREATMENT

The following bulbs need cold treatment for forced early bloom.

Allium (small types no taller than 1 foot are best)
Anemone blanda
Camassia
Chionodoxa
Convallaria majalis
Crocus (nearly all spring-blooming types can be forced, but Dutch hybrids are best)
Eranthis hyemalis
Fritillaria meleagris
Galanthus
Hyacinthus orientalis
Ipheion uniflorum
Iris (Reticulata types)
Leucojum (Israeli-grown bulbs do especially well)
Muscari
Narcissus (trumpet, large-cupped, and small-cupped daffodils; Cyclamineus hybrids)
Scilla (except *S. peruviana*)
Tulipa (Single Early, Double Early, Double Late, Triumph, and species tulips)

KEEP OUT OF THE COLD

The following bulbs do not need cold treatment, since they are native to mild-winter areas.

Anemone coronaria
Colchicum
Crocus (fall-blooming types)
Freesia
Iris (Dutch hybrids)
Ixia
Narcissus (Tazettas identified as "Paper Whites" or "indoor narcissus")
Ranunculus asiaticus
Scilla peruviana

Dutch hybrid crocus poke through openings in a ceramic pot.

Potting the bulbs

Any kind of pot with drainage holes will do for forcing, though wider-than-tall bulb pots and bulb pans are ideal. Do make sure, though, that the pot is at least twice as tall as the bulb to allow adequate space for roots. Fill the pot loosely with potting mix. If you intend to transplant the bulb into the garden after bloom, add 1 tablespoon of 5-10-5 fertilizer per 6-inch pot.

Space the bulbs close together—for example, about 15 crocuses, 6 narcissus or tulips *(Tulipa),* or 3 hyacinths *(Hyacinthus)* per 6-inch pot—and barely cover them with mix. Plant tulips with the flat side facing the outside of the pot, so that the first and largest leaf will also face that way and cover the rim of the pot. Water to settle the potting mix, but don't compact it. Label the pot with the bulb name and planting date.

Bulbs that do not need cold treatment can now be placed in a cool, well-lit spot (55° to 60°F), then moved to warmer conditions (65° to 75°F) when the buds begin to show traces of color. For bulbs requiring cold treatment, proceed according to the directions that follow.

Providing cold treatment

The hardy bulbs need a prolonged period in dark, moist, chilly conditions (35° to 50°F) to get off to a good start; without this treatment, they tend to produce foliage and no flowers. Possible cooling sites include an old refrigerator, unheated basement or garage, service porch, cold frame, or trench dug in the ground and lined with wire mesh to keep mice away. Pots kept outdoors should be mulched with leaves, sawdust, straw, or other material to protect against freezing and to exclude light. If indoor pots will be exposed to light, put them in closed cupboards or cover them (by inverting baskets over them, for example). Make sure the bulbs don't dry out.

Start checking for top growth after 12 or 13 weeks. The bulbs are ready for forcing when shoots are about 1 inch high or a little taller. The emerging leaves will be white, since they formed in the dark, but they'll color

up when exposed to light. Roots growing through the drainage holes are another sign that bulbs are ready for forcing, even if top growth isn't evident. Move the containers to a cool, well-lit spot (55° to 60°F); if you want to stagger bloom, bring them out a few at a time, every 2 weeks. When buds begin to show color, shift to a warmer, sunny location (65° to 75°F). Once flowers open, though, cooler conditions will lengthen their life. Keep plants well watered.

With the exception of amaryllis, forced bulbs cannot be forced for a second season. After bloom is over, you can set them out in the garden; in a year or two, they may build themselves up enough to flower at the normal time. Forced tulips, however, rarely bloom again.

Water culture

Some bulbs can be grown with their roots in water. Dutch hybrid hyacinth *(Hyacinthus)* and narcissus are the most familiar examples, though other choices are possible as well. Because bulbs cultivated in this manner expend all their energy, they should be discarded after bloom.

Hyacinth glass. The bulb most often grown this way is the hyacinth; in fact, it has lent its name to the special glass forcing vessel, which resembles an hourglass or egg cup. The bulb rests in the smaller upper section, while the roots grow in the larger, water-filled lower part. Other bulbs suited to this type of culture are Dutch hybrid crocus, dwarf early-flowering tulips *(Tulipa),* snowdrop *(Galanthus),* grape hyacinth *(Muscari),* squill *(Scilla),* and meadow saffron *(Colchicum).* More petite containers are sold for smaller bulbs, which would fall through the opening in the upper section of a traditional hyacinth glass.

To "plant" the glass, fill it with water to within ⅛ inch of the bulb base, then add a small piece

Hyacinth in glass

of activated charcoal to discourage the growth of algae. Place the planted glass in a dark, cool place (around 55°F) until roots are well developed and top growth has begun; add more water as necessary during this time to keep the level just beneath the bulb's base. If the water looks murky, be sure to hold the bulb in place as you change the water; don't try to take the bulb out, since you won't be able to get the roots back into the glass without damaging them. When growth is underway, transfer the glass to a fairly cool spot (65° to 68°F) with plenty of light.

Pebbles and water. This method is most often used to force the fall- and winter-blooming Tazetta narcissus varieties (such as 'Paper White' and similar types) that don't need a prolonged cool, dark period for root

growth before they send up leaves. The interval between starting and blooming is 5 to 7 weeks. Therefore, if you make your first planting in October and plant at 2-week intervals until December, you can enjoy flowering narcissus indoors over a 2-month period. Hardy narcissus varieties and Dutch hybrid hyacinths are sometimes grown this way, too.

Fill a shallow pan with pebbles, stone chips, or coarse sand. Crowd in the bulbs, anchoring them by heaping pebbles all around them, leaving only the top ½ inch or so of each bulb exposed. Then add water until the level reaches just below the base of the bulbs. As for bulbs in a hyacinth glass, start plants in a cool, dark spot, then move to a warmer, sunny spot when growth is underway. Add more water as needed.

Narcissus varieties are ideal candidates for grow *in pebbles and water.*

Forcing amaryllis

With a minimum of effort, you can bring amaryllis *(Hippeastrum)* into bloom for the winter holidays and beyond. Nurseries and mail-order firms offer bulbs already planted in special plastic containers; if you buy one of these, all you have to do is water and wait. Or buy bulbs and pot them up yourself.

Nurseries usually offer one or more types of amaryllis bulbs: African, Dutch, Giant Dutch, or Royal Dutch Hybrids. For winter holiday bloom, choose those labeled African. These are grown to blooming size in South Africa, then stored and shipped under controlled conditions. When removed from cold storage, the bulbs sprout quickly and flower in 4 to 6 weeks. For sure bloom at Christmas, plant bulbs around November 15. Most Dutch varieties are dug and shipped from Holland in September; they will bloom 7 to 8 weeks after planting. Plant bulbs every two weeks for successive winter bloom.

For each bulb, choose a container that allows 2 inches between all sides of the bulb and the container edges. Fill containers with potting mix; plant so that the neck and top half of the bulb protrude above the soil surface.

Water thoroughly after planting, then give just enough water to keep soil barely moist until active growth begins. Keep containers in a bright, warm room (70° to 75°F during the day, 60° to 65°F at night); turn the containers frequently so the flower stems will grow upright rather than leaning toward the light. As each bloom fades, cut it off to prevent seed formation. After all flowers have withered, cut off the entire stem at its base.

Leaves appear either during or after bloom. For good performance the following year, it's important to keep the plant growing vigorously; water regularly and give bimonthly applications of liquid fertilizer diluted to half strength. If you allow the leaves to wither naturally in fall, the plant will bloom at its normal time the following spring. If you'd like to schedule another bloom, however, proceed as follows. Stop fertilizing 5 to 6 months after flowering ends; then taper off watering over the next 3 to 4 weeks. When foliage yellows, cut it off; then store the dry potted bulbs in a cool closet, basement, or garage where temperatures will remain above freezing (ideally around 40° to 50°F). About 4 to 8 weeks before bloom is desired, move the pots back into a bright, warm room and water to start the next cycle of growth and flowering.

California Poppies with a Difference

Tufted poppy (Eschscholzia caespitosa) *bears small, pale yellow flowers.*

As glorious as a field of California poppies can look from the freeway, that irrepressible orange can dominate a garden. It's shockingly visible, like the fluorescent safety vests worn by highway maintenance crews. Fortunately, other varieties with the same virtues as *Eschscholzia californica*—satiny petals, ferny foliage, simplicity of care—come in softer colors.

E. californica 'Maritima', a coastal version of the orange California poppy, has clear lemon yellow flowers with small orange blotches at the throats. It's compatible with a wide range of flower colors. A true perennial, it's an excellent choice for a border.

The plant's low mounding habit also makes it handsome in meadow lawns. It reseeds freely, and it comes true from seed as long as its orange cousin isn't in the vicinity. When the two poppies cross, the orange throat blotches on 'Maritima' grow bigger with each generation until the flowers are pure orange.

'Moonglow', a cream-colored variety of *E. californica*, is mellow enough for an English garden. 'Mahogany Red', an English hybrid with deep rust-red flowers, is another attractive option.

A search through seed catalogs will turn up many other *E. californica* hybrids in a wide range of colors and as bicolors. Seed is usually sold mixed. Standouts are 'Mission Bells', semidoubles in a mix of cream, pink, and orange; 'Double Ballerina Mixed', doubles and semidoubles in shades of yellow, orange, rose, and scarlet; and 'Monarch Mixed', singles and semidoubles in a range from yellow to cerise. 'Thai Silk', a ruffled semidouble, is often available in single colors as well as in a mix of pinks.

The easiest *Eschscholzia* to blend into the garden is *E. caespitosa,* the tufted California poppy. This 6- to 12-inch-tall annual has pale yellow flowers with a faint lemon scent. Use it as an edging, mixed with other short wildflowers, or as a bulb cover.

When and how to sow poppies

In the West's mild-winter climates, sow seeds from mid-September through January (sow in fall for winter bloom or in late winter for spring bloom). In cold climates, wait until early spring to sow.

Hoe or pull weeds from areas you want to plant. Amend the soil lightly with compost, then water to force more weeds; hoe or pull this second crop.

Broadcast seeds evenly over the amended soil. Cover them lightly with additional compost or potting soil.

Irrigate to begin germination, or wait for winter rains to do it for you.

Eschscholzia californica *'Apricot Flambeau' looks like a California poppy decked out for a party. Its creamy yellow petals have ruffled edges and intense orange highlights.*

Red flowers of Eschscholzia californica *'Mahogany Red' have center tufts that echo the yellow poppies behind.*

Deterring Deer

With their soulful eyes and graceful gait, deer may be pleasant to watch, but they can make a garden ragged in no time by nipping off flower heads and nibbling tender leaves and new shoots. As wild plants dry out, deer spend more time looking for food in gardens on the fringes of suburbia. They develop browsing patterns, visiting tasty gardens regularly—most often in the evening. Fond of a wide array of flowering plants, especially roses, deer will eat foliage or fruit of nearly anything you grow for your table. Still, there are some plants that deer typically don't like. Strong-smelling and unpleasant-tasting plants will always be the last to go. But since the animals' tastes seem to vary from area to area, check with your Cooperative Extension office for a list of plants least likely to appeal to the local deer population.

Physical controls. Fencing is the most certain protection. On level ground, a 7-foot woven-wire fence will usually keep deer out, although some determined deer can jump even an 8-foot fence. A horizontal "outrigger" extension on a fence makes it harder for a deer to jump it. On a slope, you may need to erect a 10- to 11-foot fence to guard against deer jumping from higher ground. Because deer can jump high or jump wide—but not simultaneously—some gardeners have had success with a pair of parallel 5-foot fences, with a 5-foot-wide "no-deer's-land" between.

If you don't fancy a fortress garden, focus on individual plants (or areas). Put chicken-wire cages around young plants and cylinders of wire fencing around larger specimens. Cover raised beds with mesh, and use floating row covers on vegetables. It sometimes helps to keep a zealous (and vocal) watchdog in the yard, particularly during evening and nighttime hours.

Chemical controls. Commercial repellents can work if sprayed often enough to keep new growth covered and to replace what rain and watering wash away (though some repellents may make sticky, unsightly spots on flowers and foliage). Do not apply repellents to edible portions of plants unless approved by the label; some are not safe to eat. Some gardeners repel deer by hanging small cloth bags filled with blood meal among their plants; the disadvantages here are that blood meal tends to attract dogs and smells unpleasant when wet.

Some deer-resistant plants

California fuchsia (*Zauschneria californica*). Red flowers; Zones 2–10, 12–24. Blooms summer to fall.

Ceanothus gloriosus **'Fallen Skies'.** Lavender-blue flowers; Zones 4–7, 14–24. Prostrate grower, good bloomer. Quite spectacular.

Cistus crispus. Pink flowers; Zones 7–9, 12–24. It blooms a long

---

Pest protection

Where there are deer, there are usually other pests, such as rabbits, gophers, moles, and squirrels. These devices will help protect your plants.

Fence should be at least 2 feet high above ground and 1 foot below ground to stop rabbits, gophers, and moles.

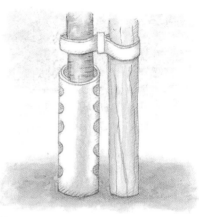

Tree guards of hardware cloth or plastic prevent rabbits from gnawing on the tender bark of young trees.

Wire basket set inside planting hole is an effective barrier, keeping tender bulbs out of reach of gophers.

Deer fence may be the only way to keep these animals out of the garden. It must be at least 7 feet tall.

time and is neat and compact. It grows over boulders, covering them like a blanket.

Coreopsis verticillata 'Moonbeam'. Yellow flowers; Zones 1–24. Continual bloomer.

Foxglove *(Digitalis purpurea)*. Various colors; all zones. Striking plant when in bloom.

Gaura lindheimeri. White or pink flowers resemble butterflies; all zones. Another continual bloomer.

Pacific Coast iris hybrids. Various colors; Zones 4–24.

Penstemon 'Beverly Johnson'. All zones.

Plumas monkey flower *(Mimulus bifidus)*. Yellow to peach; Zones 8–9, 14–24. Lovely native plant.

Rudbeckia fulgida 'Goldstrum'. Yellow; all zones. Rich color, dense bloom.

Above: Purple Verbena peruviana *and red sunrose tumble over the tops of rocks; pink common thrift and blue-eyed grass snuggle against their bases.*

Below: This deer-resistant border is filled with colorful perennials and shrubs— including poppies, yellow yarrow, purple barberry, Spiraea bumalda *'Limemound', and pink foxglove. It sweeps around the edge of the lawn and up to the house.*

Spires of pink and white foxglove rise behind a colorful mix of California poppies, multicolored Iceland poppies, and white sweet alyssum. Deer apparently don't like the taste of these bright bloomers, since they leave them alone.

TIPS FROM THE GARDEN

Use deer repellents. Young, lush plants—even some resistant plants—are attractive to deer. Spray on a bitter-tasting deer repellent and respray when new growth appears. The deer seem to get the idea that things don't taste good in the garden, so they stay away.

Place tasty plants carefully. If you want roses in deer country, train the climbers on an arbor so the foliage and flowers grow above deer's reach. (Protect young climbers by spraying them with a repellent or temporarily surrounding them with fencing.)

Brightly flowered perennials mingle with boulders. Purple Erysimum *'Bowles Mauve', yellow basket-of-gold, and pink sunrose grow in the foreground. Behind are purple verbena, light yellow sulfur flower, basket-of-gold, and moss pink.*

Living Christmas Trees to Treasure

Sawed-off trees dry out fast, their needles turning as crisp as toast before falling off. By comparison, trees in containers use nature's perfect hydration system—roots embedded in soil—to keep their foliage fresh. That's one reason living Christmas trees remain so popular.

Which trees perform best during their stay in containers and later in the garden? Which ones are favorites for decorating? While Colorado blue spruce (shown at right) wins the popularity contest, an assortment of other conifers also make lovely living Christmas trees.

Be a smart tree shopper

Pick a conifer that's as well suited to your taste in garden plants as to your taste in Christmas trees. You can expect to use the same tree in a container for four to seven years, depending on how fast it grows. If you intend to plant it outdoors eventually, be sure the variety is one that thrives in your climate.

The nursery industry offers conifers in two basic grades: sheared, well-tapered trees especially grown for sale as living Christmas trees, and landscape-grade trees that receive no special care. You may not find both grades at every nursery, but when you do you'll notice a marked difference in quality and price between trees of the same species and size. Landscape-grade trees can be rangy, but they typically cost about a third less than sheared trees. In the long run, the two grades will perform about the same in gardens. Trees of both grades are sold in various sizes in 5-, 7-, and 15-gallon plastic cans.

As you shop, you also may see trees that have been tagged with the logo of Global ReLeaf, a tree-planting program sponsored by American Forests, the nation's oldest conservation organization. Global ReLeaf encourages you to plant your tree outdoors after the holidays.

Western conifers

Coast redwoods and giant sequoias are close relatives. Redwoods are greener and not as wide at the base as sequoias; they thrive along the coast and won't take extreme cold.

Sequoias grow more slowly than redwoods, and their foliage is a grayer shade of green. These trees do best in the Pacific Northwest, mountains, and colder interior climates.

Colorado spruces have stiff branches bristling with needles in shades from bluish green to steely blue. 'Glauca' is the classic Colorado blue spruce, but its close cousin 'Hoopsii' has superior blue color and good form even when small, making it an ideal living Christmas tree.

Deodar cedar is one of the most graceful trees anywhere. Gigantic, lighted specimens line Christmas Tree Lane (Santa Rosa Avenue) in Altadena, California.

Colorado spruce
Picea pungens
'Glauca' is the standard Colorado blue spruce, but 'Hoopsii' is even bluer. Spruce aphid is a serious pest for all Colorado spruces in the Puget Sound area.
•Zones: 1–10, 14–17
•Height: 80–100 ft.

A nursery pot cover-up

Need an easy cover-up for your living Christmas tree? You can make an elegant, yet simple, one by wrapping the container in aluminum flashing, as shown at left, around the base of a Colorado spruce. Available at hardware stores in silver or gold, flashing is sold by the foot and ranges in width from 8 inches to 20 inches. Living Christmas trees are mostly sold in 5- to 15-gallon containers. Cut the aluminum to fit the size of your container and secure it at the back with silver duct tape. Shiny metallic flashing adds a festive touch, is easily removed, and can be safely stored for future use.

Best living Christmas trees for the West

AFGHAN PINE
Pinus eldarica
Also sold as Goldwater or Mondell pine, this fast-growing tree has an open habit and long needles. Good choice for desert gardens.
•*Zones:* 7–9, 11–24
•*Height:* 30–80 ft.

ALEPPO PINE
Pinus halepensis
Fast-growing tree with light green needles. Well suited for the low desert. Susceptible to dieback in Tucson and mites in Southern California.
•*Zones:* 8–9, 11–24
•*Height:* 30–60 ft.

ALPINE FIR
Abies lasiocarpa
Slow-growing tree with bluish green needles. *A. l. arizonica,* which grows in the same areas, has blue-gray needles and creamy white, corky bark.
•*Zones:* 1–9, 14–17
•*Height:* 60–90 ft.

COAST REDWOOD
*Sequoia semper*virens
Feathery leaves are green on top, grayish underneath. Relatively pest-free tree, as long as it gets enough water. A big seller in Southern California nurseries.
•*Zones:* 4–9, 14–24
•*Height:* 70–90 ft.

DEODAR CEDAR
Cedrus deodara
Nodding branches bear green needles with a bluish, gray, or golden yellow cast. Floppy top makes it hard to mount a star atop the tree. A good garden tree if you have room.
•*Zones:* 2–12, 14–24
•*Height:* 80 ft.

DOUGLAS FIR
Pseudotsuga menziesii
Soft dark green or blue-green needles. Easy to grow and shape by shearing. *P. m. glauca* is a hardy form in the Rockies. A handsome Christmas tree.
•*Zones:* 1–10, 14–17
•*Height:* 70 ft.

GIANT SEQUOIA
Sequoiadendron giganteum
Dense gray-green foliage; red bark. Widely adapted; able to tolerate colder, drier climates than coast redwood. Potentially huge tree.
•*Zones:* All zones
•*Height:* 80 ft.

KOREAN FIR
Abies koreana
Pyramidal tree with short, shiny green needles. Good choice for Southern California. Slow-growing, compact (seldom taller than 30 ft.).
•*Zones:* 3–9, 14–24
•*Height:* 10–30 ft.

WHITE FIR
Abies concolor
Symmetrical tree with bluish green needles. *A. c. 'Candicans'* has bright silvery blue needles. Good container plant.
•*Zones:* 1–9, 14–24
•*Height:* 30 ft. (eventual height when planted in the ground)

Douglas fir carpets the Pacific Northwest and grows wild down into Northern California and east to the Rockies. You can keep a Douglas fir dense and symmetrical in a container for many years using hedge shears.

Firs are classic cut trees; short-needled, well branched, and well formed, they fit everybody's mental image of a good tree. Some make outstanding living Christmas trees, but others are less than perfect as container plants: Noble fir, for instance, is one of the most popular cut trees, but it has a hard time surviving in a nursery container.

Grand, noble, and white firs often don't do well when transplanted from field to pot, but more fibrous-rooted firs like alpine, balsam, cork, and Fraser handle transplanting better.

To determine if a fir is container- or field-grown stock, ask the nursery staff or check for yourself by digging gently through the surface layer of potting soil to the root ball. If the root ball is covered with burlap, or if you find the roots growing in soil that's markedly different from the soil on the surface, the tree is field grown. If you find the same kind of soil throughout the pot, it's container grown.

Pines usually have longer needles than firs, and they often have a more open form. Most pines thrive in hotter, drier climates than firs and spruces.

Many nurseries still sell Monterey pine *(Pinus radiata)* as a living Christmas tree; if you buy one, keep it in a container and prune the roots annually to keep growth under control. Sadly, Monterey pine is no longer a viable choice as a landscape plant in California because the species is vulnerable to pitch canker, a fungal disease that has killed thousands of the trees in recent years.

How to keep trees healthy

INDOORS

■ Keep the tree in its original nursery container at least for the first Christmas. You don't want to add the shock of transplanting to the stress of its indoor stay.

■ Display the tree indoors for no longer than 10 days. Keep it away from heater vents and fireplaces.

■ Decorate with small, cool bulbs.

■ Water regularly. One easy way: Dump two trays of ice cubes onto the soil surface daily. As the ice melts, the water trickles slowly down through the root zone.

■ In cold-winter areas, before you even bring the tree into the house—and before the ground freezes—dig a planting hole in the garden (the hole should be slightly larger than the container). After its indoor stay, ease the tree's transition from the house to outdoors: First place it on a cool, bright porch for a few days; then move it to a protected place outside where the root ball won't freeze; finally, plant the tree, container and all, in the hole you dug. Spread a 5-inch layer of straw mulch over the top of the root ball to protect roots against freezing weather.

AFTER CHRISTMAS

■ Water the tree regularly year-round. Trees in containers are much more vulnerable to drying out than trees in the ground, so check often by sticking

a finger in the soil; if the top 2 inches of soil are dry, it's time to water. Always provide enough water so a little trickles out the drain holes.

■ When new growth starts in spring, feed the tree with controlled-release fertilizer (a formula that releases nutrients over a 6- to 9-month period is a good choice).

■ Each spring, before new growth starts, gently slide the tree partway out of the pot and check the roots. When they begin to circle the inside of the pot, nip them back with pruning shears, rough up the root ball, and move the tree into a larger pot.

In hot-summer areas, protect trees in black plastic nursery containers from sun; over-heated soil can injure or kill roots and eventually the tree. Transplant the tree into a lighter-colored plastic, terracotta, or wood container. Or sink the nursery container into the ground.

CUTTING GREENS FOR DECORATIONS

Cuttings from evergreens such as fir, pine, holly, mahonia, and strawberry tree make fine wreaths and swags. But don't whack off snippets indiscriminately; take advantage of this annual opportunity to prune for shape. To reveal the plant's naturally handsome form, prune from the bottom up and from the inside out. Avoid ugly stubs by cutting back to the next-largest branch or the  trunk. If the plant has grown too dense, selectively remove whole branches to allow more air and sunlight to reach into the plant.

After you've finished pruning, spray the greens with water to remove dust and insects. Trim cuttings to desired size. To keep them fresh, immerse the cut ends in a bucket of water and store outdoors in a shady spot until you're ready to decorate. Adding a commercial floral preservative to the water and spraying the cuttings with an antitranspirant such as Wilt Pruf can also help preserve their freshness. If the greens are bound for bouquets, strip foliage from the portions of the stems that will be immersed in water.

Index

NOTE: Page numbers in *italics* refer to illustrations or photographs. Page numbers in **boldface** refer to tables and charts.

Credits **Photographers and Illustrators**

AP Wide World Photos: page 172 (top).

Scott Atkinson: pages 156 (top center), 165 (top right, middle right, and bottom right), and 205 (top).

Max E. Badgley: page 118 (all).

Tom Bean: page 216.

Jerry Black: front cover (top left).

Marion Brenner: pages 104 (top), 114 (bottom left and bottom right), 136 (bottom right), 150 (left), 170 (top left), and 186 (right).

Ralph S. Byther: page 38 (right).

David Cavagnaro: pages 16 (bottom), 35 (left), 152 (top right and bottom right), and 153 (right)

Glenn Christiansen: page 20 (bottom).

Peter Christiansen: pages 79 (all), 85 (bottom left and top right), 132 (bottom right), 173 (top left and top right), 175 (top center and top right), and 223 (all).

R. Cowles: page 101 (right).

Rosalind Creasy: pages 132 (top) and 153 (left)

Claire Curran: front cover (bottom right); pages 136 (bottom center), 150 (left center and right center), 170 (bottom left), 178, and 213 (left and right).

Anthony Davis: page 209 (top).

Ken Druse: pages 33 (left) and 194 (top left).

Thomas Eltzroth: pages 33 (top right) and 138 (bottom left, middle center, and middle right).

Derek Fell: pages 20 (top), 103 (bottom), and 186 (left).

William E. Ferguson: pages 116 (top left) and 117 (top center).

Charles Marden Fitch: page 117 (bottom left).

Gardener's Supply Co.: page 156 (right).

Fiona Gilsenan: pages 82 (top left) and 116 (bottom right).

David Goldberg: page 82 (bottom left and top middle right).

Steven Gunther: pages 63 (bottom middle right and bottom right) and 158.

Lynne Harrison: page 25 (top left).

Saxon Holt: pages 34 (top), 41 (left), 43 (all), 73 (top), 84 (right), 104 (bottom left), 132 (bottom left), 133 (top), 176 (middle), 193 (top), 194 (middle left), 206 (bottom left), 207 (top), 208 (top), 210 (top), 211 (top), 212 (right), 226 (top left), 227 (top), and 228 (bottom).

Joseph Huettl: page 74 (bottom right).

Sandra Ivany: page 193 (bottom).

Debra Lambert: pages 10, 11, 12, 13, 14, 28, 29, 30, 31, 32, 46, 47, 48, 49, 50, 57 (right center), 59 (bottom), 66, 67, 68, 69, 70, 88, 89, 90, 91, 92, 108, 109, 110, 111, 112, 126, 127, 128, 129, 130, 142, 143, 144, 145, 146, 160, 161, 162, 163, 164, 170 (bottom), 180, 181, 182, 183, 184, 200, 201, 202, 203, 204, 210 M, 218, 219, 220, 221, and 222.

Janet Loughrey: pages 2 and 167 (right).

Lois Lovejoy: page 54 (all).

Maggie MacLaren: page 140.

Ray Maleike: page 101 (left).

Allan Mandell: pages 7 (left) and 99.

Charles Mann: pages 1, 7 (right), 15 (top), 25 (bottom), 34 (bottom left, bottom middle, and bottom right), 57 (right), 63 (top left), 93, 106, 136 (bottom left), 137 (bottom), 149, 150 (right), 170 (top middle left), and 207 (bottom left).

Ells Marugg: pages 103 (top) and 224 (bottom).

Jane McCreary: page 122 (bottom).

David McDonald: pages 56 and 57 (left and left center).

William T. Molin: page 82 (top middle left).

Jack Nelson: pages 231 (top and bottom) and 232 (top and bottom).

Don Normark: pages 73 (bottom left) and 212 (left).

Rik Olson: pages 52, 75, 76 (top), and 137 (top).

Mimi Osborne: pages 36 (bottom), 94, 95, 96 (top and bottom), 97, 168 (top right and bottom right), 169 (right), 214, and 230.

Erin O'Toole: page 33 (bottom right), 37 (right), 38 (left), 39, 80 (bottom), 136 (top), 154 (all), 155, 156 (left all), 157, 195, and 215.

Park Seed Co.: page 151 (top and bottom).

Jerry Pavia: page 15 (bottom), 24 (top and middle), 25 (top right), 40, 51 (top and bottom), 53 (all), 85 (top left), 152 (left), 176 (top and bottom), 194 (right), and 224 (top).

Mark Pechenik: pages 174-175 .

Pamela K. Peirce: pages 16 (top left and top right), 82 (top right, middle right, and bottom middle right), 117 (top left), and 138 (bottom center).

Chuck Place: page 172 (bottom).

Norman A. Plate: front cover (top right) and back cover; pages 3, 4, 5, 8, 18, 36 (top), 37 (top left and bottom left), 42 (top left and bottom left), 44, 58, 59 (top), 60 (all), 61 (all), 62 (all), 63 (top right and top middle right), 64, 76 (bottom right), 77 (top and bottom), 78 (top and bottom right), 80 (top right and top left), 84 (left), 85 (bottom right), 86, 98 (all), 100, 102 (all), 104 (bottom center and bottom right, 113, 114 (top), 115, 124, 131, 134 (top left), 135, 147, 156 (right), 167 (left), 168 (top left and bottom left), 169 (left), 171 (bottom), 177 (bottom), 187 (all), 188 (all), 189 (all), 190 (bottom right), 191 (all), 196 (top right and bottom right), 198, 206 (bottom right), 211 (bottom), 226 (bottom right), 229 (all), 233 (bottom), and 235 (all).

Ian Reeves: page 206 (top).

Sandra Lee Reha: page 166.

Bill Ross: page 35 (right).

Susan Roth: page 148 (left).

Lucy I. Sargeant: page 185 (all).

Alexis Seabrook: pages 233 (top) and 234 (all).

Richard Shiell: pages 17, 24 (bottom), 82 (bottom middle left and bottom right), and 197.

Steve Sibbett: page 138 (top center).

Chad Slattery: pages 74 (bottom left) and 194 (bottom left).

Lauren Springer: page 19.

Marina Thompson: pages 6, 21 (top), 22, 23, 42 (right all), 83, 119, 123, 139, and 205 (bottom all).

Michael S. Thompson: front cover (bottom left); pages 16 (middle left and middle right), 41 (right), 71, 73 (bottom right), 121 (bottom), 122 (top), 133 (bottom), 170 (bottom middle left), 177 (top), 192, 196 (left), 225 (top and bottom), 226 (bottom left), 227 (bottom), and 228 (top).

Mark Turner: page 116 (bottom left).

Alex Vertikoff: page 78 (middle).

VISIONS-Holland: page 207 (bottom right).

Deidra Walpole: page 105.

Darrow Watt: pages 134 (top center and top right), 148 (top right and bottom right), and 213 (center).

Catherine M. Watters: page 21 (bottom)

Jonelle Weaver: page 72.

Ron West: pages 116 (top right) and 117 (bottom center, top right, and bottom right).

Peter O. Whiteley: page 74 (bottom center).

Russ A. Widstrand: pages 165 (left) and 171 (top).

Doug Wilson: page 190 (top).

Tom Woodward: page 173 (bottom).

Cynthia Woodyard: page 76 (middle).

Ben Woolsey: pages 26 and 121 (top).

Tom Wyatt: page 134 (bottom all).

Linda Younker: page 55 (top and bottom).

Thomas A. Zitter: page 138 (bottom right).